THE
REFERENCE
SHELF

THE MEDIA & THE PUBLIC

Edited by CASEY RIPLEY, JR.

THE REFERENCE SHELF

Volume 66 Number 5

THE H. W. WILSON COMPANY

New York 1994

THE REFERENCE SHELF

The books in this series contain reprints of articles, excerpts from books, and addresses on current issues and social trends in the United States and other countries. There are six separately bound numbers in each volume, all of which are generally published in the same calendar year. One number is a collection of recent speeches; each of the others is devoted to a single subject and gives background information and discussion from various points of view, concluding with a comprehensive bibliography that contains books and pamphlets and abstracts of additional articles on the subject. Books in the series may be purchased individually or on subscription.

Library of Congress Cataloging-in-Publication Data

The media & the public / edited by Casey Ripley, Jr.
    p.   cm. — (The reference shelf ; v. 66, no. 5)
  Includes bibliographical references (p.).
  ISBN 0-8242-0856-0
  1. Mass media—Public opinion. 2. Mass media—United States.
3. Journalism—United States. 4. Public opinion—United States.
5. Mass media—Social aspects—United States. 6. Mass media—
Technological innovations. I. Ripley, Casey. II. Title: Media
and the public. III. Series.
P96.P832U66 1994
302.23'0973—dc20

94-19621
CIP

Cover: A Washington press corps covering an event at the White House Rose Garden.
Photo: AP/Wide World Photos

Printed in the United States of America

CONTENTS

Preface

One would be hard-pressed at this point in the mid-1990s to look at a subject such as the media and the public and come away with a positive outlook. Members of the public often complain about what they are subjected to in the way of headlines and sound bites. An important question, however, is whether the media create the agenda or merely reflect and report the preoccupations of the society at large? And does our wish to dwell at length on Nancy and Tonya, Woody and Mia, Joey and Amy, and the "Donald" and Marla—rather than on Bosnia, North Korea, or issues like health and welfare reform—say more about the media's shortcomings or the public's.

This compilation is meant to provide a range of published opinions on the relationship between the media and the public, past, present and future.

Section One deals with the current state of broadcast and print journalism. The articles examine newspapers and television, two of the chief purveyors of information, focusing on the "big business" of the media, and assess the quality of the product they provided. The short-term and long-term viability of both media are also explored.

Section Two investigates aspects of the relationship between the public and the media, such as the role that the media has played in "serving the public interest," the current state of journalism, the ethics of the "new media," and the public's responsibility as consumers of information.

Section Three takes a closer look at some of the stories and journalistic trends that define "reporting" today. These articles analyze the newsworthiness of certain high-profile events vis-à-vis what the public wants and defines as "news." These case studies include glimpses of the Gulf War, the Clarence Thomas hearings and William Kennedy Smith trial, the Los Angeles riots, tabloid and talk-show journalism, "narrowcasting" and "reality" T.V.

Section Four is devoted to the future. Technological breakthroughs and interactive media are clearly visible on the horizon. The articles explore issues of policy, availability, control, social impact, and changes in current dissemination. Every recent generation has heeded this call to progress: the Pony Express, the telegraph, telephone, radio, television, the Internet. The future is being heralded as a technological utopia, but will it be so for everyone? And if so, at what financial, social, and intellectual cost to society?

Twenty-four articles are not likely to cover all the bases of so broad a topic, and for that the editor wishes to apologize, while hoping that they convey some of the main issues in our media-oriented society.

The editor wishes to thank the H. W. Wilson General Publications staff for its assistance, and to the authors and publishers who have granted permission to reprint their material in this compilation.

CASEY RIPLEY, JR.

August 1994

I. THE MEDIA BUSINESS

EDITOR'S INTRODUCTION

The first section of this compilation is devoted to the state of print and television journalism: their history and possible directions. The articles remind us that more than ever journalism is a business and that turning a profit from television and newspapers in the competitive world of the 1990s is changing the industry and redefining the definition of news. As family and local ownership of newspapers has given way to chains and media conglomerates, as newspaper readership declines in the face of competition from television, as cable programming threatens broadcast television, every segment of "the press," as it was called, is seeking new alliances that will enable them to survive.

The first three articles, by James D. Squires in *New Perspectives Quarterly,* by Dudley Clendinen in *Lear's,* and by Doug Underwood in the *Columbia Journalism Review,* deal with the newspaper business, changes in recent years, why many have foundered, and what newspapers must do in order to stay alive in a "paperless" future. The last two articles, the first a chapter from *The Future of News* by Lawrence W. Lichty and Douglas Gomery, and the second a *Columbia Journalism Review* article by Jon Katz, are concerned with the broadcast and cable industries, and the response of the three networks to new entrants such as CNN and C-Span.

DEATH OF THE FOURTH ESTATE[1]

For all its imperfections, the "press" traditionally has been a people-oriented, privately owned, public-spirited, politically involved enterprise concerned primarily with the preservation of

[1]Article by James D. Squires, excerpt from his book *Read All About It!* ('93). Appeared originally in *New Perspectives Quarterly* 9:31–34 Fall '92. Copyright © 1992 by *New Perspectives Quarterly.* Reprinted with permission.

democracy. That in itself was a major reason it survived in basically the same form for 200 years. But the press has lost that distinctive character, which means that it now has no better chance of survival than any other business, nor should it have. Under the new order, this news medium is no longer an institution dedicated to the public interest but rather a business run solely in the interest of the highest possible level of profitability.

For two centuries the press has served as the trusted channel between the government and the governed. In keeping that moral commitment as an integral part of the system, the press has made both itself and the democracy it serves models for the rest of the world. At every crossroads in our history, nothing has been more valuable in the American experience than the incessant catalyzing of the press. It fell to the press to stir the colonies to revolution in the first place. A hundred years later, it was the newspaper voices of abolition that ultimately propelled the nation to the twin brinks of destruction and greatness over the slavery question: the Civil War. Another century later, it was dramatic press accounts of oppression in the South that produced desegregation across the land, as well as a public rebuke of the war in Vietnam. Between 1960 and 1974, the press played a vital role in an unprecedented empowerment of the citizenry: the extension of participatory rights to minorities in new civil rights legislation and a similar enrichment of women and youth by the feminist and peace movements.

In such a system, it is the reporting of unfettered truth about how things are and ideas of how they might be made better that motivates a citizenry to act and educates it to courses of action. People cannot govern what they cannot see. And whatever the imperfections, the unquestioned purpose of the old business of journalism was to provide America with an accurate reflection of itself and the understanding necessary to preserve freedom.

But since 1972, when newspaper penetration began to decline in America, the levels of public interest in and understanding of complex social and political issues has steadily declined, according to every available measurement. An authoritative study of public opinion polling by the Times-Mirror Company shows that through the 1960s, adult Americans regardless of age were equally informed about and interested in the great issues and news events of their time. But since the mid-1970s, interest and knowledge among young adults has declined until it is now only half that of older Americans. As understanding has waned, so has participation in the most important of democratic expressions: voting.

More Noise, Less News

Despite technical superiority and an unprecedented ability to disseminate information, the media of today is serving what survey after survey has shown to be the least informed, most uninvolved citizenry in the history of the republic. Rather than educating and challenging citizens, the press's purpose has become that of attracting and entertaining consumers, increasingly with distorted and unreal images that are the antithesis of those produced by good journalism.

Case in point: In the 1960s, brilliant foreign correspondents, including David Halberstam, then with *The New York Times,* and Peter Arnett, then employed by AP, reported the disturbing nature of the Vietnam War in the printed press for years without much reaction from the public. Then, the networks—still owned by old-time entrepreneurs like David Sarnoff and Bill Paley—sent their cameras out to record what Halberstam and others were writing about. Sarnoff and Paley were intent on establishing television news as a legitimate part of the free press, and it was the nightly news film dispatches of reporters like CBS's Morley Safer that set fire to the nation's conscience and burned up Lyndon Johnson's presidency. The key was the combination of the power and the accuracy of the reflection.

By contrast, 25 years later the most compelling piece of Gulf war journalism—an old fashioned press photo—could find no place in the new American news media. New York-based photojournalist Ken Jarecke, who was working the Gulf for *Time,* submitted to his editors a single grisly picture that captured precisely the essence of the entire conflict—an Iraqi soldier burned to a crisp while trying to escape a burning truck that had been bombarded from the sky. Not only did the photo not make *Time,* but the Associated Press picture editors also refused to transmit it, blaming their decision on the culture of today's press. "Newspapers will tell us, 'We can't present pictures like that for people to look at over breakfast,'" said an AP official. So much for an accurate reflection of the reality of war.

At the time when the rest of the world is realizing the importance of a free press, this most vital American institution—as intended and guaranteed by the U.S. Constitution, as preserved many times by the Supreme Court and as articulated and practiced by the important journalists of our history—is in danger of disappearing altogether from the American experience.

Journalism, the mirror through which the society has seen itself, has been drastically distorted, its practice commercialized and appropriated for a decidedly different purpose. Without much notice, its role as the information provider for the democracy is being diminished and eclipsed by a successor far more efficient at delivering information but one with neither brand-name credibility, proven conscience or character references.

An Electronic Black Hole

Like a lot of important stories, the corporate takeover of America's newspapers was long in development and did not occur without warning. Nearly a half century ago, a group funded by *Time* founder Henry Luce and headed by the great educator Robert Maynard Hutchins suggested that trends in the communications industry were threatening freedom of the press in this country. Terming this a "problem of peculiar importance to this generation," the Commission on Freedom of the Press wrote:

The modern press is a new phenomenon. Its typical unit is the great agency of mass communication. The agencies can facilitate thought and discussion. They can stifle it. They can advance the progress of civilization or they can thwart it. They can debase and vulgarize mankind. They can endanger the peace of the world; they can do so accidentally, in a fit of absence of mind. They can play up or down the news and its significance, foster and feed emotions, create complacent fictions and blind spots, misuse the great words and uphold empty slogans. Their scope and power are increasing every day as new instruments become available to them. These instruments can spread lies faster and farther than our forefathers dreamed when they enshrined the freedom of the press in the First Amendment of our Constitution.

All of that was probably true then, and even truer today. These words could have been written just as easily by 1988 presidential contender Gary Hart, jailed evangelist Jim Bakker or any American president since Franklin Roosevelt who's had a quarrel with his treatment by the press.

But like a lot of outfits formed to study things, the Hutchins Commission had the right concerns for the wrong reasons. It feared—in 1946—that the concentration of media ownership in fewer, more powerful hands would result in a monopoly of ideas and the inability of the varied elements of democracy to commu-

nicate freely with each other. At the time there were still competing newspapers in 117 cities, a dozen newspaper chains owning
seven or more papers, three separate worldwide press services,
four national radio networks, 200 separate book publishing
houses individually owned and a dozen or so big magazine em-
pires. But the trend foreseen by the commission has continued
beyond its wildest dreams. In 1990, all major media from newspapers to movies is dominated by 23 companies. Fourteen companies control half the 1,600 or so daily newspapers—down from 20
just seven years earlier. More than half the revenue from all media is collected by 17 firms. But so far, the commission's concern
that like-minded, power-hungry owners would somehow stifle the
spread of ideas and restrict access to channels through which the
country expresses itself has been unfounded.

However, in the 45 years since the Hutchins group held its
meetings, something just as insidious and threatening to democracy has occurred. What Dr. Hutchins and his colleagues could
not possibly foresee was that the 9,000 or so television sets in the
U.S. in those days would by 1960 multiply to 45 million, and by
1990 to three times that number; and that the incredible growth
of the most important communication tool ever would result in
the institution of the press being surpassed as the nation's main
source of information and be swallowed up by "the media," a
constantly expanding, earthly equivalent of a black hole.

News, which the Hutchins commission defined as "a truthful,
comprehensive, and intelligent account of the day's events in a
context which gives them meaning," was still what the press pursued when I became a reporter in 1962. And the commission of
journalism was still its overriding mission a decade later when as
Washington bureau chief of the *Chicago Tribune* I reported the
Watergate scandal and the resignation of Richard Nixon.

But during the next 15 years, the world of public-service
newspapering became a heady, high-pressure world of business,
preoccupied with cost control, return on assets and the courting
of consumers. And by the time I left the press in 1989, the definition of "news" had changed dramatically. No longer is "news"
only information that has passed through the prism of journalism
where it has been distilled by the collective judgment of professional journalists. "News" is whatever information anyone can get
placed somewhere in the vast information collection and distribu-
tion system known as "the media." That this information is important, relevant, accurate or delivered in a context that gives it

meaning is far less significant than whether it is titillating, controversial or entertaining. What people want to read, watch and listen to is now a more important value in the evaluation of "news" than any of the more traditional considerations.

Survival of the Wittiest

How much all of this ultimately matters to the enlightenment of the people, to the nurturing of ideas, to progress toward the horizon of an ideal democracy is a matter for conjecture. It can be argued effectively that ignorance cannot survive the flood of information, or, alternatively, that the size, speed and nature of the information flood assures that it will all pass too fast to soak through and nurture anything. There is ample evidence to support either.

Isn't a citizenry exposed to 10 times as much information than the old press used to deliver better informed than its predecessors, even if the sources are less credible and the information unfiltered? Perhaps. But is a citizenry that receives only those stories deemed "entertaining" and "interesting" actually better educated? Obviously not. Is a public that spends twice as much time on unsupported allegations of sexual impropriety as the charges deserve wasting time that might be spent on other, more important issues? The debate is only beginning.

Of far more certainty is that unlike the old newspaper-dominated press, the new television-dominated media business has no clearly defined, widely agreed upon and politically secure role in the political system. In recent years, journalists have lost the right to protect the identity of their sources and—ironically at the same time—the right to betray and reveal them when they turn out to be scoundrels.

If the public opinion surveys of the last few years are accurate, what has not been lost in the courts has been surrendered in a decline of public confidence in the press as a public service institution. Polls show that fewer Americans believe the news media has the right to pry into the private affairs of public officials; that in pursuit of the news journalists most often behave excessively and in their own interest; and most recently, that the government was correct in its unprecedented censorship of the press in the Gulf war.

On the horizon are even more legal conflicts between the traditional rights of the press and those rights constitutionally guaranteed to others. For example, newspapers and environmentalists have now squared off on the question of whether governments can require that newsprint be made from recycled paper. With the evolution of media still incomplete and new technology emerging daily, laws governing telecommunication and other forms of transmitting digitized data are only in their infancy. All of this insures that the parameters of free speech and the relationship between government and media will be redefined in the months and years ahead, both in the courts and Congress.

But if recent history is any indication, when the redefinition comes, the once vaunted power of the press to influence its own destiny will be concentrated on preserving its profitability, not its constitutional mandate. In Maryland in 1990, the newspaper industry exercised its clout to defeat legislation that would mandate a more environmentally sound policy of recycled newsprint. A year earlier in Florida, media companies relied on a combination of editorial-page advocacy and paid lobbyists to mount a successful political movement to repeal legislation that extended the sales tax to advertising. In Congress, the newspaper industry continues today to concentrate its resources in a single-minded effort to make sure that the telephone companies can never use their wiring monopoly to compete with newspapers. That such a feeling is so prevalent and embraces such newspapers as the *Chicago Tribune*, which once raised its voice against every attempt by government to regulate business, is proof positive that the press has finally been homogenized in its economic interest, whether its goals serve the public or not.

It's not just the camel's nose that is under the tent; the entire camel is in the tent, and for good. Corporate news media are here to stay. It is unrealistic to think that the new professional managers will ever accept smaller profits in the interest of better and more traditional journalism. Nor will it suddenly reverse itself and restore the purpose and priorities of the old press. The pressure to do so is ever so gradually being eased.

In the end, it may well be that the values and traditions of the free press will have to find refuge and nourishment in that other "public sector" of our economy—the world of non-profit foundations and educational institutions. It may be here, and here alone, that public service journalism can survive—at least in some ivory tower—so it can eventually take root in the new world of electronic information delivery.

YESTERDAY'S PAPERS[2]

Shortly after my generation started school, in 1950, two things happened that now seem important. The first was that my parents, both newspaper people, took me down into the concrete caverns where the presses stood. It was Sunday. The presses were quiet. But the ink pooled on the floor soaked through my tennis shoes and socks and into my skin. The second was that Jean Fountain's parents, who lived behind us and five houses down, bought the first television in the neighborhood. As we watched cartoons in the afternoon, TV began to soak through me, too.

It didn't matter that the hulking gray presses were silent that morning. I knew that they were mystical, that news came from newspapers, that power did, too. At the movie theaters, the news segments were introduced by headlines rolling off the presses. But I saw their power at home. On election nights, as we watched TV, my father, the editor of *The Tampa Tribune*, would turn pink and jubilant when the candidates he had endorsed won. "It's a great day for the people," he always said.

Governors-elect stopped by the house to thank him. Governors attacked for their views usually came around. This went on for decades. In Nixon's last months in office, when he'd give one of those excruciating speeches to the nation, my father would sit and watch. Afterward the phone would ring. The White House calling, wanting to know what he thought.

But even in those Watergate years, when the power of the press seemed at its zenith, it was not. It was waning, being siphoned by television, but it was a long time before newspapers and the networks realized what had occurred.

When I was first in New York, in 1980, I bumped into a familiar figure on the street. It was Steve Kroft, now of *60 Minutes*. We were both from Florida. He had been hired by CBS News. I had joined the *Times*. We immediately repaired to a bar to catch each other up.

Halfway through the second drink, he asked. "Does anyone there watch us?" It took me a minute. And then I realized that the

[2]Article by Dudley Clendinen, from *Lear's*, 5:68–71+ D '92. Copyright © 1992 by the author. Reprinted with permission.

answer was no. I had seen no one at the *Times* watch the network evening news.

Steve shook his head. "Anything that appears on the front page of *The New York Times*," he said, "we have to do a story on." That was the order. Newspapers led. Television followed.

But that was the year that Ronald Reagan, the Television President, came to office. His campaign and his whole presidential presence was programmed to the televised speech, and the network evening news. All through the '80s, he and television confirmed each other's primacy. And by this past November 3, the 1992 campaign had sealed an extraordinary change.

Nearly every day, the campaign report in *The New York Times* included a box telling the readers where to find the candidates on TV. It was, in the *Times'* quiet way, the signal of a fundamental shift. This whole remarkable election process, which was so much about feeling, about concepts and qualities like character, trust, family, values, occurred first on television. And not even on the evening news. First Perot, then Clinton and Bush, took the campaign to the "magazine" programs and talk shows, the "town meeting," "interview," and "all news" formats where there was more time and a softer focus.

It is all part of the phenomenon by which newspapers, in the last decades, have become much less relevant, but, paradoxically, immensely more profitable.

Here's one measure of the change: *The Miami Herald*, which five years ago destroyed Gary Hart's candidacy when it caught him with another woman, announced this year that its readers should no longer expect it to recommend anyone for president. Presidential choices in newspapers just don't count for much anymore, Jim Hampton, the *Herald's* editorial-page editor, wrote. There was a time, he suggested, when voters might have been deprived by the lack of a recommendation "if they got most of their political news and analysis from their newspaper. Omnipresent television, especially CNN and C-SPAN, has changed that."

To understand what is happening to newspapers in America, understand this: The percentage of people who read a newspaper every day, the amount of time they spend doing it, the number of newspapers published daily, and their circulation in proportion to the population have all been going down, down, down.

In 1972, the first General Social Survey of American habits, conducted by the National Opinion Research Center at the University of Chicago, found that 69 percent of all adults said they read a newspaper every day. According to Tom W. Smith, director of the survey, by 1991 only 51 percent of adults were claiming to read a daily paper, and that figure had remained essentially level since 1985.

But something else has changed. If readers were the lifeblood of newspapers, then advertisers have become their drug. And the advertising binge of the 1980s, which generated unheard-of profits for newspapers, has now left them largely dependent—and in the present recession, feeling the pain of withdrawal.

The modern newspaper form was created in the 19th century by the eccentric James Gordon Bennett, Sr., owner of *The New York Herald*. He understood that the spread of literacy from the elite to the masses made mass circulation possible. He chased common news by every means, a legacy his son expanded by sending Henry M. Stanley to Africa to find Dr. David Livingstone.

Most of the income from Bennett's paper came from sales. But then Joseph Pulitzer conceived mass advertising, based on circulation. Papers had another source of money. In the 20th century, advertising profits outgrew revenue from paper sales.

And in the last two decades, as the economy expanded, advertising income went up like a rocket. Leo Bogart, former executive vice president of the Newspaper Advertising Bureau, wrote that advertisers spent five times as much money to buy exposure for their products in all media available for purchase by the public in 1989 as they did in 1970. At the same time, the wave of corporate mergers and consolidations meant that fewer companies controlled the placement of those dollars.

Now, readers produce only about 20 percent of newspaper revenues. The other 80 percent, like nearly half of magazine revenues and all of on-air commercial broadcast revenues, come from advertising. When advertisers abandon newspaper readers, newspaper publishers usually abandon them, too. Thus, when national and regional advertisers deserted newspapers to buy commercial time on television or more pages in specialty-audience magazines, it killed off many of the newspaper Sunday magazines.

Television, radio, magazines, and direct mail all offer advertisers ways of reaching target audiences that seem cheaper or more effective than newspapers themselves. As product lines have multiplied, as the American consumer audience has grown but fragmented, advertisers have grown more selective and controlling. By buying space only in the leading paper in any market, advertisers have led publishers to merge and kill many of the afternoon newspapers, a trend expected to leave each metropolitan area with one main paper.

The question is what form those papers will have, and what the content will be. No one knows. Newspapers, the only business intended to produce both a profit and the public record, are in real confusion. But the decisions are going to be made by a different set of managers than before, because changes in newspaper ownership have made profit much more important than before.

James Squires, the former editor of *The Chicago Tribune* and the author of *Read All About It! The Corporate Takeover of America's Newspapers* (see previous selection in this volume) observes the following: Until about the 1960s, newspapers were owned and run by families who saw the medium as a special business, rooted in the First Amendment freedoms guaranteed by the Bill of Rights, and reflective of the culture and its events. They may have been Southern segregationists like the Hedermans of Mississippi, eccentric libertarians like Colonel McCormick in Chicago, or sober, civic-minded publishers like the Sulzbergers of New York, but their papers were extensions of their beliefs.

With no public shareholders demanding a return on investment, those owners could make whatever profit they wished, depending on how much they chose to spend on the news. For instance, by paying fewer reporters, "we could save $4 million to $5 million a year for several years, and it would drop straight to the bottom line," says Andrew Barnes, editor of *The St. Petersburg Times*. "But I'm able to say we don't have to do that."

He doesn't have to, because he may be the only major editor in the nation who votes the stock that controls the paper—a legacy of independence bequeathed by the late Nelson Poynter. That's the position owners used to have. "When I first went to work for *The New York Times* in the 1960s," says Bill Kovach, now the curator of the Nieman Foundation at Harvard University, "the Sulzbergers were content to make five percent operating profit."

No more. From the 1960s on, the Grahams in Washington, the Sulzbergers, the Chandlers in Los Angeles, the Bryans in Virginia, indeed most of the families who owned city papers, either issued stock to the public—to raise money to compete in a world going suburban, and going to TV—or they sold out to the newspaper chains that grew from the change.

As they opened their books to their investors, everyone began to realize how much money newspapers could make. With the purchase of computer systems, which saved enormous labor costs, and with the swell of advertising revenue in the boom of the 1980s, newspapers were more profitable than any industry but oil. Their share value rose.

Katharine Graham took the Washington Post Company public in 1971. An investor who bought stock after Richard Nixon resigned would have multiplied the investment over 70 times before the stock market crashed in October 1987.

The average operating profit for the newspaper industry as a whole "peaked at around twenty-one percent in 1985," said John Morton, perhaps the industry's leading analyst and broker, in an interview. Other analysts peg it at 25 percent. And that was for the industry as a whole. Some individual papers generated profits of 35 or 40 percent. "There are a lot of medium-sized papers which reached that profitability easily," said Morton. Great newspaper chains, such as Gannett, were created in the rush to buy such gold mines. Their stock prices exploded, and shareholders got rich.

"Gannett had twenty-two years of consistent quarterly earnings growth," says Squires. "It was the best record in the history of Wall Street, and what is important about that is that it set the standard for every other journalistic business in America."

During the recession, newspaper companies have shrunk their papers' size and staff in order to try to keep profits up. In the worst year of this recession, operating profits for newspapers seemed to be averaging around 11 percent.

USA Today, a paper that was created and staffed by stripping reporters from almost every other Gannett paper, and that has lost more than $100 million, nonetheless became the symbol of Gannett's success. Designed to be read by business travelers, people who already had a local paper of record to digest, it began to be widely copied by the very newspapers it was planned to supplement. The crisp, quick, conversational style of *USA Today*— a survey of news and trends and a compendium of consumer information, presented in a format as colorful, as politically concerned, and as emotionally involved as an upscale produce market—appealed to a new generation of publishers and the editors they were choosing.

These managers didn't own the paper. Some chain did. By

1985, about 71 percent of all daily newspapers nationwide were group- or chain-owned. By 1991, the figure had reached 75 percent.

With the exception of the few families who still privately own the papers where they live (as in Raleigh, North Carolina; Charleston, South Carolina; and Anniston, Alabama), or still control and run the papers they used to wholly own (as with the Sulzbergers and Grahams), the managers of papers today aren't from their paper's metropolitan area any more than most of the people who live there are. Fearful of boring or alienating the remaining readers with too much hard or critical news, many of them work to make their papers friendly, giving the readers not news—TV does that—but information, "news you can use," as the cliché has it.

The difference is that information, unlike news, can be shaped and packaged to meet the needs of advertisers. The choice is driven by two needs: to market the paper to a culture that is rapidly changing and fragmenting, and that no longer mirrors the white, male, upper-middle-class world of most newspaper editors and managers, and to maintain the huge profit margins that the marketplace has come to expect.

Like some other newspaper companies, the *Tribune*, Squires's former paper, has plans that envision a "core news section" that all its readers would get, and an array of other sections of particular interest from which they could choose. "They pick their own TV programs—they could pick the sections of the paper they want," says Colleen Dishon, the *Tribune's* senior editor and designer of the paper's successful Womenews section, which contains information and advertisements for and about women.

There are a lot of other things newspapers are trying—telephone and fax services with information for sale, and various combinations of technologies. But Roger Fidler, the director of new media development for the Knight-Ridder newspaper chain, has the most detailed technological vision around of the newspaper of the future. It is based on the development of the flat-panel display computer, a portable tablet with a televisionlike screen and computer capabilities, something the size of a legal pad that a person could hold in her hand. In it could be stored the visual form of a newspaper, with as much news and information and advertising as the computer memory could hold.

By just touching the screen, a reader could turn the pages, bring a story up close, animate a picture into a video clip of the event, or make a reservation in a restaurant she sees advertised there. No leveling of forests. No wasting of paper.

It is a captivating concept. It would make use of the most valuable assets of newspapers, which are their news and editing staffs and their familiar form of organization by page and section.

It would eliminate the slowest and most cumbersome and expensive part of newspaper publishing: the mechanical end, the trucks and, alas, the presses.

And it would use the computer to marry the two shaping forces of my youth—the newspaper and the television.

THE NEWSPAPERS' IDENTITY CRISIS[3]

Recently, readers of *The Kansas City Star* were treated to an intriguing new audio-electronic feature. In a box above a six-paragraph feature story about a rock band headed by Chicago White Sox pitcher Jack McDowell, readers were invited to dial a number to hear some of the band's music. Thirteen hundred people dialed into the newspaper's audio "StarTouch" system to hear brief samples of McDowell's songwriting, singing, and guitar playing.

These days boxed invitations abound as reporters at the *Star* strive to turn the newspaper into a "navigational tool" for readers using their telephones to gain access to the *Star*'s new audio system. "We're turning this technology over to the newsroom," says Scott Whiteside, until recently the *Star*'s vice-president for new product development. "We've told them, 'You have the privilege of redefining journalism. Nobody has done this before.'"

After decades of wringing their hands about the coming of the Information Age but doing little about it, newspaper executives are embarking on the "reinvention" of the daily newspaper—the newest buzzword in industry circles. They have been frightened into doing so by the persistence of their circulation problems, by setbacks in their fight to keep the Bell companies

[3]Article by Doug Underwood, from *Columbia Journalism Review* 30:24–27 Mr/Ap '92. Copyright © 1992 by *Columbia Journalism Review*. Reprinted with permission.

out of the information delivery business, and by the depth of the recession, which has sped the collapse of the industry's retail advertising base.

Gannett's "News 2000" program is a case in point. Editors of local Gannett newspapers are quite literally remolding their beat structures and newsroom organization to respond to perceived reader interests. The just-implemented program is part of Gannett's effort to encourage its local newspapers to pay greater attention to community issues. At the Gannett-owned daily in Olympia, Washington, for example, editors have replaced traditional beats with "hot topic" teams, slapped limits on story length and jumps, added extensive reader service lists, and replaced some reporters with news assistants who gather "news-you-can-use" data from local agencies.

Gannett has taken its cue from the trend-setting *Orange County Register,* which shook up newspaper traditionalists two years ago with its switch to reader-friendly beats like "malls" and "car culture," and from Knight-Ridder's experimental newspaper in Boca Raton, Florida, with its test-marketed formula of news nuggets, pastel hues, multiple graphics, and reader-grabbing features.

Newspapers are also experimenting once again with electronic videotext systems. Many journalists thought videotext was dead when Knight-Ridder shut down its pioneering Viewtron program in the mid-1980s because it couldn't sign up enough subscribers. These days newspapers in Albuquerque and Fort Worth are making a go of modest, low-investment videotext systems that give readers access to electronically archived material that can't be fitted into the daily newshole. At the same time, newspapers in Denver and Omaha shut down more elaborate and expensive videotext experiments, saying there was not yet a market for videotext in their cities. Meanwhile, newspaper executives are watching (nervously, in many cases) as new computer developments point toward the time when today's newspaper, television, computers, and the telephone will be blended into a single multimedia instrument.

Futurists say that all this is just the Information Age finally catching up with newspapers. Paul Saffo, a research fellow at the Institute for the Future in Menlo Park, California, argues that paper is becoming outmoded as computers become society's principal way of storing data. "We'll become paperless like we became horseless," he says. "There are still horses. But little girls ride them."

Amid all the flailing about as newspapers prepare for an uncertain tomorrow, three general strategies can be discerned: efforts to save the newspaper as it is, efforts to augment the newspaper electronically, and efforts to look beyond the newspaper-on-print.

The Future of the Newspaper-As-It-Is

In recent years, front pages with more "points-of-entry" and "scannable" news, marketing programs developed in tandem with the news department, and "news-you-can-use" and reader-written features have proliferated. And yet there is no evidence that the focus on readers—and the fixation on marketing and packaging and redesigns associated with it—has done anything to improve newspapers' prospects. Indeed, even the industry's own consultants now caution against expecting circulation growth from redesigns or the adoption of reader-driven marketing formulas.

James Batten, the chairman of Knight-Ridder, a chain known for the high quality of its journalism, launched what he called a "customer-obsession" campaign, an important part of which was the redesigned Boca Raton *News*. It showed initial circulation jumps. However, last summer the *News* dismissed two circulation managers after their departments allegedly overstated the newspaper's paid circulation—a sign of the pressure the newspaper is feeling to show results for Knight-Ridder.

Today's editors, says Susan Miller, Scripps Howard's vice-president/editorial, have come to believe that reader-driven newspapering can be a "higher calling." The vast majority of staffers are becoming accustomed to the idea that "newspapers are to be of service to readers and are not staffed by a Brahmin class that was chosen to lecture the population," Millers says, adding, "People who refuse to be service-oriented will leave in disgust and say we're pandering and will call us bad names—but they will leave."

Bill Walker, a former *Sacramento Bee* reporter, is one who left. In a piece titled "Why I Quit" in *The San Francisco Bay Guardian*, he wrote: "Nowadays, editors spend their days taking meetings in glass offices, emerging only to issue reporters instructions like this: 'Get me a 12-inch A1 box on the city's reaction to the tragedy. Talk to teachers, kids, the mayor, the bishop. Focus on the shock, the sadness, the brave determination to move on. And don't forget the homeless. We've got color art from the shelter.' Meanwhile, the promotions director is already producing a cheery drive-time radio spot to plug the story . . . . We used to have a saying: no matter how bad journalism was, it beat selling insurance for a living. But no more."

Miller, for her part, predicts that the economics of the industry will lead to a thinning of the ranks of mid-level management. At many organizations those ranks were swollen as newspapers put more emphasis on the planning and packaging of the news product. Miller thinks that the leaner newsroom of the future will mean that more power will be placed in the hands of front-line troops. Bill Baker, Knight-Ridder's vice-president/news, says that the emphasis newspaper companies will be putting on innovation will make entrepreneurial thinking in the newsroom more valued. He adds that several new information products being developed by "The Edge of Knight-Ridder," an internal product-development program, were created by veteran reporters who have "the appetite to follow through on them."

Still, newspaper managers may find it difficult to abandon the traditional hierarchy or change their ways of thinking. Publishers oriented to the bottom-line and newspaper managers who made their way up in a safe, monopolistic environment tend to be wary of creative risk-taking. The temptation to hire another consultant, order up another readership survey, or let an industry organization do their thinking for them will, in most cases, win out over coming up with their own ideas and then investing in them.

Beefing It Up Electronically

Newspapers are making a marginal profit at best in their efforts to find an audience that wants access to an electronic menu of items like restaurant and movie reviews, expanded news stories, sports scores, advance classified ads, business news, and public records. The most popular form of access has been telephone info-lines, and newspapers like *The Kansas City Star* are integrating them into the full operation of the newspaper. Videotext systems are still considered risky, but even editors at newspapers that have abandoned videotext agree that the market for electronic newspapering is growing.

That's certainly the way Gerry Barker, marketing director for the *Fort Worth Star-Telegram's* "Startext" electronic information service, sees it. "The generation coming out of school who are

very computer-oriented—these are the readers of tomorrow,"
Barker says. "People have misjudged it. It's a social revolution
that's happening out there. You can't throw dollars and technology at this and expect it to hatch. It's evolutionary. Just because we
built a few Edsels doesn't mean the car is wrong."

Many analysts attribute the failure of early videotext efforts to
the attempt by newspapers to transfer the newspaper-on-print too
literally onto the computer. "The newspaper's approach to news
has to change in order to be successful in transmitting information
electronically," says Richard Baker, director of corporate communication for CompuServe, a twenty-two-year-old computer communications company with more than 900,000 customers. "Newspapers and magazines have to embrace the concept of sharing the
creation of the news. There needs to be a willingness and openness
to let the readers have a much greater hand in determining what's
the news." Baker adds that the key to CompuServe's success is the
development of customized information and interactive "bulletin
boards."

The pressure on newspapers to become all-service information companies has grown recently as the newspaper industry has
lost court efforts to keep the telephone companies out of the
electronic information business. The experience of the French
Minitel system, which gives telephone users in France access to
telephone directories and a variety of interactive and communications services via mini-computers, is seen as the model for how
U.S. telephone companies may use their monopoly powers to
move in on newspapers' most lucrative business. Yet everything
ultimately argues for a partnership between newspapers and the
telephone companies—and that may already be happening. For
example, *The Seattle Times* (whose publisher, Frank Blethen, has
been one of the vocal critics of the Baby Bells) recently announced that the *Times* was negotiating to team up with US West
to be a data provider on the telephone company's information
network.

The Paperless Newspaper

With the coming developments in electronic data delivery,
many newspaper futurists believe the newspaper-on-print faces a
perilous future. They say videotext operations and the new
computer pagination systems—by means of which newspaper
pages are fully designed and laid out on the computer screen—

are simply crude, first steps toward the multimedia systems that will come to dominate the information industry. In software systems that are already on the market, computer users can pull from the computer's memory a variety of audio-visual material—including printed text, mobile graphics, video images, music, special effects—which let users create their own multimedia productions.

These developments—combined with the advances in computer-transmitted television—present enormous implications for both newspapers and broadcasters. Digital broadcasting—by means of which images are transmitted in a code used by computers—promises to provide a truly multimedia system that will allow text, graphics, and video images to be transmitted to the computer screen. It doesn't take a rocket scientist to see how this development will increase the pressures to blend the now-separate media forms, and companies in the U.S. and Japan have been hurrying digital technology to the marketplace much faster than many predicted.

Many communications conglomerates, now integrated across newspaper and broadcast divisions, are well structured to take advantage of those developments. Knight-Ridder officials are planning for the day (which they see happening within this decade) when these multimedia newspapers will be available on portable, touch-sensitive, flat-panel displays.

Roger Fidler, the director of new media development for Knight-Ridder, predicts a "bright future" for the "essence" of the newspaper. "I don't see print disappearing," he says. "But I see it taking a different form. The question is not whether there will be newspapers in the next century, but who will publish them. I'm not convinced the majority of the newspaper companies today will be in business in the next century."

So what will it be like to be a journalist in the brave new information world? The minimalistic journalism brought about by reader-friendly newspapering has done much to turn news into just another commodity in the marketplace. And as newspapers join the electronic competition, newspaper journalists are likely to find themselves ever more subject to the forces of technological change, the demands of perpetually updating the news for electronic services, and the pressure to think of their work in marketing terms.

As with many other professions in the go-go 1980s, marketing and the bottom-line have become the by-words of newspapering, and new information technologies offer much to encourage that trend. In the years ahead, newspaper companies—and newspaper professionals—can probably expect to bump up and down on a rocky ride of diminished profit margins, failed efforts at experimentation, and intrusions into their markets.

That's the potential dark side. But there are also reasons to be optimistic. The endless newshole promised by computers does offer an answer to the ever-shrinking news columns—and could hold hope for journalists frustrated by the design gimmicks that have increasingly circumscribed the work life of those who produce the text. Newspapers have always been at the base of the information pyramid, providing much of the in-depth information that is then compressed and marketed by the electronic information purveyors. As the explosion of information continues, there will be even more need for highly skilled journalists to root through it, filter out what's important, and help put it into perspective. The demand for more specialty reporting skills, the opportunities for more creative and analytical writing, and the chance to use data bases to do more sophisticated investigative reporting are all potential upsides of electronic newspapering.

Newspaper journalists should also take heart from the fact that virtually none of those who gaze into the future are predicting the near-term demise of the newspaper-on-print. Technology, so far, has been unable to match the efficient way the eye can scan the newspaper page or the way a newspaper can be folded up and carried around—or the way it can be read while breakfasting over coffee and bagels on a Sunday morning.

Newspapers understand their local, or their speciality, markets. And they can offer an intelligent voice in a world where the cacophony of other media seems to be drowning the public in noise it doesn't want to hear. "There are things about a newspaper that are attuned to the human spirit," says Bill Baker of Knight-Ridder, "and it'll be there forever."

MORE IS LESS[4]

In recent years television news programs have been changing as rapidly as the stories being covered. Predictable formats, epitomized by the authoritarian closing words of Walter Cronkite every evening ("And that's the way it is"), have given way to a cacophony of voices and images.

Although they provided an unprecedented window to the world, television stations and especially networks were beset by a declining market share and greatly increased competition. Shortly after all three networks—which also operate their own TV stations, most in the country's largest markets—were taken over by three new owners, their news divisions were required to cover dramatic developments around the globe. Fifty years earlier one newsreel had advertised itself as the "eyes and ears of the world." But in the late 1980s and early 1990s, television really did allow Americans in their living rooms—and citizens of many other countries—to watch dramatic changes of government in Czechoslovakia, Romania, and East Germany; a stirring challenge by students in China; and a very short war in the Middle East.

But the continuing story for the creators of news—the networks—has been their shrinking share of audience. At the beginning of the 1990s, only NBC, through its network entertainment operations, was making a substantial profit; CBS and ABC were at best breaking even. All three were still making substantial profits from stations they owned and operated. But they, like all media, suffered from a marked downturn in the economy, and increased competition from cable television and home video.

Still, NBC, CBS, and ABC remain the three largest generators of electronic media revenues. Even the other two largest cable/media conglomerates cannot challenge this network trio. Indeed, the biggest competition for news attention comes from the networks' own affiliated stations and from news-based alter-

[4]Chapter 1, by Lawrence W. Lichty and Douglas Gomery, from *The Future of News*, edited by Philip S. Cook, Douglas Gomery and Lawrence W. Lichty. (Washington, D.C.: Woodrow Wilson Center Press; Baltimore: Johns Hopkins University Press '92). Copyright © 1992 The Woodrow Wilson International Center for Scholars. Reprinted with permission.

natives to the formerly dignified—more so in retrospect—news summaries provided at the dinner hour.

Some of these new programs do not seem to provide more information. Consider the rise of "tabloid" or "trash" television. This new genre, which in format and style resembles the network evening news shows, is television's version of the *National Enquirer,* and audiences apparently love it. In a number of cities, Fox Television's "A Current Affair," a voyeur's view of the love lives of celebrities and the grizzly details of bizarre murders, or an imitator such as "Hard Copy" ranks as the most-watched program in the key early evening time period. At the same time, "Entertainment Tonight," which also spawned imitators, runs neck-and-neck in ratings with the three network evening news programs.

One response by the three networks to this new sleaze has been to include more entertainment and arts coverage in their own broadcasts—about twice as many minutes in 1990 as in 1989 or 1988. The increase came about because "there isn't anything geopolitical left" to report, according to "NBC Nightly News" executive producer Steve Friedman.

Network executives often rail against the low quality and prurient appeal of these rival programs, but they never fail to find a regular place for them on the schedule of the stations the networks own.

These new programs raise profound ethical problems for the broadcasting industry. It has long been known that in local "sweeps" months (when ratings are measured for purposes of setting local advertising rates) TV broadcasters could spike the ratings by offering programs with more than the usual amount of sex and violence. Do TV viewers differentiate trash TV from straight news, as newspaper readers have long differentiated the sports section from the hard news on the front page? In a charming twist, the struggling (eventually canceled) *USA Today's* television program in October 1988 and February 1989 even provided a daily "sweeps sleaze" update, which, in the guise of reporting, gave the show's producers an opportunity to repeat excerpts of Geraldo Rivera and Phil Donahue programs featuring nudists.

Whether all this competition will drive out all serious and significant reporting or is merely offering audiences a long-wanted choice depends finally upon the audience. As Phil Donahue mused on his experience,

It is amazing what they won't watch. They won't watch male strippers five days a week, [but] you'd better haul them out once in a while if you want to survive in the daytime arena. The audience appears to be largely interested in Madonna, not Managua. Many of our critics work for newspapers with no competition or never see our show. By the end of the year [1991] we hope for mix of entertainment and information.

The proliferation of satellites, minicams, and other new television technology has fundamentally changed news gathering, making it an around-the-clock, around-the-world operation. In the early 1960s news organizations were lucky to get film back from Vietnam in a day or so. Today, reporters cover the world—via satellite—live, in real time. As a result it is possible to program news nonstop, through the networks, Cable News Network (CNN), local stations, C-SPAN, and various other cable services.

Past As Prologue

For many people in the news business or observers of the media, these changes represent a significant evolution. The end of the 1980s was a milepost in that epoch of change. The troubles at CBS, as chronicled by several former employees, spotlight the role of individual executives. These books feature various villains—Gene Janowski, Van Gordon Sauter, Howard Stringer, Lawrence Tisch, Thomas Wyman—and present us a fascinating "inside" look at what has always been the most controversial and most chronicled broadcast news organization.

Although these personalities have had an especially important influence on specific programs and individual documentaries, outside forces have had more general influence on the networks. The people who run broadcast news are driven by a need for more profit in a world of corporate raiders, greater news competition, and increasing alternative television offerings on cable, home video, and, in the future, through high-definition television. To lay the foundation for some conclusions and predictions for the 1990s, let us review recent key changes in the industry.

In March 1987 while Dan Rather worried about the budget and staff cuts at CBS News, Av Westin at ABC took a different tack. In an eighteen-page memo he wrote, "Too many resources, too much money, has undone network news, leaving it vulnerable to indiscriminate cost-cutting from above and unable editorially, creatively, and distinctively to meet the fierce competition from increasingly aggressive and inventive news operations at local stations." After comparing early "Days of Penury" at ABC with more recent "Days of Affluence," he concluded that planned reductions were not so much cuts as elements of "redesign." Westin was really calling for more thought about news and less chasing after stories. The former largess "must be replaced by editorial direction based on thoughtful journalism, insight, and creativity." He went on, "If carried out with care, 'redesign' will result in the building of a superior instrument of electronic news gathering and reporting which will ensure that network news will be around for a long time."

In a *New York Times* op-ed article, Dan Rather grappled with the same issues in different language. Pondering CBS's firing of some two hundred news employees he wrote:

> Our concern, beyond the shattered lives of valued friends and colleagues is: How do we go on? How do we cover the world? Can we provide in-depth reporting and analysis with resources so severely diminished? Can we continue to do our job in the finest tradition of this great organization? In the tradition of Edward R. Murrow, Walter Cronkite, Douglas Edwards, Charles Collingwood? . . . I have said before that I have no intention of participating in the demise of CBS. But do the owners and officers of the new CBS see news as a trust . . . or only as a business venture?

The same criticism has, of course, been made of newspapers, the wire services, and magazines as they have responded to the economic forces of the marketplace. In March 1989, James D. Squires, editor of the *Chicago Tribune,* told members of the American Society of Newspaper Editors, "The pressure of the marketing challenge forced editors to decide they'd better tear down the barriers and learn to master the whole paper or be totally at the mercy of the business side. It is in no way a compromise of editorial integrity. It is in fact the assurance of it."

The "old world" of television news used to begin and end with the continuing profitability of the three networks. In the 1980s came new owners, new competitors, and new methods of operation. Several months before he was "kicked upstairs," the president of the CBS Broadcast Group, Gene Janowski, noted, "I love what I do and I'm not looking to go anywhere. But something my father told me years ago is that the trick is to be an owner."

The networks, despite recent blushes, are not in great financial trouble. Under Lawrence Tisch, CBS sits on nearly $1 billion in cash, principally from the sale of its records division to Sony. Capital Cities/ABC has skillfully hedged its loss in network viewership through cable investments, in particular ESPN. NBC developed its own cable service, CNBC, in April 1989. In the end, what keeps the networks in their special niche is their singular ability to offer sizable audiences to major bulk advertisers. The complete domination of the "good old days" of the networks is over, but no one knows how far network audience shares will shrink. The most important implication of the economics of the 1980s for network operation (news or otherwise) in the 1990s is a management emphasis on "the lean and mean." Make profits now; worry about the long run later.

The networks are giants compared with their independent or cable rivals. Consider the millions involved in the "musical chairs" of news stars in 1989, when Diane Sawyer moved to ABC and Connie Chung moved to CBS. Reportedly, Sawyer earns $7.5 million under her five-year contract; Chung somewhat less. And bidding for talent is not restricted to the networks. In 1989 CBS's "owned and operated" station in New York hired Ernie Anastos from ABC's local station for more than a million dollars a year.

However, the 1990-91 recession forced change. For the first time in memory, local stations did not renew the contracts of highly paid anchors and asked reporters and anchors alike to take salary cuts. Even some network stars were asked to take substantial pay cuts. In part, this was another lesson of the competition of CNN, especially during the Gulf War. In the long run, it is not the news presenter, but the news itself that is the star. According to one executive, networks have begun to ask, "How much will he be missed if he goes? . . . how much will it hurt me when he ends up on the competition?"

Owners and managers of the networks continue to pursue the reporter/anchor/star who can attract the crucial eighteen- to forty-nine-year-old viewers who bring the premium advertising rates. A small move up in the ratings for news can mean millions of extra dollars in revenue, easily enough to cover the high salaries and still generate millions more in profits. Today's "million-dollar club" of TV news stars includes Dan Rather, Tom Brokaw, Peter Jennings, Ted Koppel, Barbara Walters, Bryant Gumbel, Mike Wallace, and the top anchors in the major markets from New York to Chicago to Los Angeles.

Network Audiences

The future of broadcast news rests, as always, with audiences—the TV viewers across the country—and network audiences are eroding. *Newsweek* summarized the problem in apocalyptic terms in an October 1988 "Special Report: The Future of Television":

> With many rivals gnawing at their franchise, ABC, CBS, and NBC have seen their combined share of the prime-time audience plummet from 92 to 68 percent in just 10 years. Even the networks seemingly invincible supremacy over electronic journalism is in jeopardy. Local affiliate stations have suddenly discovered that they don't need the networks anymore to cover the world. . . . According to some prophecies, the nightly network newscast—perhaps the most ritualized manifestation of our teleculture—could be a mere memory by the century's end.

The TV writers' strike in the fall of 1988 further eroded network audiences. Independent stations, on average, now account for about 20 percent of all TV viewing; advertising-supported cable accounts for another 12 percent or so.

When the network audience share during prime time slipped to two-thirds for the thirty-week 1988 season, *USA Today* trumpeted that for "the first time the network share has dropped below 70 percent." For a number of months in the past few years (in particular during the summer), however, the networks' share has occasionally dropped below 60 percent. During the 1988 political conventions, the networks scored their lowest prime-time share ever: less than 50 percent. Indeed, only about one-third of the television audience watched the convention coverage.

Did the 1991 season end the slide, or, more precisely, the rate of decline? We don't know. The three networks had averaged a 63 percent share during prime time—or 74 percent if the Fox (which behaves and advertises itself as a network, but is not a "network" under FCC rules) programs were considered. That is still a very impressive portion of viewer attention when many viewers have more than a hundred alternatives. On the one hand, in the daily press the end of the networks is near. Tom Shales, for the 1991–92 season, announced "TV's Sinking Net Worth " as "The End of an Era."

Yet it seems to us that cable growth—measured in terms of new subscribers, share of viewing, and advertising generated—has slowed and soon may reach a dead calm. No other advertising medium comes close to providing network television's advertising reach and efficiency. The problems of the three networks may be numerous, but each still had revenues in excess of $2 billion.

The networks' main problem is multiple competition. More than half the nation's households have cable service (many with thirty or more channels) plus home video. Still, two-thirds of the audience usually tunes to one of the three networks in prime time. Even in the half of U.S. homes that have cable, the three networks command a remarkable 50 percent share compared with 33 percent for all cable choices.

We agree with most network officials who predict that the network audience slide has begun to level off. Projections for 1995 still give the networks more than a third of all TV advertising dollars, down slightly from today's 37 percent. During the same period advertising dollars for cable are expected to grow from about 5 percent to 7 percent, but the networks will still be the big players on the television block.

Playing of rented or purchased videotapes at home has cut into the network TV audience, particularly for the next generation of adult viewers, today's teenagers and children, but to date at least, most households use home taping as "time shifting," to view a favored program at a different time. Thus, although home video recording certainly has had an effect, it may not be so big a threat to broadcast television as was first thought.

At the end of the 1980s, the go-go world of media takeovers had slowed for several reasons, including the difficulty of determining real value in the face of increased competition among cable companies, networks, and independents, and the threat of government reregulation. The market for the nation's 650 network-affiliate stations appears to have peaked. With single-digit growth expected for advertising and the competing attraction of new television technologies, the over-the-air television business is simply not as good as it once was.

These numbers will remain the order of the day even as the number of television households continues to increase. (By 1995 we should be nearing 100 million television households.) Weep not for the networks; they will survive because they continue to offer the advertiser the best value and reach for the money. There simply is no viable alternative on the horizon.

News Competition

With regard to news competition, our conclusions may be summarized as follows:

• There will always be several national newscasts.
• There will be one newscast on each of the three "traditional" national networks (ABC, CBS, NBC).

• Total news time (morning, evening, late night, weekends, specials) will expand on these three networks.

• It will be a long time indeed before there is less time devoted to news than there is now.

• Expansion will take place outside prime time.

• The greatest growth will be in news/information and magazine formats, especially those providing specific categories of information or appealing to special audiences, such as business, entertainment, and health programs.

• All news-gathering organizations, especially the networks, will seek more cooperative deals, alliances, and exchanges among themselves in order to reduce costs further.

• Networks will continue to seek ways to earn additional income from their news gathering and other current activities—providing news to local stations and worldwide, selling footage and videotapes of coverage, and producing special and historical programs.

"Local" news will follow a different path. The relationship between local newscasts and network news has always been complementary. It is now possible for local stations to use their own or rented satellite uplinks and to send reporters and anchors to cover important stories. Hundreds covered Mikhail Gorbachev's visit to Washington in December 1987, several presidential primaries, and both political conventions in 1988. Despite all the talk about the supremacy of CNN, coverage of the Gulf War reminded many viewers of the primacy of the networks in providing international news. Furthermore, dozens of local stations sent their own reporters and camera crews to Saudi Arabia. Virtually all this effort was for promotional reasons: Local stations covered these stories primarily to build the credibility of anchors and reporters. Some of this reporting may be excellent and useful, but it provides no real competition for the networks on a day-to-day basis.

Circumstantial evidence clearly supports the notion that network news audiences and local news audiences are closely linked. Statistical analysis shows the most important determinants of local news ratings for individual stations are, first, the rating of the network news program that follows it, and second, the rating of the preceding program.

Analysis of early evening news programs on fifty-seven stations in major, medium-size, and small markets by Raymond L. Carroll shows that the early evening newscast on these stations devoted an average of less than three minutes (15 percent) to national and world news, compared with more than fourteen minutes (82 percent) to local and state items. Satellite feeds from the networks to local stations, broadcast before the network evening news is on the air, are really important only for the occasional, big, breaking stories, especially sensational crimes and disasters.

The trend to longer, one- and two-hour, early evening newscasts by network affiliates is one (small) factor in the decline of network news audiences. The effect has been greatest in the West and at the largest market stations. The majority of stations throughout the country still offer only thirty minutes of local news in the early evening.

The local late-night newscasts are heavily dependent on edited network news stories narrated by the local anchors. To meet the competition of other syndicated news services, the networks have increased their own "feeds" of news material using stories not needed for the evening newscast, material from other news programs (such as the early morning), and material provided by affiliate stations.

A vivid, if self-serving illustration of the interrelationship between station and network is provided by the frequent use by late-night local newscasts of "news stories" directly related to preceding entertainment programs. Especially during sweeps, the networks give affiliates a few extra seconds before the end of entertainment programs that precede the late local news for promotion of upcoming news items. The networks also suggest local stories that tie in to the preceding network dramas. NBC, for example, prodded affiliates to inject "news" stories on "how the rich and famous in your area live" to follow an NBC movie about a Hollywood star who was killed. NBC also suggested that a story on "colorful and flamboyant lawyers in your area" follow a "Perry Mason" TV movie. Memos to stations prepared by a "Sweeps Task Force," according to one network executive, sought to exploit the "great impact on both the lead-in show and your late news, if you find a common thread of promotion."

Since the early 1980s, cable has clearly been cutting into the ratings for local news. Research by James Webster shows that between 1982 and 1987 local news audiences declined about 6 percent in larger markets in homes with basic cable and nearly 20 percent in homes with pay cable as well. The loss of audience was even greater in smaller markets.

Newscast competition is likely to be keener among stations in the same market than between affiliates and networks. This competition is evident in the growing use by local stations of video footage created by amateurs. For example, Seattle TV stations aired the first footage ever of the FBI apprehending a fugitive on its "Most Wanted List." (The person who tipped off the FBI also alerted a friend who appeared on the scene with his personal camcorder.) The camcorder has become a staple of Fox Television's "A Current Affair," which has aired footage ranging from tapes of "preppy" murderer Robert Chambers, out on bail and partying, to a child's recording of his toys being bounced around in a California earthquake.

TV news organizations, under budget and competitive constraints, now recognize the nation's 2 million camcorder owners as a pool of 2 million potential stringers. Some actively solicit footage. No one rejects unique coverage, whatever the quality, of a disaster or crime in progress, and most organizations pay little more than a token fee ($100).

CNN has been the most aggressive. Since January 1987 CNN has been promoting its "News Hound" service, encouraging viewers to call a toll-free number if they have a scoop. CNN has used about four submissions per month, including scenes of a train wreck in Sacko, Montana, and a tornado in Hilton Head, South Carolina. An amateur with a camera was on the scene when the Aloha Air Boeing 737 made its miraculous landing in Maui, Hawaii, after its fuselage had ripped open. While professional news media were flying in to cover the aftermath, CNN airlifted the VHS cassette to the island of Hawaii, where it was converted to three-quarter-inch tape and sent by satellite to CNN headquarters in Atlanta.

The most explosive recent examples include a March 1991 tape of Los Angeles police officers beating a suspect—a tape shot from a balcony overlooking the scene. In Washington, D.C., robbers even videotaped their own crimes—the tapes were shown at the trial and many times on national and local newscasts. Anyone who has vacationed recently has a good idea of the millions of portable video cameras available to catch almost any dramatic event.

At the local level the CBS-owned and -operated station in Philadelphia, WCAU, has had "Channel 10 Newswatchers" since June 1988. One "Newswatcher" classic was submitted by two college students who witnessed a tractor-trailer accident that closed

Interstate 95, the main East Coast artery. The accident was the lead story of the day, and WCAU had an exclusive. Frank N. Magid Associates, the broadcast news consultant firm, has urged its local station clients around the nation to set up similar operations.

Put simply, local news is important to stations because it is profitable and it is virtually the only programming that originates with the local stations. Thus local news makes money, distinguishes these stations from the cable networks, and helps build an image in the local market. The ratings and shares for local television news remain impressive; in New York City, the local CBS, NBC, and ABC stations, all owned and operated by the networks, generate $100 million in revenue annually.

The topic of revenue brings us back to the need to recruit and pay "talent." Consider the results of talent raids in St. Louis in recent years. In 1986 the third-ranking CBS affiliate KMOV challenged the second-place ABC affiliate by hiring a new anchor, a new consumer reporter, and a new weekend anchor. Soon KMOV was challenging the top-ranked station. According to Arbitron, KMOV's 5 P.M. news broadcast rose from a 9 rating in May 1986 to a 15 early in 1989. The 10 P.M. news (late night in the central time zone) went from a 13 rating to a 17. In St. Louis, where anchors typically earn $200,000 to $250,000 a year, those rating increases were worth several million dollars in ad revenue.

Members of Congress certainly understand the new environment of local news and, in recent years, have become even more sophisticated in their use of television, creating "interviews" that air on local stations in their districts.

Congress has long maintained studios on Capitol Hill, but until recently they were rarely used for breaking news stories. Instead, shows were taped days in advance and carefully scripted, to be broadcast on Sunday morning public affairs shows, not the nightly news.

Now, however, the Senate and House recording studios have satellite links to beam live shows to local stations. Increasingly, the studios are taking a backseat to the productions of the National Republican Campaign Committee, the Democratic Congressional Campaign Committee, the Senate Republican Conference, and the Senate Democratic Policy Committee.

The Senate Republican Conference set the pace in 1985 when it installed a microwave tower atop the Hart Senate Office Building. The Democrat's flagship facility, which had opened a year

earlier, did not establish a satellite link until 1987. It is located in
the Democratic Congressional Campaign Committee's $3 million
Harriman Communications Center in the basement of Democratic Party Headquarters on South Capitol Street.

Every Wednesday afternoon when Congress is in session, the
National Republican Campaign Committee positions a camera
crew on the lawn outside the Capitol and invites Republican members of Congress to stop by and make "news" for local stations
back home. One by one, members appear before the camera, and
"field" questions posed by their own press secretaries. Later the
same day (in time for the evening news) the National Republican
Campaign Committee beams the appropriate portions of the tape
to the local stations that have been alerted for the satellite feed.
Viewers are not told that these are not typical interviews in which
an objective reporter asks questions. Local stations pay nothing
for these submissions, and many news directors not only use them
but request them.

The Changing Network Newscast

Network owners have begun to bring in new managers to
redesign their nightly news. Some of these managers have come
from outside the television field, as is the case with NBC News,
headed since July 1988 by a veteran print journalist, Michael
Gartner. Controversy has swirled around him ever since. Upon
the appointment of new presidents for the CBS Broadcast Group
and CBS News in July 1988, Lawrence Tisch was quoted as saying, "If we can't win the war with this bunch, then it's my fault."
He seems to have lost the initial battle, for his new chief of news
operations lasted only two years.

The war was being fought under new rules of engagement.
The deregulation of American broadcasting, begun under President Carter and accelerated in the Reagan years, enabled the
networks in general, and the news departments in particular, to
operate simply as profit-making sectors of major economic institutions. NBC News (and the other networks) made deep staff cuts
while General Electric, unhindered by federal regulators, diver-
sified NBC by moving into the cable television business. The networks were no longer "single-product" companies delivering
their wares via the "public" airwaves. They had become part of
big business, aiming at profits and caring little about "public interest" obligations fostered by earlier administrations in Washing-

ton. As always, the networks were locked in an all-out struggle for higher ratings.

Most striking has been the rise of ABC News since the appointment of Roone Arledge as president in 1977. ABC's news audience has expanded along with ABC's entertainment audience. More recently, ABC has been aided by the growing stature of anchorman Peter Jennings, by the addition and retention of a number of veteran correspondents (while others were being fired at CBS), and by the growth of other news programs, in particular "Nightline," "Good Morning America," and "This Week with David Brinkley." Arledge is often praised by "insiders" for his ability to recognize and build "talent" like Jennings, Ted Koppel, and more recently, the morning news anchors, Paula Zahn (who left for CBS) and Forrest Sawyer. But "Primetime Live," featuring Diane Sawyer and Sam Donaldson, took much longer to find its audience.

From the time the special chemistry of Chet Huntley and David Brinkley was discovered at the 1956 political conventions and Walter Cronkite began his rise to evening news anchorman at the 1960 political conventions, the networks have considered the quadrennial elections as the "Super Bowl" for news ratings. The primaries are the seasons, the conventions the playoffs, and election night is the championship. Probably because of higher prime-time network ratings, NBC won top ratings for four of five important election events in 1988 when the three networks were on the air at the same time (but lost to ABC on election night 1990).

For all the problems of the three network evening news shows, their share of audience (the percentage of homes with the set on watching a specific program) has remained about the same for five years—about 60 percent of all viewing during the hour in which they are broadcast. Much competition among them is waged with dueling anchors. Dan Rather stayed steadily in place after replacing Walter Cronkite. For several years Peter Jennings seemed poised to move into first place. Even NBC's Tom Brokaw said that Jennings "has the better élan" and is a "better performer" than himself or Rather. "World News Tonight," the ABC evening newscast, was briefly in first place in the spring of 1988 and again in the spring of 1989. By early 1990 Jennings began to be ahead most weeks, with NBC most frequently third. During the Gulf War the audiences of all three evening news programs increased, and special coverage was often the highest rated of all programming during the week. The Gulf coverage seemed to solidify ABC's hold on first—critics and viewers often noted Jennings's greater foreign experience and ABC's broader range of news stars. More than ever before it is a very close race tallied weekly in most major newspapers and all trade publications. Often less than a single, sometimes only a tenth, of a rating point separates the triad.

Special Promotions

Note the appeals of these CBS news promotions:

• Rather: "You know your mother always told ya—stand up, look 'em in the eye, and tell them what you know. That's what we do on the 'CBS Evening News.'"
• Rather: "A good evening news broadcast includes the following: what you need to know, what you want to know, perspective, context, and maybe a new way of looking at a story you already know about."
• Announcer (over pictures of Dan Rather reporting from Mississippi, Georgia, Vietnam, Cuba, Mexico City, and Moscow): "Dan Rather, he's been there, he'll be there."
• Announcer (over a picture of Dan Rather in Vietnam, 1966): "Before Dan Rather went to the front desk he went to the front lines."

Although these promotions illustrate the image that CBS seeks to project for Walter Cronkite's successor, Rather has become the most controversial of TV news anchors as a result of a series of incidents—including a six-minute sulk away from the anchor desk in September 1987 when CBS tennis coverage ran over its projected time and the interview-turned-shouting match with candidate George Bush in January 1988. *TV Guide* even built a recent article around the observations of a few "therapists" who were asked to comment on Dan Rather.

According to several surveys, Rather is the most popular with the general public. He wrote in his first autobiography, "I am not, never have been, a natural smiler." But particularly during the 1988 presidential campaign he tried, strained even, to be homey and personal. Can anyone image Walter Cronkite's making any of the following comments Rather made?

• "An Iceland chill back in the air . . . close but no cigar . . ." (on the summit in October 1986).

• "One of the candidates saw the light at the end of the tunnel, and the light was out" (referring to Pat Robertson).

• "You talk about your blowouts . . . the big train, George Bush, keeps rolling along."

• "What's at stake has always been the sizzle" (concluding a "48 Hours" segment about auto racing).

One week, Rather ended the broadcast with "Courage"; later he tried "That's some of the world today"—as if he was still searching for a persona to replace Cronkite with his familiar closing. These are minor points but from just such trivialities network news programs rise and fall.

Most journalists and TV critics would like newscast content, rather than presentation, to be the most important part of television reporting. Executives and producers are undecided on the relative weight of each, but all agree on the value of anchors, star reporters, sets and visuals, story order, and the rest. It is an evolving business and with the large audiences for TV news (at least relative to other news media) and the high salaries have come the public attention that most serious journalists disdain.

One of the first acts of David Burke, who moved to CBS News from ABC in the summer of 1988 and was let go two years later, was to read the riot act to employees about leaking stories and talking to the press. Tom Brokaw also has suggested that the news organizations should be allowed to do their business in "private." Howard Stringer, who moved up from CBS News president to head of the CBS/Broadcast Group, has given a number of speeches arguing that the network's salvation is "good programming and ratings which generally increase sales." He proposes "nurturing the creative process" and working more closely with the Hollywood producers who provide the bulk of prime-time programming. Presumably, a stronger network means a larger budget for the news division and more money to the affiliates. In 1991, Stringer argued that another solution was to "find ways to get the costs down." The network's continued economic problems reemphasized the dependence of TV news on the entertainment part of the business.

Within the news division at CBS another evolving strategy has been to project a single "news presence" across all programs. Note these examples:

• For several years an increasing number of reporters, especially those from Washington, have gone to New York to present their stories and sit across from Rather to chat or exchange small talk.

• "60 Minutes" reporters were used as special correspondents on the evening news as an experiment for several weeks.

• Charles Kuralt assisted Rather in reporting from Moscow and Japan.

• When President Bush traveled to Japan for Emperor Hirohito's funeral, CBS used a staff of more than one hundred and had segments related to Japan and the trip, many with Rather's presence, on all the news and magazine documentary programs.

• During the Gulf crisis a special war room set was built, Rather traveled to the Middle East several times, appeared on many special reports, and usually was the primary interviewer of the network's expert consultants.

Will President Robert Wright of GE allow NBC, the top-rated network overall, to remain clearly in third place in evening news and other prime-time information formats? Will CBS quietly let ABC-Jennings-Koppel inherit the mantle of first place in news? As though goading the others, ABC, using the cumulative ratings of its news programming, has advertised that "more people get their news from ABC than any other source."

Over the years the single most striking feature of the network evening news programs has been their sameness. In a sample of network evening news programs during 1988 we found that all three had the same lead story more than one-third of the time, and the initial stories were different on all three only one-fifth of the time.

A clear recent trend is for each program to try for distinctive, longer-than-average features; both ABC and NBC have regular end-of-the-week features—"Person of the Week" and "Assignment America," respectively. After the election in November 1988 ABC's newscast began offering a regular "in-depth" segment labeled "The American Agenda." NBC has had such features since the 1970s.

In September 1990, "NBC Nightly News" began offering a feature report each night under the rubric "Daily Difference." These were suspended during much of the Gulf War, but began again in March 1991. CBS had been less routine in this regard; except for stories divided into several parts or major excursions

involving Rather, such features are confined to weekend shows
such as "Inside Sunday." In April 1991 CBS instituted "Eye [the
CBS logo] on America." Rather explained: "We try to bring you
interesting stories each night about important issues facing our
country." We wonder what this definition says about the other
stories in the newscasts. But the trend is obvious, as the networks
cut budgets, fire personnel, and close foreign and local bureaus.
The emphasis will remain, according to an NBC spokesperson,
"on analysis and interpretation of news.". . .

Cable Television

Almost every major cable network boasts some news or information during the day. Programmers as varied as C-SPAN, the
Discovery Channel, the Arts and Entertainment Cable Network,
the CNBC, ESPN, Black Entertainment Television, Movietime,
Showtime, HBO, MTV, VH-1, the Weather Channel, the Travel
Channel, and localized "News 12 Long Island" offer some information programming. Surveys indicate that once cable has been
in a household for a while, these information/news services become important to the typical subscriber.

There have been innovations in news reporting on cable television, particularly with the rise of CNN, both its regular and
headline service; the financial and weather channels; and the two
C-SPAN channels, which telecast the proceedings of the United
States Senate, the House of Representatives, and other govern-
mental and nongovernmental activities, both in the United States
and abroad. Cable news networks, which now reach more than
half the nation's households, offer television watchers significant
viewing alternatives, thus forcing news offerings to compete even
more strongly for audiences.

CNN achieved recognition at the two political conventions in
1984. Executives at the three major network news organizations
(and many other news-gathering offices) now stay tuned to CNN
Headline News service all the time. CNN may not be an equal
competitor, but it is certainly a growing—and profitable—force.
CNN runs a lean operation, based on nonunion (save in New
York, Washington, and Los Angeles) young workers. To quote
executive vice-president Ed Turner (no relation to Ted), "We
don't have the fat that accumulates with any organization that is
20 or 30 years old like our friends at the other networks." CNN
has more than one thousand employees and bureaus in cities

around the world, including Madrid, Brussels, Geneva, Athens, Manila, Seoul, and Santiago. In 1991 it added offices in India, Brazil, and Jordan.

While the Gulf coverage momentarily boosted CNN's popularity in the United States, the lasting effects are not yet measurable. CNN was already well established; its position is now assured. Most important, during the war CNN was introduced to many new viewers worldwide; often stations carried CNN in lieu of their own programming during the most dramatic incidents.

CNN's highest ratings have been tied to disasters and major breaking stories. The highest rating CNN had received before the Gulf War was a 7.4 for its October 16, 1987, coverage of infant Jessica McClure's entrapment in a well in Midland, Texas. Next highest was a 7.0 rating for the August 2, 1985, Delta airlines crash in Dallas and the April 14, 1984, bombing of Libya by the U.S. Air Force. At the beginning of the Gulf air war, January 16, 1991, CNN was being watched in nearly a fifth of all cable homes, but this sum, however impressive, still did not equal the ratings for any of the three networks. The networks still had a much larger potential audience (only 61 percent of all households received cable). Nonetheless, with three reporters in Baghdad telephoning the only reports of the first night of bombing to the outside world, and with its later, controversial, live coverage by Peter Arnett from Baghdad via satellite, CNN clearly received a significant boost. But many critics did note that after this dramatic beginning, CNN's halo seemed to dim. Several studies did indicate, however, that a growing share of viewers thought CNN had provided the "best coverage." Clearly, the Gulf War marked a beginning; CNN is poised to be the television news organization of the future.

CNN was evolving in other ways as well. According to Paul Amos, executive vice-president in charge of news programming, "As we mature, we are beginning to look at ourselves more as a program-driven network than [as] a generic news network." By May 1988, almost 40 percent of CNN's weekday schedule consisted of five and a half hours of talk programming and four hours of show business, financial, and sports news programs, plus repeats of programs.

For a year leading up to the 1988 presidential election, CNN presented a nightly thirty-minute program of campaign news. The program did not have a large audience—in the East and Midwest it competed with the network evening news in most markets—but it helped establish the network image. It was also a feast for political news junkies. Live coverage of a number of events, including congressional hearings, have similarly shaped the public's view of CNN. Some recent research indicates that people often think of CNN on a par with the older networks when a big story breaks.

To counter CNBC, CNN Headline News began early in 1989 to put a business ticker at the bottom of the frame, and inserted more business news into its features. With CNN Headline News promoting the regular headlines on the hour and the business news as well, CNN aims to function more like a magazine. To quote Ed Turner again, "Any good magazine offers room for many different departments. But the glue that holds it all together is the news of the day."

In covering the news for cable TV, CNN dominates but it is not alone. C-SPAN has become more than simply a television record of the activities of the United States Congress, especially during 1990–91 with live coverage of state and defense department briefings and a plethora of other special wartime coverage. Indeed, of the more than 17,000 hours of programming on C-SPAN each year, Congress now accounts for only 2,000 hours. C-SPAN's viewership has broadened in recent years. The highest percentage of viewers among the 42 million subscribers comes from people between the ages of twenty-five and fifty-four. The 1988 election pushed up viewership; indeed, between 1984 and 1988 C-SPAN's audience grew 184 percent. In 1989, C-SPAN stepped up its promotion with advertising campaigns in major national publications, and it has wooed cable operators with behind-the-scenes tours of Washington.

A unique local cable news program is "News 12 Long Island," a unit of Rainbow Programming Enterprises, which is a subsidiary of Cablevision and NBC Cable. Launched on December 15, 1986, "News 12" took a local access channel and brought news to an area that had been inadequately served by the New York stations. In the first year, "News 12"'s goal was simply to persuade people to tune in. In 1988 the goal was to gather advertisers. "News 12" serves more than a half-million subscribers on Long Island. The same concept may be tried in Connecticut, New Jersey, and Westchester County.

"News 12" programming mimics all-news radio on television. From 6 A.M. to 9 A.M., viewers get a glimpse of the news headlines, sports, weather, and traffic conditions. Cameras positioned along major highways into New York City provide traffic news. Every fifteen minutes, the segments are repeated. From 9 A.M. until 5 P.M., "News 12" offers a series of breaking news reports, features, interviews, and weather information. From 5 P.M. to 10 P.M., "News 12" summarizes the day's events on Long Island, as well as presenting world news from the CONUS World Network and Worldwide Television News. The staff, including technicians, tops one hundred. Although "News 12" is clearly the most ambitious local news service, hundreds of individual cable systems also provide area news, albeit less comprehensively.

A number of other regional all-news cable programs have been proposed. By October of 1991, however, only those in Orange County, California, and Washington, D.C., are actually operating. A European all-news satellite service operated from London but was available only on a limited basis and seemed in grave financial trouble.

The smallest changes often indicate the bigger trends. In 1991 first CNN, then NBC and CBS each began to display its network logo—the stylized CNN, a peacock, and an eye—at regular intervals in the bottom right hand of the corner of the screen. Station call letters had been used before to remind cable viewers what station they were watching—because one station was often found on different cable "channels" on different systems. Such devices are the equivalent of radio stations' constantly repeated call letters and slogans. This practice may remind us how interchangeable the news formats and personnel are, but it says more about the audience. With remote tuners, viewers can zip from channel to channel.

The Survival of News Programming

To conclude, let us return to the changing economics of network news. The enormous investment in news by the three networks, estimated to be $750 million per year, assures the continued dominance of network news, but a growing variety of continual news will probably be offered by a multitude of sources. CNN, C-SPAN, and CNBC/FNN, to name but three, will tender information around the clock. Television news will never approach the narrow casting formulas of today's radio industry, but the cable subscriber will be able to watch more news than anyone thought possible during the heyday of the three television networks two decades ago.

This proliferation, however, will continue to have its downside. Some form of news as entertainment, in a changing format, will always be with us. Talk shows may go out of fashion, and tabloid TV will certainly not maintain the ratings it enjoyed in the late 1980s.

Exactly how evolving technology will affect the television news business remains unpredictable. As recently as 1974, when the Vietnam War was winding down, film still had to be flown out, and satellite time had to be booked in advance.

During the Gulf War, however, live coverage from all over the globe served the world twenty-four hours a day. It is safe to predict that, as the technology improves, the effects of television news will be felt in ways we cannot yet anticipate. Television news will continue to change, if only because its role in society and in the economy will continue to be redefined.

BEYOND BROADCAST JOURNALISM[5]

It isn't fashionable to like TV, but there seems to be no stopping it. If kids aren't playing interactive video games on the screen, parents are shopping on it, ordering movies, watching Congress vote, or tuning in continual weather forecasts and up-to-the-second sports. We can see Nelson Mandela walk out of jail, watch Cruise missiles roar over Baghdad, sit in on public discussions of public officials' sexual behavior, join jurors in once-forbidden courtrooms.

Yet television's very success has knocked one of its crown jewels—broadcast journalism—off its pins. It no longer seems feasible for news to compete in its current form with all the other things that can now be done with/on/via a television set. In fact, commercial broadcast news, network and local, is struggling to survive in its native habitat.

For broadcasters in general, and broadcast journalists in particular, the worst is by no means over. In the coming months, new technological Godzillas will be stirring. The '90s will see additional evolutionary leaps for the box that dominates our living rooms.

[5]Article by Jon Katz, first appeared in the *Columbia Journalism Review* 30:19–23 Mr/Ap '92. Copyright © 1992 by Jon Katz. Reprinted by permission of Brandt & Brandt Literary Agents, Inc.

Some changes will be instantly apparent, on display in stories like the presidential campaign. Others will evolve less noticeably. But news media already battered by recession, defecting youth, cable and VCR competition, and tabloid telecasts have little relief in sight.

The challenges described below are not simply economic—they strike at the heart of how issues are identified and examined, at what viewers see, at what a news medium is and does. Broadcast journalism may have to redefine its mission, its fundamental sense of purpose and reason for being.

Local Cable News

Later this year [1992], when Time Warner plugs in its twenty-four hour cable news operation—New York One News—in New York City, a new age of truly local television news will dawn. A few states and major cities (including Washington) already have local cable news channels, but New York's will be the largest and most visible. Individual TV stations have always called their news programs local, but few are. Most are regional outlets whose newscasts air a mere dozen daily stories, plus sports and weather. Grass-roots news—fires, city council elections, zoning board flaps, high school football—has been the almost-exclusive province of daily and weekly newspapers.

Local cable news operations will change that. Programming around the clock, they'll have more news time to fill in one day than a network news division or local commercial station gets in weeks. They have the air time already, and satellite trucks and ENG (electronic news gathering) vans—which send microwave signals back to station receivers—have given cable operations the cost-effective technology with which to originate live from anywhere: a Christmas Eve concert by your local church choir, the high school's commencement ceremonies. Soccer league championships will come to television in the same manner that the Olympics now do—live and at considerable length. Imagine the viewership when your township council debates whether or not to double your property taxes, or the board of education decides whether or not to offer free condoms to high school students, and the local cable channel invites you to register your opinion via touch-tone phone.

If all politics is local, news is even more so. The existing mainstream media, broadcast and print, will have to contend with live news not just from Moscow but from Main Street. Television will be able to tell you where all those sirens are headed, and show you the fire as well.

Local cable will pose serious news challenges for advertising and marketing departments, since retailers—furniture stores, home appliance chains, discount houses—will find broadcast advertising opportunities more affordable and appealing.

Time Warner has also recently begun signing up subscribers to the country's first 150-cable channel operation in Queens, New York. Called Quantum, and described by company officials as a "video highway" into the home, the new channel brings an additional technological dimension and potential to television. It offers about half again as many additional channels as the largest systems now in operation, providing cable companies the means to offer specialized experimental, informational, educational, and other services. The system includes fifty-seven channels for pay-per-view movies and special events, with sixteen different movies available at all times—there's even a NASA channel. Quantum will eventually offer new high-definition television, interactive voice technology, and links with computers, fax machines, and a new generation of PCNs—personal communications networks.

The Video Culture Will Expand

More than 40 million home entertainment systems— Nintendo, Sega, Genesis—are now installed in American homes. New services like the Miami-based Video Jukebox Network allow subscribers to dial up their own music videos. The network now has 13 million subscribers. Sports channels are experimenting with interactive controls that would permit viewers to choose from a variety of camera angles, in effect making each viewer his or her own director. Specialized programming will join with Baby Bell computer systems and home entertainment programs to ensnare anyone with a TV set.

In January, the Federal Communications Commission designated a special radio frequency for interactive over-the-air television services. The frequency would allow television users to order take-out food from local restaurants, pay credit card and utility bills, and call up sports scores by operating remote control devices.

MTV, the cable music channel, has its own daily and weekend news broadcast and a staff of reporters and broadcasts. While MTV news concentrates on rock music, it has also aired stories on politicians like David Duke and non-music issues like AIDS and human rights. The video culture has spawned its own print publications as well. *Entertainment Weekly,* one of the fastest-growing magazines in America, often skillfully and professionally crosses the line between traditional issues and popular culture, especially in areas where the two fuse. The magazine recently devoted a cover story to sexual harassment in the entertainment industry, and another to the controversy surrounding the movie *JFK.*

Pay-Per-View

The Olympics have always been considered a quasi-news event, a marriage between geopolitics, a nationalism, and sports. The 1972 terrorist attack on the Israeli Olympic team in Munich and the barring and readmission of South Africa from competition make it clear that world sports and world politics can merge.

But this year [1992] NBC will make broadcasting history by presenting 1,080 hours of Barcelona Olympics on pay-per-view cable channels, along with the network's free coverage. The cost will vary, depending on how many events viewers subscribe to watch, but network officials estimate the average cost will be $125. Regardless of whether sports addicts or regular Olympics fans will pay extra to watch more complete coverage of specific events, pay-per-view presents a significant challenge to the already pressed commercial networks. Many mainstream journalists have viewed the approach of pay-per-view television with horror, concerned that the free dissemination of information that characterized broadcast journalism will be impeded. Possibly, but another option is that busy, distracted Americans will be able to choose the type of news and special-event programming they want, when they want it.

C-SPAN

Cable's public service channel will become one of the most important sources of government and political news in America, probably during this presidential election year. C-SPAN already is on all day in many news bureaus, lobbyists' and bureaucrats' offices, and public interest group headquarters, broadcasting congressional debates, key policy speeches, and discussions. During the presidential campaign—when the networks all say they will send fewer people, devote less airtime, and spend less money—C-SPAN will be offering round-the-clock mainstream press conferences, call-ins, debates, and conferences with no journalists to get in the way. When it isn't airing congressional debates, it might air the Russian Evening News, as it does every day at 6 P.M., go live to Portsmouth, New Hampshire, for President Bush's address to the local Rotary Club, invite *Washington Post* reporter Bob Woodward to take calls about the series he recently co-authored with David Broder on Vice-President Dan Quayle, broadcast *JFK* producer Oliver Stone's luncheon address to the National Press Club, or air Joint Congressional Economic Committee Hearings on a proposed "Marshall Plan for America." "The networks used to be the video record of the campaign," said Tim Russert, senior vice-president of NBC News, in an interview with *The New York Times* in December. "Now C-SPAN has taken that role."

Trawlers

One of the most-feared new phenomena in broadcasting is the growing tendency of switcher-armed viewers to "trawl" through the channels on cable and commercial networks, skimming past one broadcast after another, pausing only briefly. Networks refused to release surveys they've commissioned that disclose precise numbers on the enormous audience shifts, and for good reason: one of the annoyances viewers no longer need endure, even for a second, is commercials. Subscribers pay for cable, guaranteeing cable operators some revenue aside from commercial time, but networks have no such fallback.

Trawling presents serious public policy implications, as well as electronic ones. One network executive conceded that during the gulf war, "our overnights [ratings] told us that millions of people would shift to CNN the second a commercial came on. Often they wouldn't come back. It's amazing, but on a given night when there's a big story, you have literally millions of people—huge chunks of the country—jumping back and forth to avoid commercials or boring guests." It also raises the question of whether Americans will have the patience to focus on serious issues—health care, homelessness, violence—when it's so easy to hop to movies around the clock.

The Baby Bells

Newspapers and broadcasters had been dreading—and lobbying against—the unleashing of these potential communications
monsters for years. They've lost. The federal courts have freed
these companies—calling them babies is like calling the Terminator "Toodles"—to enter the information market with computers
that access financial and other information, and with message
systems that will expand Americans' ability to chat electronically
with like-minded people nationwide. This technology has existed
for some years, but the Baby Bells, which already own and operate many of the telephone lines and transmission systems the
technology requires, have the marketing and economic muscle to
make them attractive to consumers.

Sometime in the next year the Baby Bells are expected to
offer information ranging from sports scores to stock market
quotations, from electronic storage of medical and dental records
to home banking and shopping and video services that allow students to view school lectures from home. The technology will
enable users to control appliances remotely and to display electronic Yellow Pages, which newspaper publishers dread will displace classified advertising. Telecommunications analysts believe
Congress will eventually allow the Baby Bells to compete directly
with cable companies by offering television programs.

Live Real-Time Coverage of Everything

You Were There and you will be there more and more frequently. The gulf war, the aborted coup in the former Soviet
Union, the Clarence Thomas-Anita Hill confrontation, and the
William Kennedy Smith trial highlighted an emerging pattern in
big-story coverage, one that is born of TV technology but functions almost independently of traditional journalistic notions.

All these stories were covered live, in "real time." All connected the viewer in unprecedentedly direct ways. The role of the
correspondent seemed much diminished. Reporters and anchors
were hosts, telling us where we were and, most of the time, where
we were going, but seeming to know little more than the rest of us
about what was really happening, or what it meant.

In the William Kennedy Smith trial, cable continued to shoulder aside the technological, legal, and cultural barriers that have
blocked TV from many of the country's courtrooms, demonstrat-

ing again how specialized cable news coverage can provide airtime not available to commercial broadcast news, and in the case of specialized channels like the Court Channel, specialized expertise about subjects like the law as well.

Even when the biggest stories erupt—the gulf war, Clarence Thomas—the commercial networks can't afford to air them as extensively as cable. It costs too much now for the networks to junk hours of prime-time entertainment, but covering live news is precisely what cable is set up to do.

The challenge for broadcast news has never seemed more fundamental: at a time when television technology can take us almost everywhere to cover almost anything, what precisely is the new role of the broadcast journalist? To introduce live coverage? Or to explain, shape, and comment on it?

Retrenchment For Most Fixed-Time Newscasts

The great fixed-time newscasts of network and local news—America's common bulletin boards through the '60s, '70s, and mid-'80s—are fragmented and in disarray. With cable news on the air around the clock, why should we wait for half an hour of evening news? And even if we wanted to sit down and watch, everybody's too busy.

Breaking hard news will become the virtually exclusive province of cable news channels, which have no expensive entertainment broadcasts to preempt when war or scandal breaks out. In vivid contrast to the expensive, cumbersome anchor-bureau model of the networks—which kept correspondents and producers sitting around in distant bureaus with nothing to do much of the time while paying anchors millions of dollars a year for appearing on the air about eight minutes a day—cable news organizations like CNN are models of efficiency. There are no multimillion-dollar anchors; many more reporters and producers make a lot less money; and because the network is on twenty-four hours a day, its bureaus can be used more regularly and efficiently.

These days the networks all seem headed in different directions, GE—NBC's new owner—has drawn enormous fire within NBC and in other news media for its sometimes heavy-handed and brutal cost reductions, so much so that it is reportedly considering selling the network to one of the giant entertainment conglomerates like Paramount or Disney. That is especially ironic, because GE seemed to understand from the beginning that information technology would alter journalistic function. NBC recently acquired the Financial News Network and began its own video wire service, the News Channel. In the long run, from an economic standpoint, NBC seems the best equipped to survive in the fragmented, cable-driven world of TV news.

ABC, on the other hand, appears to be the best positioned for the short run. Its news division seems the likeliest to stay in the evening news business. Of the Big Three, its owner—Capital Cities—seems to best understand the broadcast culture, managing to quietly make its news division more efficient while acquiring and leaving intact its most visible symbols—including the strongest lineup in broadcast journalism.

CBS News, which has settled down somewhat since the relentless and highly public bloodletting of Laurence Tisch's early regime, seems quieter but still adrift. It has yet to publicly articulate a new sense of direction to replace the institution Tisch decimated. It has not moved in new directions, as NBC has, or beefed up its anchor stable, as has ABC. Aside from *48 Hours,* broadcasting's flagship news division still seems stunned by years of layoffs and budget cuts, a raccoon lying in the road as the car speeds away.

Newsmagazines Will Grow

Network news has no choice but to back away from hard news. News divisions, pressed to find revenues for their tight-fisted new owners and showcases for their news personalities, will continue to retreat to the new generation of prime-time newsmagazines. These broadcasts make sense both economically—they cost a fourth of a prime-time entertainment broadcast—and journalistically; they are less hide-bound than evening news broadcasts, freer to use dramatic video and range away from reporter-clogged institutions like the White House and the State Department.

CBS has finally stopped bouncing the gritty, dramatic *48 Hours* from one time slot to another, and the broadcast has boosted its ratings as viewers have finally been able to figure out where to find it. *ABC News* has also stuck with its new newsmagazine, *PrimeTime Live,* giving it time to recover from its disastrous and over-hyped start nearly three years ago. There are reports that Sam Donaldson, co-anchor of *PrimeTime Live,* will leave the broadcast to anchor his own new newsmagazine program, and that NBC News will bring out its own newsmagazine this spring.

The newsmagazines' great but closely guarded secret is that they are much closer to the highly successful tabloid telecasts like *Hard Copy* and *Inside Edition* than they are to traditional news division newscasts or documentaries. With their emphasis on crime, sensationalism, and celebrity, they are mining territory the evening news always considered unworthy. For the newsmagazines to continue to compete with the booming tabloids, they will have to get even racier. They will. For better or worse, commercial broadcast news will make its last stand here.

The news media persist—at their peril—in covering this revolution as an amalgam of toys, or as more bad habits for kids. It is, in fact, a new culture of information, profoundly reshaping the leisure time and information habits of tens of millions of Americans.

At least some of these changes will be evident during the presidential campaign. When the Bush campaign wanted to expose its embattled vice-presidential nominee to a skeptical nation in 1988, aides simply walked Dan Quayle over to the anchor booths at the Republican convention for chats with Bernard Shaw, Dan Rather, Peter Jennings, and Tom Brokaw. In 1992, with the possible exception of CNN, there won't be anchors at the Republican convention or on the scene at key presidential primaries.

The three commercial networks have announced that their anchors will cover only the Democratic convention in New York, a cheap limo ride across town from their headquarters. They will also scale back the number of reporters, producers, and camera persons assigned to the primaries, the campaign, and the election, all of which will get less airtime. The networks can't afford to cut deeply into prime-time entertainment revenues and can't compete directly with the ubiquitous, lower-paid, more mobile legions of CNN.

It is unclear how politicians will get their messages across in a system as fragmented as broadcast journalism. Challengers without the power of a president to command media attention will have a more difficult time than ever getting through to a public mesmerized by a staggering array of video choices. It is also unclear how journalists will transmit *their* messages. Just as newspapers were—many still are—reluctant to concede television's permanence and relevance, so broadcast news executives and producers have been slow to react to the manner in which technology has made news instantaneously available.

Whether broadcast news does or doesn't respond, this technology will continue to supplant, thus alter, one of the most basic functions of the reporter: to take us where we can't go ourselves.

Like much of the mainstream print media it has challenged and in some ways supplanted, broadcast journalism tends to equate the status quo with responsible, ethical journalism and to view the new video culture as a cross between prostitution and Armageddon. Because it has been so slow to respond to the evolution of its own medium, to permit real diversity of opinion and creatively distinct news programming, broadcast journalism has allowed itself to be perceived as dying, in a constant state of retrenchment and cutback. Yet television news is hardly becoming extinct; it is spreading all over the place.

In one sense, commercial broadcast journalism is freer to experiment and innovate than at any time since its inception. News divisions may have lost much of the virtual monopoly on the daily presentation of news they came to hold through their evening newscasts, and they may no longer be able to compete effectively on breaking stories. But that leaves a lot of room—for real commentary, more reports, and reporting away from the media clusters in Washington and New York, a revival of investigative units looking at crime, waste, and corruption, and closer looks at largely untapped subjects like science, technology, popular culture, and religion.

As for the tube itself, we may like it or not, but we can probably all agree that, whatever its shortcomings, there is one thing it will continue to do brilliantly: grow.

II. MEDIA EVOLUTION & CRITIQUE

EDITOR'S INTRODUCTION

The articles in this section explore the symbiotic relationship between the media and the public. Does the media decide what is news? Does their selection of stories and manner of presenting them really serve the public interest? Do the media appeal to the so-called lowest common denominator in order to please their advertisers? Should we hold the media—or ourselves—accountable for what we are subjected to: a barrage of re-creations, video images without context, an evening news of snippets and sound bites, celebrity escapades, and the dominance of salacious crime reporting?

The first three articles take a look at the history of the media-public relationship. In the first article, reprinted from his book *The Great Society and Its Legacy,* Charles Green reexamines the civil rights movement, Vietnam, and Watergate to demonstrate that during these eras, it was events, and not the media, which set the public agenda. In the second article, reprinted from the *Journal of Communication,* Donald C. Hallin discusses the collapse of the "political consensus," formed between the 1930s and 1960s, and how that collapse has affected both journalism and the society in which it operates.

Carl Bernstein's *New Republic* article—part history, part critique—discusses his own well-known journalistic involvement in Watergate, and contrasts it with the present role of the media. He finds his profession lacking in responsibility to society at large. Two other well-known television journalists, Dan Rather and Bill Moyers, writing respectively in *The Humanist* and *New Perspectives Quarterly,* also offer their opinions on the state of journalism. Finally, Michael Parenti, in another article from *The Humanist,* looks at how the entertainment industry's films and television programs shape how we think about race, gender, politics, and society.

THE ROLE OF THE MEDIA IN SHAPING
PUBLIC POLICY[1]

"The role of the media in shaping public policy: 1964 to 1984" is, of course, an impossibly broad subject. It ranges from the flowering of the civil rights movement through the Vietnam War to the "Me Generation" era, and spans five presidents. There's an old author's trick that says when you're faced with an impossibly broad subject, the only safe course is to expand it still further. Thus, let's begin on 18 December 1917 by quoting a famous article published on that date in the *New York Evening Mail:*

A NEGLECTED ANNIVERSARY

On December 20 there flitted past us, absolutely without public notice, one of the most important profane anniversaries in American history—to wit: the seventy-fifth anniversary of the introduction of the bathtub into these states. . . . Bathtubs are so common today that it is almost impossible to imagine a world without them . . . and yet the first American Bathtub was installed and dedicated so recently as December 20, 1842.

Curiously enough, the scene of its setting up was Cincinnati, [by] Adam Thompson. . . . [His] trade frequently took him to England, and in that country, during the 1830s, he acquired the habit of bathing.

The bathtub was then still a novelty in England. It had been introduced in 1828 by Lord John Russell and its use was yet confined to a small class of enthusiasts.

Moreover, the English bathtub, then as now, was a puny and inconvenient contrivance—little more, in fact, than a glorified dishpan—and filling and emptying required the attendance of a servant. Taking a bath, indeed, was a rather heavy ceremony, and Lord John in 1835 was said to be the only man in England who had yet come to doing it every day.

Thompson, who was of inventive fancy . . . conceived the notion that the English bathtub would be much improved if it were made large enough to admit the whole body of an adult man, and if its supply of water, instead of being hauled to the scene by a maid, were admitted by pipes from a central reservoir and run off by the same means. Accordingly, early in 1842 he set about building the first American bathroom in his Cincinnati home.

. . . In this luxurious tub Thompson took two baths on December 20, 1842—a cold one at 8 A.M. and a warm one some time during the after-

[1]Article by Charles Green, from *The Great Society and Its Legacy: Twenty Years of U.S. Social Policy,* 1986, edited by Marshall Kaplan and Peggy Cuciti. Copyright © 1986 by Duke University Press. Reprinted with permission.

noon. The warm water, heated by the kitchen fire, reached a temperature of 105 degrees. On Christmas day, having a party of gentlemen to dinner, he exhibited the new marvel to them and gave an exhibition of its use, and four of them, including a French visitor, Col. Duchanel, risked plunges into it. The next day all Cincinnati . . . had heard of it, and the local newspapers described it at length and opened their columns to violent discussions of it.

The thing, in fact, became a public matter, and before long there was bitter and double-headed opposition to the new invention.

. . . The noise of the controversy soon reached other cities, and in more than one place medical opposition reached such strength that it was reflected in legislation. Late in 1843, for example, the Philadelphia common considered an ordinance prohibiting bathing between November 1 and March 15, and it failed of passage by but two votes. . . .

. . . Dr. Oliver Wendell Holmes declared for the bathtub and vigorously opposed the lingering movement against it. . . . The American Medical Association held its annual meeting in Boston in 1859 and a poll of the members in attendance showed that nearly 55 percent of them now regarded bathing as harmless and that more than 20 percent advocated it as beneficial. At its meeting in 1850 a resolution was formally passed giving the imprimatur of the faculty to the bathtub. . . .

But it was the example of President Millard Fillmore that, even more than the grudging medical approval, gave the bathtub recognition and respectability in the United States . . . on succeeding to the presidency at Taylor's death, July 9, 1850, he instructed his secretary of war, Gen. Charles M. Conrad, to invite tenders for the construction of a bathtub in the White House. . . . This was installed early in 1851.

Most of us are already familiar with most of these "facts" that were a staple of newspaper features and fillers for more than a half-century. Most of us also know that each "fact" was a total fraud generated by the beguiling mind of the article's author, H. L. Mencken.

As Mencken himself confessed in a 23 May 1926 article, his tongue-in-cheek article, buttressed by its rich if imaginary detail, lodged itself deeply in the popular culture:

It was reprinted by various great organs of the enlightenment. . . . Pretty soon I began to encounter my preposterous "facts" in the writing of other men. They began to be used by chiropractors and other such quacks as evidence of the stupidity of medical men. They began to be cited by medical men as proof of the progress of public hygiene. They got into learned journals. They were alluded to on the floor of Congress. . . . Finally, I began to find them in standard works of reference. . . .

I recite this history not because it is singular, but because it is typical. It is out of just such frauds, I believe, that most of the so-called knowledge of humanity flows. What begins as a guess—or, perhaps, not infrequently, as a downright and deliberate lie—ends as a fact and is embalmed in the history books.

As a practicing journalist for many years, I have often had close contact with history in the making. I can recall no time or place when what actually occurred was afterward generally known and believed. Sometimes a part of the truth got out, but never all.

Mencken's article is a legend among journalists precisely because it illustrates the staying power of misunderstanding—as well as the chronic inability of corrections to catch up with error, whether deliberate or inadvertent. Let a story contain an erroneous assertion and it will be faithfully clipped and filed in newspaper morgues and public libraries throughout the country—from which it is resurrected by diligent researchers and incorporated anew into more articles, which in turn are filed away to await a new generation of researchers. The correction, or in more serious cases the debunking article, seems in contrast always destined to lie below the fold under someone's birdcage, its nagging presence unseen, unwanted, and unquoted.

It's worth remembering Mencken's hoax today for reasons that go beyond comic relief. Today's media myths have lost none of their power to endure, although they often today assume less amusing forms. Today the prevalent myth is of the Imperial Media, an awesome force that somehow bestride the republic like a colossus, working their will and whim upon a passive populace.

I do not deny that the news media collectively played an important, even a vital role in the unfolding of public policy in the last two decades. But however important that role was, I suggest it was also primarily though not wholly passive. How can we be both powerful and passive? You need look no further than the nearest public address system for an analogy. The amplifier may increase the range of power of the speaker's words, but it has no control over what goes into it.

In a nutshell, we did our job, and generally, we did it very well. We recorded and sometimes catalyzed the great events of these two decades. But we did not cut them from whole cloth.

Let's begin with the most obvious myth, one that even sometimes finds adherents within the communications industry itself: that the news media drove President Richard Nixon from office. This is no place to recount in detail the sordid history of Watergate. But the belief that the news media were somehow the decisive actors in the events that by and large they faithfully recorded flourishes with a strength directly proportional to the believer's misunderstanding of the constitutional process.

It was, after all, federal judge John Sirica who struck the first decisive blow against the Watergate cover-up by sentencing the original burglary defendants to long prison sentences, then commuting them when they broke their conspiracy of silence about the instigators of their squalid caper. The next great acts were the hearings of the House and Senate judiciary committees. While these televised hearings made folk heros of the likes of Senator Sam Ervin and Representative Elizabeth Holtzman, they were not media events devoid of a broader power. They were acts of the most profound constitutional meaning, which the media were privileged to attend and report.

Finally, the U. S. Supreme Court cast the decisive blow by unanimously ruling against President Nixon on the question of the tapes. That set off the final act in this drama in which two of the coequal branches of the federal government, Congress and the judiciary, exercised their classic "checks and balances" role to terminate an unlawful act within the executive branch.

Admittedly, this is one occasion where the notion that the media's role is primarily passive seems contradicted by their own exertions. Obviously, the *Washington Post* exposed many of the early lies with which the White House had tried to sweep the burglary and cover-up under the rug. *Time* magazine and the *New York Times* reported on the wiretapping. The *Baltimore Sun* unearthed irregularities within the Internal Revenue Service. The Dita Beard–ITT connection received considerable attention in our own *Denver Post,* among other outlets. The television networks, while plowing little new ground themselves, did keep the nation's attention riveted on the unfolding events.

But all this activity only highlights the true power of the much-misunderstood "power of the press" on major public policy issues. The media do have power to focus public attention on a problem, to put a subject on the national agenda. But this is distinctly not a power to punish the wicked or to reward the just, save for what good or ill feeling the subjects of a story may privately derive from it. Such punishment or reward must come from other persons and institutions making their independent judgment upon those media revelations. We do not indict, we do not acquit. Newsrooms do not write laws, and paperboys do not enforce them.

Thus it is simply silly to say the media hounded Nixon from office. That gives us far too much credit. The truth hounded Nixon from office. The media merely reported the truth. Congress did not grovel before the pens of outraged editorial writers.

It acted because its own investigations, however much they may have been spurred by media revelations, had stirred its own outrage.

The story of the news media and public policy throughout the rest of the 1964–1984 period is much the same—as indeed it was for centuries before and will doubtless be for generations to come. Our power, and it is a great one, is basically the power to put an issue on the public agenda. We are not the sole possessors of that power. But even when we do not initiate the discussion of an item on the public agenda, our decisions as to the reporting of that item can greatly shape its direction, amplifying or diminishing its importance.

That becomes clear if we turn back to the beginning of the era in question, when the great civil rights movement was stirring. The media did not instigate its seminal protest, the Montgomery bus boycott. That began when a black woman, Rosa Parks, had had enough of indignity one day and refused to move to the back of a bus. The media merely reacted, rather laggardly when one considers the scope and duration of the underlying social policies, to a great event already unfolding.

The institution most responsible for putting the question of black dignity on the national agenda was one with which we share the first amendment, the church. Beginning with black religious leaders such as the Reverend Martin Luther King but swiftly spreading to those of white Christian and Jewish groups, ministers and rabbis began denouncing a system of laws and customs violently at war with our Judeo-Christian tradition.

Obviously, the coverage in print and on television of the protests at Selma, Birmingham, and Ole Miss, of such martyrdoms as those of Goodman, Chaney, and Schwerner, and above all the impassioned dignity of King helped arouse the conscience of the American people.

But it's worth noting again that our role was essentially passive. However strongly we might sympathize editorially with their goals and however far we might spread their words, we did not create the Selma marchers. Moreover, victory was theirs only after the other great institutions of American public opinion—the church, the academy, business, labor unions, and political parties—had weighed their message, found it just, and marched by their side.

In debunking the myth that the media exercise awesome power in public affairs, I do not wish to belittle the role we do play.

But it is quite clear that however effectively we may serve as amplifiers, and occasionally as catalysts, we are generally not leading actors in the dramas we report and have very little power to determine their outcome.

The contrast between the power to focus public attention on an issue and the power to influence the outcome of the resulting political process is vividly apparent in the very different outcomes of the black civil rights movement and the similar quest a decade later by homosexuals for equal rights. It can be argued that the media gave comparable and fairly respectful coverage to the demands of gay and lesbian leaders. But with the exception of a few scattered local ordinances, homosexuals have had much more limited success in changing their standing in either the law or public opinion than blacks did. In the latter case, our reporting and commentary have simply not convinced the other opinion-molding institutions of society or the public at large to embrace the gay cause. The media can lead the public policy horse to water, but we can't make it drink.

Oddly, the myth that the media somehow determine the outcome of the public agenda hides and obscures just how great our real power is in terms of forming that agenda itself. The power to put an item on the public agenda—or to keep it off—is more than enough power for any one institution in a free society.

Mussolini once mused, "If you give me the power to nominate, you can vote for whomever you please." We similarly tell our readers that we can't tell them what to think. But we have a great deal of influence in deciding what they think or don't think about.

That power is at its most absolute when exercised in the negative. Every day in the newsrooms of print and broadcast media in this country thousands of stories come in begging for a few seconds of airtime or a few inches of print. We select only a small fraction of them. You may disagree vigorously with the opinions or purported facts we do present—but you have little means of knowing about the more numerous items we did not transmit. The latter may well have been the more critical.

As a very simple example, consider the coverage given to the massacre of Moslem refugees in Beirut by Christian Phalangists. Much criticism was vented upon Israel for not acting more decisively to prevent such slaughter. The day the Israelis released their own official report on the massacre—one that sharply criticized their own government for its indirect complicity—our wire services at the *Post* bulged with nearly seventy different accounts of that report.

I don't think we really need to write editorials and columns saying that the Beirut massacres were bad. People in general don't like massacres and if the question, "Should we stop massacres in Beirut?" is put on the public agenda, then the answer is inevitable. But why was there no similar outcry over the massacres at Ad Judayl or Hama?

Ad Judayl is—or more precisely, was—a town in Iraq where, on July 11, 1982, someone made an assassination attempt on Iraqi dictator Saddam Hussein. According to a five-inch article in the London magazine *The Economist* five months later, Hussein responded much as Hitler did in destroying the village of Lidice, Czechoslovakia, after the assassination of Reinhard Heydrich.

The British newsmagazine reported: "There were about 150 casualties in the two hours of fighting that followed the attempted assassination. After that, 150 families simply disappeared. The remaining men were sent off to northern Iraq, the women and children were sent south. Bulldozers then demolished the town."

A check of *Post* wire services and a computerized data-base search of American newspapers and magazines produced absolutely nothing about this event. We did base an editorial on the *Economist* article and what little we were able to learn from our own independent sources about the Ad Judayl massacre. But it is clear that the general decision to regard the massacre in Iraq as non-news and the massacre in Beirut as news had a profound effect on U. S. foreign policy in the region.

Little more attention was given in American media to a far worse massacre in Hama, a city in Syria where the Moslem Brotherhood had mobilized opposition to the rule of Hafez Assad. Assad surrounded the city with troops and opened fire with artillery rather indiscriminately. Reports that reached us through Japanese newspapers later indicated that between 5,000 and 10,000 people died—mostly innocent people caught in the crossfire. Yet U. S. media paid very little attention to the event.

Such events are not suppressed as a result of a conscious conspiracy. But they do reflect a sense of what journalists think is important in selecting items for the public agenda, and those choices do influence the outcome of public policy. If every Israeli misdeed is to be analyzed in exhaustive detail and every atrocity of its most bitter foes is to be overlooked, it can be safely predicted that ultimately the U. S.-Israeli "special relationship" will be undermined.

Paradoxically, it is the fairly open societies, such as Israel, that receive the often unwelcome microscopic examination. Reporters can get into the country, talk to victims and survivors, film with only a minimum of censorship, and report in voluminous detail. Contrast that to the fact that it took five months for even the most minimum account of the Ad Judayl massacre to leak out of the tightly closed Iraqi society. When such facts do emerge, they are difficult to verify and have lost much of their timeliness.

Still, I think the media in general do a fair job of setting that public agenda. It is fortunate that the media in this country are quite numerous and diverse. Thus critical issues have a way of being thrust upon us by our own brethren. Much of the intellectual agenda actually comes from small journals of opinion, such as the *National Review, Commentary, The New Republic,* or the numerous outpourings of liberal and conservative think tanks such as the Brookings Institution or the Heritage Foundation. Their readership is small but highly concentrated within the mass media.

To a substantial degree the initiatives of the Great Society were a success. But because the media used its agenda power in a negative way, the public was left with an overriding impression that they failed. That, in turn, may have profoundly influenced the political climate to usher in the so-called "Reagan revolution" of the 1980s.

Let me quote from John Schwarz, associate professor of political science at the University of Arizona, in *The New Republic:*

> The War on Poverty decisively changed the living conditions facing the poor. Programs such as food stamps virtually eliminated serious malnutrition among low-income children and adults in America. Medicaid and Medicare greatly increased the access of low-income Americans to health care. In turn, the enlargement of both the nutritional and medical programs led to a decline in the infant mortality rate among minority Americans of 40 percent between 1965 and 1975, a drop that was eight times larger than the decline that had taken place in the ten years prior to 1965. The expansion of governmental housing programs helped to reduce the proportion of Americans living in overcrowded housing from 12 percent in 1960 to 5 percent in 1980. Those living in substandard housing declined from 20 percent to 8 percent.

> If that's true, then how did the popular impression emerge that the War on Poverty was a failure? That impression did much to aid the success of Reagan's attack on what he called "the failed policies of the past."

To a great extent, such success stories just did not make good copy. Editors and reporters did not aggressively pursue them. The negative side of our policy role showed its power because people were not made aware of these successes.

Of course, it must be said that one reason the media did not declare a victory in the War on Poverty is because its own generals were so busy crying defeat. The Pentagon doesn't march into a congressional budget hearing and loudly proclaim that the Red Army couldn't fight its way out of a wet paper bag. The administrators of the War on Poverty were no less canny in the bureaucratic infighting, trying to bestir Congress to increase their budgets by focusing on the magnitude of yet unsolved problems. Many minority leaders, fueled by a sense of frustration over what remained undone, similarly belittled the genuine progress that had been made. Once again we see the media's role in public policy being essentially the passive one of transmitting the ideas of others—even when exercising our greatest power of deciding what stories to ignore.

Let's close by discussing issues great and issues small: the tragedy of Vietnam and Gerald Ford's tendency to bump his head. Taking the latter first, we get a small glimpse of the fairly inadvertent exercise of media power.

Ford was actually our most athletic president since Teddy Roosevelt. It's a fact that even the best skiers fall down occasionally, let alone one of his age. The rule that the exceptional tends to make news dictated that those pictures would be given disproportionate play—and that the public would pay more attention to them than to shots showing the president gliding smoothly down a slope. Thus an impression was created of clumsiness—which then led photographers and the public to watch eagerly for more such inevitable incidents, which reinforced the erroneous stereotype. The image became a kind of metaphor for his administration.

The same rule applies, of course, to the verbal "faux pas." James Watt actually did say some sensible things in his stormy tenure. But his love for the vivid and polarizing remark soon had everyone waiting to pounce upon further controversial remarks. A public figure who gets into too many controversies simply reaches a point where he can't avoid them because he's subjected to an intense scrutiny by journalists looking for a "there he goes again" story.

The power to stereotype and to ridicule has a potent effect on the course of public policy. Once again however, a media image need not in itself be decisive to a politician who carefully tends his base. Jesse Helms has certainly received a generous dose of such treatment, yet he succeeded in his 1984 race for Senate reelection.

What then of the seminal media issue of this turbulent period: Vietnam. Its complex history shows evidence of all the issues we have discussed so far. Obviously, the news media didn't put the war itself on the agenda. Presidents Kennedy and Johnson deployed the troops. By and large, the media didn't begin the chorus of protest either, though that protest was often carefully crafted to attract the attention of the press.

But the power of setting agenda still showed at key points. The Viet Cong and North Vietnamese terror campaigns that killed thousands of local leaders and their families received scant attention in American media. But the picture of General Loan executing the Viet Cong suspect went worldwide. The My Lai massacre was intensely reported, as it should have been. But once again, a relatively open society found its warts displayed before the world while a closed one basically limited the message of its atrocities to those they were intended to terrorize. The power of stereotype and ridicule showed clearly in coverage of the inept South Vietnamese regimes, particularly in the era of frequent coups that followed the assassination of Ngo Dihn Diem.

In retrospect, it is clear that the Tet offensive of 1968 was an enormous military defeat for the Viet Cong which lost so much of its cadre that it had to turn over the main battlefield role to North Vietnamese main force units. But it was a tremendous psychological victory for the National Liberation Front and North Vietnamese and broke the back of American public support for the war. Many media critics have used this as a key example of how ignorance of military history, sensationalism, and the rush to deadlines in the media can distort the path of public policy.

Even more basic, many thoughtful analysts argue that the U.S. defeat in Vietnam stemmed from its being the first war fought in the living room. Advances in technology made it very easy to cover the war and plaster ugly images across the nineteen-inch color screen.

Yet even the lessons of Vietnam are at least ambiguous. It's worth noting that even before the Tet offensive the United States had been involved in Vietnam longer than our entire fighting role in World War II. And Tet was hardly the first time we'd been caught with our pants down by a supposedly beaten enemy. Remember the Battle of the Bulge? Yet the Nazi Ardennes offensive only served to stiffen American resolve to destroy the Hitler regime. Why did Tet weaken our resolve in Vietnam?

One of the best analysts of that war, Colonel Harry Summers, Jr., has argued,

> Our failure in Vietnam mostly grew out of a lack of appreciation of military theory and military strategy, and especially the relationship between military strategy and national policy.
> By failing to mobilize the national will behind the Vietnam War, our national leaders ignored Clausewitz's precept that war is a continuation of national policy by other means.
> American leaders deliberately excluded people from their role in selecting the political object—the reason for fighting the war. Not only did the Johnson administration fail to declare war; it sought to commit American troops to combat as imperceptibly as possible, lulling the American people into forgetting that a war was on. It was not surprising that Washington's resolve collapsed after Tet-68. What is surprising is that it did not collapse much earlier. We must relearn that public support is critical to American military strategy.

Former secretary of state Dean Rusk has stated that President Johnson deliberately forswore stirring up patriotic sentiment over Vietnam because he was afraid of arousing a conservative political tide that would hinder his liberal Great Society programs domestically. Whether that would have happened is debatable. What is not debatable is that the president called the people to arms with an uncertain trumpet. The media did not create this ambiguity in public policy. They could not and should not have avoided reporting it.

After all, technological flourishes aside, the media today aren't really so different from their predecessors in their power to inform and arouse emotion. Someone once quipped that "Marshall McLuhan says the printed word is obsolete. He wrote eighteen books to prove it."

Can it really be said that it took television to expose the horror and ugliness of war? Did Stephen Crane write *The Red Badge of Courage* for nothing? Didn't *All Quiet on the Western Front* and other works expose the stupidity and slaughter of World War I? Didn't Emie Pyle and a generation of combat reporters expose all too vividly the horror of Guadalcanal, of Tarawa, of Omaha Beach? Yet the public bore the burden of those wars because the same media that reported their horror were used by their political leaders to justify their necessity.

In summation, I should say that as the Mencken piece shows an enduring myth takes on a kind of reality of its own. It is an overstatement to say that in politics the perception of power is power, because there can be power in the unperceived as well. But while the media's power in public policy is both misunderstood and overrated, the very fact that politicians and others themselves tend to believe in it tends to reinforce it. They may overrate our ability to influence public opinion, as distinct from reporting it, but they do assign some weight to our opinions.

But in the end, it is the broader reality that we try to report that decides the outcome of public policy, not reporting itself. Just ask President Thomas E. Dewey.

THE PASSING OF THE "HIGH MODERNISM" OF AMERICAN JOURNALISM[2]

My first encounter with a professional journalist was an interview with Peter Arnett, then at the Associated Press. It was the late 1970s, and I was a bearded graduate student at Berkeley writing my dissertation on the media and Vietnam, a story that Arnett had covered since the early 1960s. He assumed from my background that I would want to know why journalists hadn't taken a stronger stand against the war; this was the era when advocacy journalism enjoyed a heyday of sorts—quite brief and marginal, really—as a challenger to the journalistic mainstream. So he launched into an articulate defense of what he called "Establishment journalism." Just by reporting the facts, he said journalists had contributed more effectively to ending the war than they could have done in any other way.

What impressed me the most in this interview was the sense of wholeness and seamlessness in Arnett's vision of journalism, or to put it the other way around, the absence of a sense of doubt or contradiction. I remember being quite surprised by this, which I suppose reflects my very different generational experience, as

[2]Article by Daniel C. Hallin, from *Journal of Communication* 42/3:14–25 Summ '92. Copyright © 1992 by Oxford University Press. Reprinted with permission.

someone who came of age politically just as the polarization that
ended the 1960s reached its height. Arnett's view reflects very
well the consciousness of American journalism at the peak of the
country's power and prosperity: This was an era when American
journalists felt they had overcome all the basic contradictions that
historically have troubled the practice of journalism. And in
fact—consciousness never fundamentally standing apart from
material reality—they had achieved resolutions of these contradictions that for the moment seemed solid and stable.

Politically, it seemed possible for journalism to be independent of party and state, and yet fully a part of the "Establishment." Thus James Reston [in *Deadline: A Memoir* ('91)], the premier journalist of the era, recounts delivering through his column
a threat of nuclear war if the Soviets failed to back down in Berlin,
the exact wording approved by President Kennedy but presented
on Reston's own authority. With John Foster Dulles, secretary of
state under Eisenhower, who "liked . . . philosophical wanderings
with a fellow Presbyterian," Reston had a continuing relationship
of this sort. These kinds of ties were not entered into without an
occasional pause to weigh their implications. But they were not
seen by journalists as a conflict of interest or surrender of independence. They were, after all, voluntary agreements in which
the journalists gained extraordinary access to the inner workings
of politics. The journalists felt they had bargaining power of their
own, could criticize without losing access, and indeed could uphold the old ideal of press as a scourge of the powerful. "When
they tried to bully our reporters," Reston writes, "I reminded
them that we had been around before they arrived, and would
probably still be in Washington when they were gone." But most
important, they felt confident that all of it was done in the defense of the Free World, a cause that stood above politics.

In their internal organization, the news media seemed to have
resolved the twin problems of private ownership and personal
bias. Owners had largely ceded day-to-day control of the news
columns to the journalists. With the shift of the *Los Angeles Times*
toward neutrality in the 1960 election and the death of Henry
Luce in 1967, the last important survivors of the days when the
news media were essentially political tools of their owners were
gone.

The journalists, for their part, had accepted the bureaucratic
hierarchy of the newsroom and the constraints of the professional
norms of neutrality and "objectivity." [In *The Media Elite: America's*

New Powerbrokers ('86)] Lichter, Rothman, and Lichter found contemporary journalists much less likely to complain about editors interfering with their news judgment than the journalists of the 1930s, when Leo Rosten [*The Washington Correspondents* ('37)] found a majority complaining that stories had been altered or killed for "policy" reasons. They interpret this as an indication that individual journalists now have more or less complete autonomy. But I think it reflects something else, besides the undeniably greater professional autonomy of the contemporary journalist. Contemporary journalists have internalized the constraints of professionalism far more than the 1930s writers had done, and are also far less politicized than their predecessors. They are committed more strongly to the norms of the profession than to political ideas.

We know, of course, that politics never disappeared. It was there all along, in sources, in routines, in consensus assumptions that major political actors didn't disagree about, and which therefore weren't seen as political. Still, we shouldn't allow the critique of objectivity, which has occupied so much of the media scholarship of the last couple of decades, to obscure the real historical change represented by professionalization. Journalism took on a role in this period that felt to most of those involved and appeared to most of the society to be genuinely "above politics."

Finally, in economic terms, prosperity meant that the "profane," commercial side of the news organization, didn't have to conflict with its "sacred," public-service side. Not that everything was well with every paper. Newspapers, in fact, were dying right and left. But the ones that remained were for the most part so prosperous in their new, usually monopoly status, that journalists could think of themselves more as public servants or as keepers of the sacred flame of journalism itself than as employees of a profit-making enterprise.

It was the same at the television networks, where the separation of the news divisions from the commercial side of the enterprise was reinforced by the regulatory injunction that broadcasters serve the public convenience and necessity. The prosperity of these organizations was closely connected with their universality: Their audience knew no bounds of class, politics, or any other social distinction. And that prosperity lifted both the status and income of the individual journalist. Think of the change in the journalist's image in popular culture, from the rowdy, corrupt, politically-entangled ambulance-chasers of "The Front Page" to the altruistic professionals of "All the President's Men."

This was the high modernism of American journalism, an era when the historically troubled role of the journalist seemed fully rationalized, when it seemed possible for the journalist to be powerful and prosperous and at the same time independent, disinterested, public-spirited, and trusted and beloved by everyone, from the corridors of power around the world to the ordinary citizen and consumer. Two major social conditions made this possible. The first was political consensus, rooted in the New Deal and the Cold War. The second was economic security, both for the society at large and for media industries specifically. Both have substantially broken down. How far their disintegration will go or what new political and economic forces will replace them we cannot know. But it is clear that the changes underway are already shaking up the profession of journalism. I will organize the remainder of my discussion around these two broad themes: the collapse of political consensus and the intensification of economic competition.

The Collapse of Political Consensus

From the beginning of World War II to the late 1960s, political debate in the United States was extremely muted. In domestic politics the liberal policies of the New Deal commanded a majority solid enough to leave the far left marginalized and the conservatives with little choice but to join the fold. In foreign policy, wartime consensus was converted into the bipartisan policy of Cold War containment, whose basic outlines came essentially to define the bounds of political reason. Consensus was accompanied by a high level of public confidence in political institutions. In this environment, it was possible for social scientists to proclaim the "end of ideology" and to put forward a vision of social science as a source of neutral expertise, closely tied to governing institutions, and at the same time serving society as a whole. And in a similar way consensus made it possible for journalists to feel that they could be part of the political "Establishment" and yet remain neutral and independent.

A series of major changes in political life have undermined this consensus. First, and probably most basic, the New Deal majority has broken apart, destroyed by racial and other social divisions and by economic conditions. Second, the Cold War consensus has disappeared, first undermined by Vietnam and détente, and now made irrelevant by the collapse of the Soviet bloc. Third, public confidence in political authorities declined. To a large extent, this had probably been a by-product of the general decline of political consensus. But I think it also has a more specific and simple cause, namely that the instrumental attitude toward communication developed during wartime became institutionalized, and officials were caught again and again in blatant falsehoods, from the U-2 incident to the Dominican invasion to Watergate.

Finally, important institutional changes have taken place in the relations among major political actors. The political system has become increasingly fragmented, individualized, and adversarial, with central structures weakened and individual actors looking out for themselves. The parties have weakened substantially: Voters identify with them far less strongly, they exercise less discipline in Congress, and their organizations play a diminished role in the electoral process. Relations between the president and Congress are more adversarial and, as Samuel Kernell [*Going Public* ('86)] has shown, presidents bargain less with congressional leaders and rely more on the mobilization of public pressure.

As this last point suggests, changes in political communication were central to these developments. It is likely, for instance, that the advent of television was an important factor: Television made it much easier for presidents to go "over the heads" of congressional leaders by appealing directly to the public, and gave candidates a new way of reaching the voters without relying on the old party ward leaders. And certainly public communication—or if one likes, propaganda—became more central to the political process.

And the news media were affected by the changes in ways similar to other political actors: Their relations with those actors became more adversarial, less bound by a sense of reciprocal obligations. Gone is the clubby atmosphere of the Roosevelt years, when the president met with reporters every week and the reporters agreed not to print photographs showing his leg braces. Press conferences are far rarer today, and are less occasions for give-and-take between the president and the press corps than they are confrontations staged by the president to impress the television audience. And the media are more reluctant to honor politicians' wishes about what will be publicized: Consider the networks' decision to broadcast tape of President Bush vomiting in the lap of the Japanese prime minister.

More Mediated Forms of Journalism

All of this was beginning to change journalism substantially by the late 1960s. Journalists were becoming bolder about challenging political authority, as they did most dramatically by publishing the *Pentagon Papers*. And more profoundly, the old model of "objective journalism" was giving way to a more active, mediated, journalist-centered form of reporting, which I have described in some detail in ["Sound Bite News: Television Coverage of Elections, 1968–1988," *Journal of Communication*, 42, '92]. I will not recapitulate that argument here, but I would like to go on to address some of its broader implications.

First, a qualification. It is important not to exaggerate the extent to which American journalism has become either more adversarial toward political authority or more interpretive in mode of presentation. The relation between the news media and political power is still tight and symbiotic; and it seems to me that the news media are still very much the junior partner. The statistics on news sources, for instance, have changed little since the early 1970s, when Leon Sigal [*Reporters and Officials* ('73)] found that about half the sources in front-page stories in *The New York Times* and *The Washington Post* were U.S. government officials. The large percentage of these that are unnamed suggests the degree of trust that still prevails between reporters and officials. And one has only to think of the way the media image of Saddam Hussein's regime changed as he shifted from ally to enemy to realize how much official policy still shapes the news. American journalists, moreover, remain far more comfortable with the role of reporter than that of commentator.

Still, the changes that have taken place since the 1960s are substantial. And there are reasons to think they may continue to develop. One such reason is the end of the Cold War. It was the Cold War above all that made a relatively passive, state-centered model of journalism appear reasonable. Truth and power seemed united in the Washington headquarters of the free world, and the basic job of the reporter, in a phrase I have often heard from reporters covering national security policy, was to "reflect the thinking" of official Washington. Given the prestige of the national security beat, moreover, this model of journalism tended to influence the rest of the profession, just as the national security paradigm influenced the rest of political thought. (We still talk about a war on drugs and argue for education or economic reform on the grounds that they will promote national security. This is one of the only ways we have of talking about the public good.) As foreign policy consensus has broken down, reporters have had to think for themselves much more, about which voices to listen to, for example, and how to synthesize for their audience a political reality that is not black and white. The end of the Cold War raises the prospect that this will become a normal condition.

Another reason to expect continuing change has to do with the anguished state of electoral politics, which became a major subject of discussion following the 1988 election with subsequent polls showing intense voter dissatisfaction with political leadership. It is naive, of course, to imagine that there was once a golden age when political discussion in America was a model of reason. But I do think it is true that there have been periods when the political identities of the two parties were relatively clear, and when the bulk of the electorate felt represented by one or the other. This was the case during the New Deal era, and it made the journalists' job relatively easy, as covering politics meant, above all, relaying to the voters what the candidates were saying about whatever issues they chose to stress. Since the breakup of the New Deal coalition in 1968, however, the identities of the parties have become muddled. This has interacted with—perhaps it opened the way for—the domination of campaigning by professional consultants, to produce the substanceless politics of 1988.

And the latter in turn has provoked considerable discussion among journalists about how to cover elections. Should journalists, as *The Washington Post's* David Broder has proposed, take a more active role in defining the agenda of the campaign, or is that, as others argue, a presumptuous and unrealistic usurpation of the role of the parties and candidates? So far, coverage of the 1992 campaign seems to have moved modestly in the direction Broder has advocated. *The New York Times* recently ran as its right-hand lead a story under the head:

> DEMOCRATS VYING IN '92 RACE OFFER
> PAINLESS RECOVERY
> ECONOMISTS ARE SKEPTICAL
> Except for Tsongas, Candidates are Avoiding Remedies
> that Might Antagonize Voters

No candidate was quoted until the 10th paragraph.

Journalism and Civil Society

For the most part, the changes of the last two decades have made American journalism better, and I think we should welcome the prospect of further change, especially in the direction of greater independence from the state, greater sensitivity to diversity of viewpoints, and more sophisticated interpretation. But the changes also confront American journalism with some rather difficult questions about its role.

One way to think about what has happened is this: Key institutions of political debate and interpretation in America have weakened in recent years. The presidency, in particular, has lost credibility (even as it has become more aggressive and sophisticated in the practice of public relations); and the parties—especially the Democrats—have fragmented and lost a sense of what they stand for. The interpretive role of the journalist has expanded to fill part of the vacuum.

Up to a point this is fine. Better the journalists than the flacks. But in many ways journalists are neither well positioned nor well qualified to fill the void of political discussion. They remain, for one thing, too much insiders, too close to the powerful institutions whose actions need to be discussed.

And they are too constrained by the need to avoid offense to any major political faction or, most powerfully, to the majority sentiment of the moment. In the case of elections, again to summarize what I have developed at greater length earlier [in "Sound Bite News"], journalists tend to steer the discussion in the direction of technical questions that don't seem political: Which candidate is running the most *effective* campaign? A similar thing happened, by somewhat different means, during the Gulf War—the kind of emotional political issue that arouses the most intense fears in the media of being on the wrong side of public opinion. The television networks hired as consultants retired military and defense department experts, who could provide seemingly neutral technical analysis and who also had a base of authority outside journalism, and turned over much of the interpretation directly to them.

This problem—the emptiness of the American public sphere—is not one that can be solved solely or primarily by the news media. It is first of all a political problem. But assuming it is not going to disappear quickly or easily, journalism will have to adapt to it. And it seems to me that this may require journalism to be reattached to the all-but-forgotten republican notion of citizenship. This is too large a problem for me to explore fully here. But I would like to make two points about what it might mean in practical terms. First of all, journalists need to move from conceiving their role in terms of mediating between political authorities and the mass public, to thinking of it also as a task of opening up political discussion in civil society, to use the term popular in the new democracies of Eastern Europe. If the candidates in an election campaign, for instance, don't seem to have much to say, why not look for someone else who does? Because Broder's critics are ultimately right: Journalism has a thin political skin, and if it blows itself up too big, it will burst.

Second, it might be time for journalists themselves to rejoin civil society, and to start talking to their readers and viewers as one citizen to another, rather than as experts claiming to be above politics. I am not arguing here for a revival of advocacy journalism. That kind of journalism has an important role to play, and it is too bad that forms like the "authored" documentary have become so marginalized. But the front page of a monopoly newspaper is not the place for it.

I am also not arguing for the kind of pseudo-populist identification with popular sentiments that is often seen today on television news (more on this in a moment). All I am arguing is that the voice and judgment of the journalist may have to be more honestly acknowledged. The style of modern American journalism, with its attributions, passive-voice constructions, and its substitution of technical for moral or political judgments, is largely designed to conceal the voice of the journalist. But as journalism has become increasingly interpretive, it seems to me this form has become increasingly problematic—both alienating, in the wall it throws between the journalist and the reader, and fundamentally dishonest. Journalists used to speak sometimes in the first person— listen to Edward R. Murrow or Bill Shirer. Perhaps it wouldn't be a bad thing if that practice came back.

The Commercialization of News

Economics, meanwhile, has eroded the barrier between journalism and the profit-making business of selling audiences to advertisers. And this is likely to bring into question both the notion of journalism as a public trust and the existence of the common public culture that news once provided. To some extent, all news media have been affected by these changes, as declining audiences and the proliferation of new advertising media have squeezed the bottom line, and as the news media have increasingly become part of media conglomerates for which news is only one more form of "software." But the changes have been most dramatic by far in television, and I shall focus here on that medium. Newspapers remain in the calm before a storm that is likely to hit when a technological alternative to the printing press emerges.

News never was "the core of the asset" (Jack Welch, CEO of NBC-owned General Electric, quoted in [Ken Auletta's *Three Blind Mice* ('91)] in television as it was in the newspaper industry. But it did have a privileged and insulated place in the networks for a relatively brief period, from about 1963 until the mid-1980s. That special position was based primarily on two things: the secure profitability of the networks, and the fact that broadcasting was a regulated industry. A series of developments beginning in the 1970s have eroded it.

In the first place, local TV news emerged as a highly profitable form of programming, far too important to the bottom line of local stations to be left under the control of journalists. It has since evolved into a powerful hybrid of news and show business. It is also the main training ground for network journalists, who in earlier days were trained in radio or print. Then in the 1980s, the advent of cable and the VCR threw the television industry into a period of intense competition which has seen the network share of the television audience decline from near 90% to near 60%. Broadcasting, meanwhile, was being substantially deregulated, and all three networks were taken over in deals that involved the assumption of substantial debt by the new parent companies. All of this combined to force both budget cutbacks and increased pressure to worry about the ratings.

The character of the evening news has already changed substantially. Its pace has come to resemble more closely the pace of the rest of commercial television, with 10-second sound bites and tightly packaged stories. The agenda of news has changed, with fewer traditional political stories and more stories that "tug at the heart strings." And the pressure is far greater today for the stories to have high "production values," both narrative and visual: drama, emotion, and good video. These changes are not all bad; and the common view that sees television history as a simple decline from the supposed Golden Age of Murrow and Cronkite (extremely different eras, actually!) seems to me seriously mis-leading. News in the "classical age" probably was, for example, far too centered on Washington; and I see nothing wrong with a switch toward greater attention to health or family life or other subjects that are both closer to the lives of the viewers and signifi-cant political issues in their own right.

Still, many changes that have taken place in television news are indeed disturbing. If the news agenda has been democratized in certain ways, it has been trivialized in others, with more atten-tion to stories like celebrity trials and beached whales. The net-works have also, to some extent, adopted the local news practice of dropping neutrality and presenting the journalist as a "regular person" who shares and champions the emotions of the audience. This is an old practice of the tabloid press, with its language of outrage and pathos. In TV news it is most common in stories of crime, heroism, or tragedy that are at least on the surface non-political. But it often spills over into the political arena when emotions are high and consensus seems present. There was plen-ty of it at all levels of American television during the Gulf War. Often the temptation in TV news is to push a political story into the arena where consensus prevails, so war becomes a story not of political decisions but of individual heroism, and the journalist, like the politician, can ride the crest of the emotions that pour into such a story. This is what I referred to earlier as "pseudo-populism," its danger being that it heightens emotion and makes black and white what is in fact far more ambiguous.

Tabloid News and the Fragmentation of Audience

The network news divisions, of course, still have one foot firmly planted in the traditional profession of journalism. But they now face competition that is purely commercial, and it is possible that this will have a profound impact eventually on the nature of television news. One of the most significant effects of deregulation and the proliferation of television outlets is the growth of what is often called "trash television." The term has been applied to a number of different kinds of programming, and may be unfair to some of it. It includes, for example, popular daytime talk shows, some of which combine sensation with a sig-nificant amount of serious social content and might be seen as a democratization of the talk-show format, which used to be reserved for discussions among Washington's movers-and-shakers, with journalists prominently included.

But the ones that seem to me most likely to affect television journalism are the "tabloids," seen in most markets in the evening, at the beginning of prime time: "A Current Affair," "Hard Copy," and "Inside Edition." These shows are both cheap to produce and successful in the ratings. They borrow the form and aura of journalism—"Hard Copy" uses a typewriter ball in its promotional imagery—but are produced purely as commercial products. And they involve an intertwining of "real" and "fictional" material: They report on "actual events" using a combination of documentary material and re-creations, the lines between the two blurred by a heavy use of music and visual effects.

The tabloids are, it seems to me, a deeply problematic development for American culture. They exist, for one thing, primarily in the emotional realm of *fear*. Violent crime, often linked to sex, is their most cherished material, and they handle it in a way that maximizes the feeling of omnipresent threat. One typical recent story, for example, about a transvestite stockbroker who murdered a client, ends with the principal character saying, "Do I have to live in fear until that man gets caught?" This line comes over video of the killer in a courtroom, turning toward the camera—that is, the viewer—with a smile; his gaze is then frozen for a moment at the end of the segment. They are also pervaded by irrationalism both in their content, which is full of UFOs and ghosts, and, probably most important, in form: The core of what they say is not stated directly, but insinuated in cryptic lines and visuals (they are much like political commercials in this respect).

Perhaps these shows should be dismissed as "just entertainment," with no relevance for understanding American journalism. But I doubt that this will prove correct. A number of them are produced, for one thing, by people who have moved over from the network news divisions, and it seems likely that personnel movements will continue to cross-fertilize the different programming forms. The tabloids, moreover, are simply too successful not to be tempting to those in local and network television news who are also, in the new language of television, in the business of "reality-based programming."

It is also possible that significant parts of the public will one day be exposed to no other sort of "news" than the tabloids. And this brings me to my final point. In the period I have called the high modernism of American journalism, the news audience was close to universal. The metropolitan newspaper and the network evening news provided rich and poor, political and apolitical alike with a source of relatively serious reporting on public affairs. These media served some members of the audience better than others, to be sure; but most everyone was at least part of the audience. It is not clear that this common audience will survive. Newspapers have lost circulation generally. But it is likely to be in television that a really dramatic change takes place, reproducing something like the split in the newspaper market of many European countries between the quality and mass press.

Serious public affairs programming was never economically rational, at least in a narrow sense, for the television industry. It developed for reasons of prestige and regulatory pressure, and it is not likely to survive unmodified the combination of increased competition and deregulation. Some form of serious television journalism will certainly survive. CNN is doing well with its low-budget operation, and it seems likely that at least one network will continue to produce a major evening news show. But there is already considerable talk in the television industry about whether three such programs can survive.

If they do not, "the public" will become fragmented in a way that is potentially very significant for American politics and culture. Fragmentation of the news audience might not necessarily be a bad thing. One can imagine a system in which, for example, distinctive forms of journalism emerged for middle-class and working-class audiences (and subgroups of these), reflecting the different tastes and concerns of the audiences but providing each with serious discussion of the world of politics in the widest sense. (Public broadcasting has long served to provide the educated middle class—but not other groups, who were assumed to be served adequately by commercial television—with a specialized kind of news programming that the market does not deliver.) Unfortunately, this is not what is likely to happen. What is likely instead is a division of the audience into one part, mostly wealthier and better educated, that "consumes" news of perhaps a higher quality than we have yet seen, and a large part—poorer, less educated, and substantially drawn from minority ethnic groups—that consumes nothing but "A Current Affair" and a sort of soft tabloid style of local news. And this would mean not only a widening of cultural barriers, but also an intensification of the knowledge gap.

THE IDIOT CULTURE[3]

It is now nearly a generation since the drama that began with the Watergate break-in and ended with the resignation of Richard Nixon, a full twenty years in which the American press has been engaged in a strange frenzy of self-congratulation and defensiveness about its performance in that affair and afterward. The self-congratulation is not justified; the defensiveness, alas, is. For increasingly the America rendered today in the American media is illusionary and delusionary—disfigured, unreal, disconnected from the true context of our lives. In covering actually existing American life, the media—weekly, daily, hourly—break new ground in getting it wrong. The coverage is distorted by celebrity and the worship of celebrity; by the reduction of news to gossip, which is the lowest form of news; by sensationalism, which is always a turning away from a society's real condition; and by a political and social discourse that we—the press, the media, the politicians, *and* the people—are turning into a sewer.

Let's go back to Watergate. There is a lesson there, particularly about the press. Twenty years ago, on June 17, 1972, Bob Woodward and I began covering the Watergate story for *The Washington Post*. At the time of the break-in, there were about 2,000 full-time reporters working in Washington, D. C., according to a study by the Columbia University School of Journalism. In the first six months afterward, America's news organizations assigned only fourteen of those 2,000 men and women to cover the Watergate story on a full-time basis. And of those fourteen, only six were assigned to the story on what might be called an "investigative" basis, that is, to go beyond recording the obvious daily statements and court proceedings, and try to find out exactly what had happened.

Despite some of the mythology that has come to surround "investigative" journalism, it is important to remember what we did and did not do in Watergate. For what we did was not, in truth, very exotic. Our actual work in uncovering the Watergate story was rooted in the most basic kind of empirical police report-

[3]Article by Carl Bernstein, from *The New Republic* 206:22+ Je 8 '92. Copyright © 1992 by Carl Bernstein. Reprinted with permission of the author.

ing. We relied more on shoe leather and common sense and respect for the truth than anything else—on the principles that had
been drummed into me at the wonderful old *Washington Star*.
Woodward and I were a couple of guys on the Metro desk assigned to cover what at bottom was still a burglary, so we applied
the only reportorial techniques we knew. We knocked on a lot of
doors, we asked a lot of questions, we spent a lot of time listening:
the same thing good reporters from Ben Hecht to Mike Berger to
Joe Liebling to the young Tom Wolfe had been doing for years.
As local reporters, we had no covey of highly placed sources, no
sky's-the-limit expense accounts with which to court the powerful
at fancy French restaurants. We did our work far from the en-
chanting world of the rich and the famous and the powerful. We
were grunts.

So we worked our way up, interviewing clerks, secretaries,
administrative assistants. We met with them outside their offices
and at their homes, at night and on weekends. The prosecutors
and the FBI interviewed the same people we did, but always in
their offices, always in the presence of administration attorneys,
never at home, never at night, never away from jobs and intimida-
tion and pressures. Not surprisingly, the FBI and the Justice Department came up with conclusions that were the opposite of our
own, choosing not to triangulate key pieces of information, because they had made what the acting FBI director of the day,
L. Patrick Gray III, called "a presumption of regularity" about
the men around the president of the United States.

Even our colleagues in the press didn't take our reporting
seriously, until our ordinary methodology turned up some extraordinary (and incontrovertible) information: a tale of system-
atic and illegal political espionage and sabotage directed from the
White House, secret funds, wiretapping, a team of "plumbers"—
burglars—working for the president of the United States. And
then of the cover-up, an obstruction of justice that extended to
the president himself.

It is important to remember also the Nixon administration's
response. It was to make the conduct of the press the issue in
Watergate, instead of the conduct of the president and his men.
Day after day the Nixon White House issued what we came to call
the "non-denial": asked to comment on what we'd reported, Press
Secretary Ron Ziegler, House Minority Leader Jerry Ford, or
Senate Republican leader Bob Dole would attack us as purveyors
of hearsay, character assassination, and innuendo without ever

addressing the specifics of our stories. "The sources of *The Wash-ington Post*" are a fountain of misinformation," the White House responded when we reported that the president's closest aides controlled the secret funds that had paid for the break-in and a pervasive cover-up (not to mention John Mitchell's inspired words to me: "If you print that, Katie Graham's gonna get her tit caught in a big fat wringer . . . ").

Rather than disappearing after Watergate, the Nixonian tech-nique of making the press the issue reached new heights of clever-ness and cynicism during the Reagan administration, and it flour-ishes today. Hence Reagan's revealing statement about the sad and sorry events that ravaged his presidency in the Iran-contra affair: "What is driving me up the wall is that this wasn't a failure until the press got a tip from that rag in Beirut and began to play it up. This whole thing boils down to a great irresponsibility on the part of the press."

And now in George Bush we have still another president ob-sessed with leaks and secrecy, a president who could not under-stand why the press considered it news when his men set up a faked drug bust in Lafayette Square across from the White House. "Whose side are you on?" he asked. It was a truly Nix-onian question. This contempt for the press, passed on to hun-dreds of officials who hold public office today—including Bush, may be the most important and lasting legacy of the Nixon ad-ministration.

In retrospect, the Nixon administration's extraordinary cam-paign to undermine the credibility of the press succeeded to a remarkable extent, despite all the post-Watergate posturing in our profession. It succeeded in large part because of our own obvious shortcomings. The hard and simple fact is that our re-porting has not been good enough. It was not good enough in the Nixon years, it got worse in the Reagan years, and it is no better now. We are arrogant. We have failed to open up our own institu-tions in the media to the same kind of scrutiny that we demand of other powerful institutions in the society. We are no more forth-coming or gracious in acknowledging error or misjudgment than the congressional miscreants and bureaucratic felons we spend so much time scrutinizing.

The greatest felony in the news business today (as Woodward recently observed) is to be behind, or to miss, a major story; or more precisely, to seem behind, or to seem in danger of missing, a major story. So speed and quantity substitute for thoroughness and quality, for accuracy and context. The pressure to compete, the fear that somebody else will make the splash first, creates a frenzied environment in which a blizzard of information is presented and serious questions may not be raised; and even in those fortunate instances in which such questions are raised (as happened after some of the egregious stories about the Clinton family), no one has done the weeks and months of work to sort it all out and to answer them properly.

Reporting is not stenography. It is the best obtainable version of the truth. The really significant trends in journalism have not been toward a commitment to the best and the most complex obtainable version of the truth, not toward building a new journalism based on serious, thoughtful reporting. Those are certainly not the priorities that jump out at the reader or the viewer from Page One or "Page Six" of most of our newspapers; and not what a viewer gets when he turns on the 11 o'clock local news or, too often, even network news productions.

"All right, was it really the best sex you ever had?" Those were the words of Diane Sawyer, in an interview of Marla Maples on "Prime Time Live," a broadcast of ABC News (where "more Americans get their news from . . . than any other source"). Those words marked a new low (out of which Sawyer herself has been busily climbing). For more than fifteen years we have been moving away from real journalism toward the creation of a sleazoid info-tainment culture in which the lines between Oprah and Phil and Geraldo and Diane and even Ted, between the *New York Post* and *Newsday,* are too often indistinguishable. In this new culture of journalistic titillation, we teach our readers and our viewers that the trivial is significant, that the lurid and the loopy are more important than real news. We do not serve our readers and viewers, we pander to them. And we condescend to them, giving them what we think they want and what we calculate will sell and boost ratings and readership. Many of them, sadly, seem to justify our condescension, and to kindle at the trash. Still, it is the role of journalists to challenge people, not merely to amuse them.

We are in the process of creating, in sum, what deserves to be called the idiot culture. Not an idiot *sub*-culture, which every society has bubbling beneath the surface and which can provide harmless fun; but the culture itself. For the first time in our history the weird and the stupid and the coarse are becoming our cultural norm, even our cultural ideal. Last month in New York we witnessed a primary election in which "Donahue," "Imus in the Morning," and the disgraceful coverage of the *New York Daily News* and the *New York Post* eclipsed *The New York Times, The Washington Post,* the network news divisions, and the serious and experienced political reporters on the beat. Even *The New York Times* has been reduced to naming the rape victim in the Willie Smith case; to putting Kitty Kelley on the front page as a news story; to parlaying polls as if they were policies.

I do not mean to attack popular culture. Good journalism *is* popular culture, but popular culture that stretches and informs its consumers rather than that which appeals to the ever descending lowest common denominator. If, by popular culture, we mean expressions of thought or feeling that require no work of those who consume them, then decent popular journalism is finished. What is happening today, unfortunately, is that the lowest form of popular culture—lack of information, misinformation, disinformation, and a contempt for the truth or the reality of most people's lives—has overrun real journalism.

Today ordinary Americans are being stuffed with garbage: by Donahue-Geraldo-Oprah freak shows (cross-dressing in the marketplace; skinheads at your corner luncheonette; pop psychologists rhapsodizing over the airways about the minds of serial killers and sex offenders); by the Maury Povich news; by "Hard Copy"; by Howard Stern; by local newscasts that do special segments devoted to hyping hype. Last month, in supposedly sophisticated New York, the country's biggest media market, there ran a craven five-part series on the 11 o'clock news called "Where Do They Get Those People . . . ?," a special report on where Geraldo and Oprah and Donahue get their freaks (the promo for the series featured Donahue interviewing a diapered man with a pacifier in his mouth).

The point is not only that this is trash journalism. That much is obvious. It is also essential to note that this was on an NBC-owned and -operated station. And who distributes Geraldo? The Tribune Company of Chicago. Who owns the stations on which these cross-dressers and transsexuals and skinheads and lawyers for serial killers get to strut their stuff? The networks, the Washington Post Company, dozens of major newspapers that also own television stations, Times-Mirror and the New York Times Company, among others. And last month Ivana Trump, perhaps the single greatest creation of the idiot culture, a tabloid artifact if ever there was one, appeared on the cover of *Vanity Fair.* On the cover, that is, of Condé Nast's flagship magazine, the same Condé Nast/Newhouse/Random House whose executives will yield to nobody in their solemnity about their profession, who will tell you long into the night how seriously in touch with American culture they are, how serious they are about the truth.

Look, too, at what is on *The New York Times* best-seller list these days. *Double Cross: The Explosive Inside Story of the Mobster Who Controlled America* by Sam and Chuck Giancana, Warner Books, $22.95. (Don't forget that $22.95.) This book is a fantasy pretty much from cover to cover. It is riddled with inventions and lies, with conspiracies that never happened, with misinformation and disinformation, all designed to line somebody's pockets and satisfy the twisted egos of some fame-hungry relatives of a mobster. But this book has been published by Warner Books, part of Time Warner, a conglomerate I've been associated with for a long time. (*All the President's Men* is a Warner Bros. movie, the paperback of *All the President's Men* was also published by Warner Books, and I've just finished two years as a correspondent and contributor at *Time*.) Surely the publisher of *Time* has no business publishing a book that its executives and its editors know is a historical hoax, with no redeeming value except financial.

By now the defenders of the institutions that I am attacking will have cried the First Amendment. But this is not about the First Amendment, or about free expression. In a free country, we are free for trash, too. But the fact that trash will always find an outlet does not mean that we should always furnish it with an outlet. And the great information conglomerates of this country are now in the trash business. We all know pornography when we see it, and of course it has a right to exist. But we do not all have to be porn publishers; and there is hardly a major media company in America that has not dipped its toe into the social and political equivalent of the porn business in the last fifteen years.

Many, indeed, are now waist-deep in the big muddy. Take Donahue. Eighteen years ago Woodward and I went to Ohio on our book tour because we were told that there was a guy doing a syndicated talk show there who was the most substantive interview in the business. And he was. Donahue had read our book. He had charts, he knew the evidence, he conducted a serious discussion about the implications of Watergate for the country and for the media. Last month, however, Donahue put Bill Clinton on his show—and for half an hour engaged in a mud wrestling contest that was even too much for the studio audience.

Donahue was among those interviewed for the WNBC special report about "Where Do They Get Those People . . . ?," and on that report he uttered a damning extenuation to the effect that as Oprah and the others get farther out there, he too has to do it.

Yes, we have always had a sensational, popular, yellow tabloid press; and we have always had gossip columns, even powerful ones like Hedda Hopper's and Walter Winchell's. But never before have we had anything like today's situation in which supposedly serious people—I mean the so-called intellectual and social elites of this country—live and die by (and actually believe!) these columns and these shows and millions more rely upon them for their primary source of information. Liz Smith, *Newsday*'s gossip columnist and the best of a bad lot, has admitted blithely on more than a few occasions that she doesn't try very hard to check the accuracy of many of her items, or even give the subjects of her column the opportunity to comment on what is being said about them.

For the eight years of the Reagan presidency, the press failed to comprehend that Reagan was a real leader—however asleep at the switch he might have seemed, however shallow his intellect. No leader since FDR so changed the American landscape or saw his vision of the country and the world so thoroughly implanted. But in the Reagan years we in the press rarely went outside Washington to look at the relationship between policy and legislation and judicial appointments to see how the administration's policies were affecting the people—the children and the adults and the institutions of America: in education, in the workplace, in the courts, in the black community, in the family paycheck. In our ridicule of Reagan's rhetoric about the "evil empire," we failed to make the connection between Reagan's policies and the willingness of Gorbachev to loosen the vise of communism. Now the record is slowly becoming known. We have, in fact, missed most of the great stories of our generation, from Iran-contra to the savings and loan debacle.

The failures of the press have contributed immensely to the emergence of a talk-show nation, in which public discourse is reduced to ranting and raving and posturing. We now have a mainstream press whose news agenda is increasingly influenced by this netherworld. On the day that Nelson Mandela returned to Soweto and the allies of World War II agreed to the unification of Germany, the front pages of many "responsible" newspapers were devoted to the divorce of Donald and Ivana Trump.

Now the apotheosis of this talk-show culture is before us. I refer to Ross Perot, a candidate created and sustained by television, launched on "Larry King Live," whose willingness to bluster and to pose is far less in tune with the workings of liberal democracy than with the sumo-pundits of "The McLaughlin Group," a candidate whose only substantive proposal is to replace representative democracy with a live TV talk show for the entire nation. And this candidate, who haş dismissively deflected all media scrutiny with shameless assertions of his own ignorance, now leads both parties' candidates in the polls in several major states.

Today the most compelling news story in the world is the condition of America. Our political system is in a deep crisis; we are witnessing a breakdown of the comity and the community that has in the past allowed American democracy to build and to progress. Surely the advent of the talk-show nation is a part of this breakdown. Some good journalism is still being done today, to be sure, but it is the exception and not the rule. Good journalism requires a degree of courage in today's climate, a quality now in scarce supply in our mass media. Many current assumptions in America—about race, about economics, about the fate of our cities—need to be challenged, and we might start with the media. For, next to race, the story of the contemporary American media is the great uncovered story in America today. We need to start asking the same fundamental questions about the press that we do of the other powerful institutions in this society—about who is served, about standards, about self-interest and its eclipse of the public interest and the interest of truth. For the reality is that the media are probably the most powerful of all our institutions today; and they are squandering their power and ignoring their obligation. They—or more precisely, we—have abdicated our responsibility, and the consequence of our abdication is the spectacle, and the triumph, of the idiot culture.

JOURNALISM AND THE PUBLIC TRUST[4]

A public journal is a public trust. This is true whether you are talking about a newspaper or a magazine or a radio station or a television news program. I've always been fond of the maxim—slightly paraphrased here—that it's the journalist's duty to report the news and to raise hell. I was taught early on that one of the fundamentals of being a good journalist is to play no favorites, pull no punches, and—insofar as humanly possible—have no fear of the results.

Having said that, I'm pretty sure that, when I'm sitting in my rocker at the old folks' home or fishing my last river, among my regrets will be that I didn't raise enough hell—not that I raised too much. Believe me, there's plenty to raise hell about, and too few reporters left who believe in asking the tough questions—in raising a little hell. I do like the fact that, lately, that diminishing number of good reporters has been asking some pretty tough questions about leadership. *Time* magazine put it most bluntly last fall with a cover story asking the question: "Is Government Dead?" It went on to sum up the problem in a nutshell: "Unwilling to Lead, Politicians Are Letting America Slip into Paralysis."

David Broder recently expanded this discussion in the *Washington Post.* The headline to his column read: "Nation's Capitol in Eclipse as Pride and Power Slip Away." Broder laid the blame at the feet of those politicians who are too weak, he said, to exert American influence in a time of global change. "There's a lot of talk around Washington these days . . . about an allegedly pussy-footing Congress and a President who refuses to lead from the front." (Mark well, I'm quoting.) Most recently, the *New York Times* devoted a series to the fact that leadership in government has been replaced by an obsession with public opinion polls. Michael Orkesis, the *Times* reporter, came up with some pithy quotes. From Congressman David Obey: "Is American politics so brain dead that we've been reduced to having political shysters manipulate symbols?" From Congressman Mickey Edwards: "We've tended to trivialize issues to the point where meaningful debate has

    [4]Article by Dan Rather, from *The Humanist*, 50:5–7+ N/D '90. Copyright ©
1990 by the American Humanist Association, 1990. Reprinted with permission.

become almost impossible." From Lee Atwater: "Bull permeates everything."

That level of frustration and cynicism from government officials is disturbing. It is also news. It's good, honest reporting—the kind of tough questioning we're supposed to do to bring important issues to the public's attention. Personally, I don't think we need to apologize when our questions turn out to be disturbing. We're supposed to be honest brokers of information; our job certainly isn't to please the people we're covering, nor is it always to make America feel good about itself.

But as we in journalism ask these tough questions, honesty demands that we also face some facts about ourselves. One of those facts is that, when it comes to leadership, we aren't in a very good position to be casting stones. I'm reminded of the cartoon showing a politician on the stump saying, "If it's demonstrated to me that the American public wants leadership, then, by God, I'll give them leadership." Journalists *should* denounce government by public opinion polls. But we also ought to acknowledge that our own coverage of the news is more and more driven by this same kind of market research. "What kind of news are you most interested in hearing? Are you more interested in medicine, consumer affairs, the Trumps, or Tiananmen Square?" The networks have already gotten into the habit of screening news programs for "focus groups" in order to find out which stories are the most popular. Not which stories are the most *important*—which are the most *popular*. And focus groups have long been used by many newspapers as well.

Market research tells us that the public isn't clamoring for more news about government. Stories about the national debt and the national trade deficit—so we're told—don't sell newspapers or attract advertisers to broadcasts. And so too many of us use that rationale to avoid covering the issues that will shape our lives and the lives of our children—indeed, the very future of our country. Market research also tells us that international news is not of paramount concern to the public; and, sure enough, the trend in coverage is *away from* foreign news stories, the incredible events of 1989 notwithstanding. Last fall, one of those fancy think-tanks in New York which seems to specialize in bashing television news (at least from my standpoint) published a study entitled "The International News Hole: An Endangered Species." This study documented how deeply 10 of our most acclaimed newspapers have slashed foreign news coverage over the past two decades. In 1971, over 10 percent of their editorial space was devoted to foreign news. In 1988, their foreign news coverage dropped to *one-quarter* of that—2.6 percent. And this is in our best newspapers: 2.6 percent of their editorial space devoted to foreign news coverage at the very time it has become indisputably clear that America's future depends upon our having a better understanding of that great big world beyond our shores. Foreign news coverage was slashed by our best newspapers at the very time when we watched our economy falter in the face of foreign competition.

I do not bring this up in order to pat myself on the back. We make a lot of mistakes on the "CBS Evening News," and in some important ways it's true that the "CBS Evening News" is not even as good as your average newspaper, particularly when it comes to depth, perspective, and context. But here's the point: in television, too, there are powerful forces arguing against foreign news coverage. Consultants continually tell news directors at local stations that foreign news is a turn-off. As a result, you don't see much foreign news on local station newscasts. "But that's okay," you may respond, "that's not their province; the networks, with their greater financial and material resources, will take care of foreign news coverage." However, these days the networks are aswarm with cost-paranoid accountants damning what they see as the comparatively high price tag on foreign news coverage. Too often now the question comes up: "Why do you need all those foreign bureaus and foreign correspondents? Why not just buy news footage from somebody—anybody—and narrate the stories from New York?" It's kind of ironic; for years, newspaper reporters asked the right question, which was: "Why do we allow the nation's priorities to be set by broadcast journalists—all those anchor men and managing editors cooped up in windowless rooms on the west side of Manhattan?" Now our accountants pose a different question: "Come on, Dan, do you *really* have to leave New York? Can't you just report the news from here?"

As journalism becomes more and more competitive, all of us—whether in broadcast news or in print (some may want to argue that this is true more of broadcast news, and I perhaps wouldn't want to debate that)—are falling back on the tried and true local news formulas. We have, by and large, accepted the proposition that people don't care about foreign news, don't really care much about hard news at all—that "feel-good" news, entertainment, "infotainment," features, and gossip sell better than anything serious and certainly sell better than anything too disturbing.

I believe that kind of talk is wrong. I believe that kind of talk is dangerous. And I know that kind of talk has nothing to do with leadership and public service. Using public opinion polls, focus groups, and other market research techniques in a limited role as *informational tools* is one thing; using them as an excuse to duck our responsibility to the public trust is quite another. And for journalists to become slaves to market research—like the politicians before us—is, I submit, most dangerous of all. Where are the publishers, editors, and reporters of grit, gumption, and guts? Where are the ones who will follow their conscience or even their "nose for news" instead of the public opinion polls? Harry Truman once said that, if Moses had taken a public opinion poll, he would never have left Egypt.

Of course, there is one special problem for those of us who earn our living reporting the news that others make. Leadership requires definite opinions on which course to take, what path to follow; but those of us in the mainstream media are trained to set our opinions aside as far as humanly possible. We try to keep open minds; by and large, we aren't joiners. We know (often better than we're given credit for) that we don't have any secret formulas for answering the important questions. So we can justifiably ask: "How are we to lead?" I think a lot of politicians are ducking this very question. I *know* that we in the media are. George Bernard Shaw once observed that newspapers are unable to distinguish between a bicycle accident and the collapse of civilization. Today he might say that we are unable to distinguish between the breakup of the Trump marriage and the breakup of the communist empire. For us, leadership should be the willingness to distinguish between what's merely interesting and what's vitally important.

Now, when someone says that some stories are more important than others, he or she is often labeled an elitist, someone who just doesn't understand what "real people" care about. This is, of course, the familiar defense for trash television and trash tabloids. And it's also the reason given for reducing foreign news coverage, as well as coverage of political campaigns. There are a lot of people in the business who say "'real people' won't care unless it bleeds or burns. There are a lot of news doctors and market researchers out there who insist that "real people" care only about entertainment, sex, and cats. According to these "experts," "real people" don't care much what happens in the rest of the world—they want the words *American* and *the United States* plastered all over their news like flags crowding a campaign platform.

Well, I don't buy it. I come from a family of people who worked with their hands, who put their backs into it. Sam Houston State Teachers College (where I went to school) has about as much ivy on it as your average McDonald's. I did not grow up with or go to school with any of these "real people" that the news consultants are so knowledgeable about. I also travel a good deal and talk to a lot of people, but none of them fits that description either. The people I meet are concerned about their jobs and their families and their country. They want their lives to have meaning, and they're worried that their children's lives may not be better than theirs. They are struggling to understand the changes that they know are happening all around them. They can separate bull shine from brass tacks—and often a whole lot better than we journalists who are supposed to be experts at it. These "real people" know what's going on, and they have a thirst to understand and come to grips with it. And I think they'd be offended to hear what some editors and reporters, taking their cue from the market researchers and the news consultants, say they care about. Those who say that "real people" care only about trash television and tabloids are the ones who are out of touch. *They* are the elitists.

In Search of Excellence became a runaway bestseller because it spoke to the actual concerns of real people. America's "real people" want a country of excellence and quality and principle. A friend of mine told me a story: he's building a house in upstate New York, not an area of the country that has been experiencing any great economic boom. One day, not too long ago, my friend paid a visit to his contractor. After the usual chat about the weather, the contractor started talking about Nelson Mandela. For the next half hour, my friend says, the discussion with the contractor and the plumber and the plumber's assistant was about South Africa, Mikhail Gorbachev, and how long Fidel Castro can hold out.

For these "real people," television has become much more than a means of entertainment and information. Like it or not, we have all become part of a kind of worldwide electronic democracy. We saw the English language banners in Tiananmen Square. And we heard "We Shall Overcome" in front of the Berlin Wall.

Television has become a kind of visual two-way telephone. We talk to the world, and the world talks back. But if we keep shutting down one end of the conversation—because it doesn't sell newspapers or because the ratings go down when we're overseas—forget about leadership. We may make money, we may increase our ratings or our circulation, but we won't *lead*. And, as a result, we will have prostituted the public trust.

"Okay," you say, "so what are your answers?" Well, for one, as simple as it may sound—and I hope it sounds simple because it is something we can accomplish—we need to *rededicate* ourselves to original reporting and analysis by first-rate writers, journalists, and thinkers. Sometimes that will mean paying more money for reporters with better minds and giving them the chance to do what they do best. Broadcast news and newspapers are in danger of sinking into a miasma of mediocrity, with a new generation of hacks turning out cliched images which match their cliched writing, in formats rapidly degenerating into trite and stale formulas.

Make no mistake: we are in considerable danger of losing our appeal to the best and the brightest of the next generation. Journalism is now attracting more than its share of lightweights and careerists instead of writers, reporters, and dreamers. We're attracting too many people who love the limelight and too few people who love the news. Too many of us are becoming known as news *packagers*, not news gatherers. Once we had the reputation of working for organizations that would pay any price, go any distance to get an important story; now we have the reputation of working for a bunch of bean counters in yet another news factory.

We in print and broadcasting can dish it out—and we should. Many politicians are not doing their jobs at either end of Pennsylvania Avenue nor around most state capitals nor around most city halls or courthouses. The *Time* magazine cover is dead on the money: "Unwilling to Lead, Politicians Are Letting America Slip into Paralysis." But we in journalism can't lay the blame exclusively at the feet of the politicians. There *is* such a thing as journalistic leadership. It has nothing to do with arrogance or self-righteousness, with journalists setting themselves up as some kind of shadow government. Nor does it have anything to do with ratings or circulation or bigger profits. It has to do instead with nobler ideals: with public service and caring and, yes—I don't flinch from the word—patriotism. The *Time* article talks about a "frightening inability to define and debate America's emerging problems. A *now-nowism*. Our collective short-sightedness." And it concludes that the list of missed opportunities and challenges is already much too long: "The sooner government sets about doing its job again, the better." To which I say, "Amen," but add that the sooner we in journalism set about doing *our* job again, the better.

OLD NEWS IS GOOD NEWS[5]

Mine is the reporter's perspective—one small fish in that vast ocean we call the media. I want to put in a word for the craft, for reporting, the old-fashioned kind.

When I began working for *Harper's* in 1970, I though I understood what the word "news" meant, where information stopped and entertainment began; what newspapers did that was different from television. Since then, we have witnessed a media explosion, the effect of which is like standing at ground zero seconds after the explosion of the atomic bomb. Walter Lippmann told us that journalism is a picture of reality people can act upon. What we see today is a society acting upon reality refracted a thousand different ways.

Where is America's mind today? It's in the organs, for one thing. Now folks can turn on a series called *Real Sex* and watch a home striptease class; its premier was HBO's highest-rated documentary for the year. Or they can flip over to NBC News and get *I Witness Video*. There they can see a policeman's murder recorded in his cruiser's camcorder, watch it replayed and relived in interviews, complete with ominous music. Or they can see the video of a pregnant woman plunging from a blazing building's window, can see it several times, at least once in slow motion. Yeats was right: "We have fed the heart on fantasies, and the heart's grown brutal from the fare."

I wonder if *Real Sex* and *I Witness Video* take us deeper into reality or insanity? How does a reporter tell the difference anymore in a world where Oliver Stone can be praised for his "journalistic instincts" when he has Lyndon Johnson tell a cabal of generals and admirals: "Get me elected and I'll get you your war."

Rolling Stone dubs all this the "New News." Straight news—the

[5]Article by Bill Moyers, from *New Perspectives Quarterly* 9:35–37 Fall '92. Copyright © 1992 by *New Perspectives Quarterly*. Reprinted with permission.

Old News by *Rolling Stone's* definition—is "pooped, confused, and broke." In its place a new culture of information is evolving—"a heady concoction, part Hollywood film and TV, part pop music and pop art, mixed with popular culture and celebrity magazines, tabloid telecasts, cable and home video." Increasingly, says the magazine, the New News is seizing the function of mainstream journalism, sparking conversation and setting the country's social and political agenda. So it is that we learn first from Bruce Springsteen that the jobs aren't coming back. So it is that inner-city parents who don't subscribe to daily newspapers are taking their children to see the movie *Juice* to educate them about the consequences of street violence; that young people think Bart Simpson's analysis of America more trenchant than many newspaper columnists; that we learn just how violent, brutal and desperate society is, not from the establishment press, but from Spike Lee, Public Enemy, the Geto Boys and Guns N' Roses.

I don't want to seem a moralist. The public often knows what's news before we professionals do. But there's a problem: In this vast pounding ocean of media, newspapers are in danger of extinction. I don't mean that they're going to disappear altogether—but I do feel that we are in danger of losing the central role the great newspapers have historically played in the functioning of our political system.

Once newspapers drew people to the public square. They provided a culture of community conversation. The purpose of news was not just to represent and inform, "but to signal, tell a story and activate inquiry." When the press abandons that function, it no longer stimulates what the American philosopher John Dewey termed "the vital habits" of democracy—"the ability to follow an argument, grasp the point of view of another, expand the boundaries of understanding, debate the alternative purposes that might be pursued."

I know times have changed, and so must the newspapers. I know that while it's harder these days to be a reporter, it's also harder to be a publisher, caught between *Sesame Street* and Wall Street—between the entertainment imperatives that are nurtured in the cradle and survival economics that can send a good paper to the grave.

I sense we're approaching Gettysburg, the moment of truth, the decisive ground for this cultural war—for publishers especially. Americans say they no longer trust journalists to tell them the truth about their world. Young people have difficulty finding anything of relevance to their lives in the daily newspaper. Non-tabloid newspapers are viewed as increasingly elitist, self-important and corrupt on the one hand; on the other, they are increasingly lumped together with the tabloids as readers perceive the increasing desperation with which papers are now trying to reach "down-market" in order to replace the young readers who are not replacing their elders.

Meanwhile, a study by the Kettering Foundation confirms that our political institutions are fast losing their legitimacy; that increasing numbers of Americans believe they are being dislodged from their rightful place in democracy by politicians, powerful lobbyists and the media—three groups they see as an autonomous political class impervious to the long-term interests of the country and manipulating the democratic discourse so that people are treated only as consumers to be entertained rather than citizens to be engaged.

That our system is failing to solve the bedrock problems we face is beyond dispute. One reason is that our public discourse has become the verbal equivalent of mud wrestling. The anthropologist Marvin Harris says the attack against reason and objectivity in America today "is fast reaching the proportion of a crusade." America, he says, "urgently needs to reaffirm the principle that it is possible to carry out an analysis of social life that rational human beings will recognize as being true, regardless of whether they happen to be women or men, whites or blacks, straights or gays, Jews or born-again Christians." Lacking such an understanding of social life, "we will tear the United States apart in the name of our separate realities."

Taken together, these assumptions and developments foreshadow the catastrophe of social and political paralysis. But what's truly astonishing about this civic disease is that it exists in America just as a series of powerful democratic movements have been toppling autocratic regimes elsewhere in the world. While people around the globe are clamoring for self-government, millions of Americans are feeling as if they have been locked out of their homes and are unable to regain their rightful place in the operation of democracy. On the other hand, those same millions want to believe that it is still in their power to change America.

The Center for Citizen Politics at the University of Minnesota reports that beneath America's troubled view of politics "is a public that cares very deeply about public life. This concern is a strong foundation for building healthy democratic practices and new traditions of public participation in politics."

People want to know what is happening to them, and what they can do about it. Listening to America, you realize that millions of people are not apathetic; they want to signify; and they will respond to a press that stimulates the community without pandering to it; that inspires people to embrace their responsibilities without lecturing or hectoring them; and that engages their better natures without sugarcoating ugly realities or patronizing their foibles.

THE MAKE-BELIEVE MEDIA[6]

Make-believe. The word connotes the playful games and fantasies of our childhood—a pleasant way of pretending. But in the world created by movies and television, make-believe takes on a more serious meaning. In some way or other, many people come to believe the fictional things they see on the big and little screens. The entertainment media are the make-believe media; they make us believe.

Today, instead of children's games, storytelling, folk tales, and fables of our own making, we have the multibillion-dollar industries of Hollywood and television to fill our minds with prefabricated images and themes. Nor are these just idle distractions, for such images often have real ideological content. Even if supposedly not political in intent, the entertainment industry has been political in its impact, discouraging critical perceptions of our social order while planting pictures in our heads that have been supportive of U.S. militarism, armed intervention abroad, phobic anti-communism, authoritarian violence, consumer acquisitiveness, racial and sexual stereotypes, vigilantism, simple-minded religiosity, and anti-working-class attitudes.

Remarking on the prevalence of media-induced stereotypes of African-Americans, Ellen Holly put it well: "Again and again, I have seen black actors turned down for parts because they were

[6]Article by Michael Parenti, from *The Humanist* 50:18–20 N/D '90. Copyright © 1990 by the American Humanist Association. Reprinted with permission.

told that they did not look the way a black person should or sound the way a black person should. What is this business of 'should'? What kind of box are we being put into? I have seen black writers told that the black characters they put down on a page were not believable because they were too intelligent."

Studies show that women, too, are put in a box: portrayed mostly in subsidiary roles and depicted as less capable, effective, or interesting than the more numerous white male principals. To be sure, things have changed somewhat. Women can now be seen playing lawyers, judges, cops, executives, professionals, and sometimes even workers, but the questions of gender equality and the fight for feminist values are seldom joined. Likewise, the struggles of sleep-starved, underpaid single mothers trying to raise their children and survive in an inhospitable environment are not usually considered an appropriate theme for prime-time television or Hollywood.

Working people of both genders and whatever ethnic background are still underrepresented in the media. With few exceptions, such as the movie *Norma Rae,* they play minor walk-on roles as waiters, service people, gas station attendants, and the like in an affluent, upper-middle-class, media-created world. Blue-collar people are portrayed as emotional, visceral, simple-hearted and simple-minded, and incapable of leadership or collective action against the injustices they face in their workplace and community. Their unions are depicted as doing more harm than good for them. Given the hostility that network and studio bosses have manifested toward organized labor in the entertainment industry, it is small wonder that labor unions are almost always portrayed— if at all—in an unsympathetic light.

Generally speaking, whether it's a movie about factory workers, cops and crime, or the invasion of galactic monsters, it is individual heroics rather than collective action that save the day. Solutions and victories are never won by ordinary good people, organizing and struggling for mutual betterment, but by the hero in self-willed combat, defying the odds and sometimes even the authorities to vanquish the menace and triumph.

In as great a supply as the heroes of the make-believe media are the purveyors of violence and macho toughness: the military man, cop, counterinsurgency agent, spycatcher, private investigator, and adventurer. From Dirty Harry to Rambo, it's all helicopter gunships, screeching car chases, and endless shoot-em-ups and punch-em-outs. Check the movie ads in your newspaper and count the number of weapons displayed. Flip your television dial during prime time and count the number of guns or fistfights or other acts of violence and aggression. They are even more numerous than the commercials.

To be sure, iconoclastic opinions and images get through now and then. Liberal and even strongly progressive themes can be found in an occasional movie or television episode. Underdog and dissident voices are heard for rare moments. But these are the exceptions. As media critic Erik Barnouw concludes: "Popular entertainment is basically propaganda for the status quo." And sociologist Hal Himmelstein believes that television has become "one of our society's principal repositories of {conventional} ideology."

Do these media images and themes have any real effect on us? Indeed they do. In modern mass society, people rely to a great extent upon distant image-makers for their cues about a vast world. In both entertainment and news shows, the media invent a reality much their own. Our notion of what a politician, a detective, a corporate executive, a farmer, an African, or a Mexican-American is supposed to be like; our view of what rural or inner city life should be; our anticipations about romantic experience and sexual attractiveness, crime and foreign enemies, dictators and revolutionaries, bureaucrats and protestors, police and prostitutes, workers and communists—all are heavily colored by our exposure to movies and television shows.

Many of us have never met an Arab, but few of us lack some picture in our minds of what an Arab is supposed to be like. If drawn largely from the mass media, this image will be a stereotype—and most likely a defamatory one. As Walter Lippmann noted almost 70 years ago, stereotypic thinking "precedes reason" and "as a form of perception [it] imposes a certain character on the data of our senses." When we respond to a real life situation with the exclamation "Just like in the movies!" we are expressing our recognition and even satisfaction that our media-created mental frames find corroboration in the real world.

The media images in our heads influence how we appraise a host of social realities, including our government's domestic and foreign policies. If we have "learned" from motion pictures and television series that our nation is forever threatened by hostile alien forces, then we are apt to support increased military spending and warlike interventions. If we have "learned" that inner-city denizens are violent criminals, then we are more apt to support

authoritarian police measures and cuts in human services to the
inner city.

Audiences usually do some perceptual editing, projecting
something of their own viewpoint upon what they see. But this
editing itself is partly conditioned by the previously internalized
images fed to us by the same media we are now viewing. In other
words, rather than being rationally critical of the images and
ideologies of the entertainment media, our minds—after prolonged exposure to earlier programs and films—sometimes become active accomplices in our own indoctrination.

We are probably more affected by what we see than we realize.
Jeffrey Schrank notes that 90 percent of the nation's adult viewers consider themselves to be "personally immune" from the appeals of television advertisements; yet, this same 90 percent accounts for about 90 percent of all sales of advertised products.
While we might think it is always other people (less intelligent
than ourselves) who are being manipulated by sales appeals and
entertainment shows, the truth might be something else.

Media critic Jerry Mander argues that electronic images are
"irresistible," since our brains absorb them regardless of how we
might consciously perceive such images. Children believe that
what they are seeing on television and in the movies is real; they
have no innate capacity to distinguish between real and unreal
images. Only as they grow older, after repeated assurances from
their elders, do they begin to understand that the stories and
characters on the big and little screens do not exist in real life. In
other words, *their ability to reject media images as unreal has to be
learned.*

The problem does not end there, however. Even as adults,
when we consciously know that a particular media offering is
fictional, we still "believe" it to some extent—that is, we still accu-
mulate impressions that lead to beliefs about the real world. When
drawing upon images in our heads, we do not keep our store of
media imagery distinct and separate from our store of real-world
imagery. "The mind doesn't work that way," says Mander.

The most pervasive effect of television—aside from its actual
content—may be its very existence, its readily available, com-
manding, and often addictive presence in our homes, its ability to
reduce hundreds of millions of citizens to passive spectators for
major portions of their lives. Television minimizes interactions
between persons within families and communities. One writer I
know only half-jokingly claims, "I watch television mainly as a way

of getting to know my husband and children." Another associate of mine, who spent years in Western agricultural regions, relates how a farmer once told her: "Folks used to get together a lot. Now with television, we see less of each other."

Claims made about the media's influence sometimes can be unduly alarmist. It is not all a matter of our helpless brains being electronically pickled by the sinister tube. But that is no excuse for dismissing the important impact the media do have. The more time people spend watching television and movies, the more their impressions of the world seem to resemble those of the media. Academic media critics George Gerbner and Larry Gross found that heavy television users, having been fed abundant helpings of crime and violence, are more likely to overestimate the amount of crime and violence that exists in real life. They are also more apt to overestimate the number of police in the United States, since they see so many on television. "While television may not directly cause the results that have turned up in our studies," conclude Gerbner and Gross, "it certainly can confirm or encourage certain views of the world."

In sum, it is not just a matter of the entertainment industry giving the people what they want but of playing an active role in creating those wants. As any advertiser knows, supply not only satisfies demand, it helps create demand, conditioning our tastes and patterning our responses. The single greatest factor in consumption is product availability. For every ounce of quality programming and quality movies made available to us, the media also give us a ton of mind rot.

Those who produce images for mass consumption exercise an enormous power, but they are not omnipotent. They are not entirely free from public pressure. The viewing audience is sometimes more than just a passive victim. There are times when popular agitation, advances in democratic consciousness, and changes in public taste and educational levels have forced the media to modify or discard the images that are served up. The public has to keep fighting back. We got rid of Amos 'n' Andy and Sambo; we can get rid of Dirty Harry and Rambo.

More important than eliminating the bad shows is demanding better ones—for our children and ourselves. Viewing movies like *Glory* and television series like "Roots" are a far better way to learn about the African-American experience than watching shows like "The Jeffersons." A movie like *Salt of the Earth* tells us more about the realities of the labor struggle and blue-collar life than the clownlike Archie Bunker on "All in the Family." A film like *Born on the Fourth of July* tells us more about the heart-wrenching realities of war than all the John Wayne and Rambo flicks put together. Better entertainment can be produced that is not only intelligent and socially significant but also capable of attracting large audiences. But at present there is not enough of it, and the little there is usually gets poorly distributed and modestly advertised— if at all.

There is nothing wrong with mindless relaxation in front of a viewing screen now and then. What is wrong is when it becomes a way of life, preempting our experience and taking over our brains, providing us with a prefabricated understanding of what the world is supposed to be. And this it does for too many people. A better awareness of how we are manipulated by the make-believe media might cause us to waste fewer hours of our precious lives in front of both the big and little screens and allow us more time for reading, conversing, relating to our friends and families, criticizing social injustice, and becoming active citizens of our society and the effective agents of our own lives.

III. STORIES, TRENDS

EDITOR'S INTRODUCTION

To understand American journalism and its relationship to the public, it is important to look at the events that have helped define what is news today. Just as JFK's assassination, the Vietnam war, and Watergate were watershed events of the not-too-distant past that greatly affected American society by the manner in which they were presented to us, so too are the many events discussed in this section.

What we consider news or "newsworthy" has not totally changed: wars, disasters, and political indiscretions have always been "front page" material. What is different now is the ubiquitous existence of videotape, which so often seems to offer images at the expense of understanding.

The articles in this section deal primarily with the medium that Americans use as their main source of information, television. The first three articles look at some of the biggest news stories of the early 1990s. Tom Engelhardt, writing in *The Nation*, comments on the birth of "total television;" that is, a "real-time" event packaged for viewers as a "T.V. Special" rather than as reportage. Engelhardt's viewpoint has proven prophetic, in light of the recent coverage of O.J. Simpson's attempted escape from authorities on a California highway, which was packaged as a sports spectacular. The event—which included anchor-type commentary on the "game," side-line spectators, and even "cheerleaders"—transfixed 95 million viewers to their T.V. sets. Correspondent Christopher Hanson under the pseudonym "William Boot" recounts in the *Columbia Journalism Review* the media's role and the public reaction to it during the Clarence Thomas–Anita Hill controversy; and Charles Oliver, in an article from *Reason*, discusses reportage of the 1992 Los Angeles riots.

The article "Naming Names," written by Barbara Kantrowitz and reprinted from *Newsweek*, explores the ethics involved when the media choose to reveal or withhold the names of rape victims. Jon Katz's article "The Plugged-In Voter," reprinted from *Rolling*

Stone, looks at the "New News": Larry King, CNN, Donahue, Oprah, C-Span, and a panoply of emerging news sources.

Elayne Rapping, writing about "Court T.V." in the *Progressive,* and Jon Katz, writing about the syndicated show "Cops" in the *Columbia Journalism Review,* explore the coverage of not only these two phenomena, but also coverage on legal and police activities in general, and find that these programs have merits beyond their "narrowcasting" appeal to niche audiences. In the final article, however, Krista Bradford, writing in *Rolling Stone,* takes a look at tabloid television and reveals the business to be about as smarmy as its critics charge.

THE GULF WAR AS TOTAL TELEVISION[1]

Here we've just cruised past the first anniversary of the bombing of Iraq—Gulf-War-plus-one (plus)—and the packs of Desert Storm bubblegum cards are long gone from newsstand counters. The war to re-establish war, American-style, seems to have vaporized even before Gen. H. Norman Schwarzkopf (retired) could get his memoirs into print. All that's left here of that twenty-four-hours-a-day, eye-burning, blood-pumping, high-tech, all-channel media event are self-satisfied military men and resentful journalists, both acting as if the initial bombing run on Baghdad had had CNN's outpost at the Al-Rashid Hotel as its target. But those who now claim that the media were the "losers" in the Gulf War, that censorship, press pools and military handlers galore represented an epic Bush Administration triumph over reportorial independence, still can't see the screen for the pixels.

What we viewed last year was less the death of independent media than the birth of "total television," a new co-production process to which normal labels of media critique and complaint largely don't apply. The Gulf War can, in fact, be seen as the ur-production of the new media conglomerate. For it, the war proved promising exactly because the boundaries between military action and media event broke down in such a way that military planning could become a new form of media reality.

[1]Article by Tom Engelhardt, from *The Nation* 254:613+ My 11 '92. Copyright © 1992 by The Nation Company, L.P. Reprinted with permission.

Total television can be seen to have its antecedents neither in traditional war reportage nor in American war mythology. It was not even the child of Vietnam, which was not (as is so often said) our first television war but our last nontelevision one in its inability either to adhere to precise scheduling or achieve closure. Instead, total TV was born in certain mesmeric moments in the eighties when the whole nation seemed to have been mobilized at couchside to stare at the same images across many channels.

Starting with the Iran hostage crisis of 1979–81 and running through the Gulf War, these glimpses of total TV generally had the theme of America or Americans held hostage—most humiliatingly in Iran; most tragically in various terrorist plane-nappings and murders; most pathetically in the Challenger disaster, in which a schoolteacher's life was hostaged to the failure of American technology; most absurdly in the little girl hostaged to the elements by her fall down a well shaft in Texas; most triumphantly in the images of students kissing American soil after their ostensible rescue from Grenada.

From the media's point of view, most of these events were, fortunately, quite limited. One kidnapped plane on an airport runway; one embassy surrounded by a crowd; a few film clips of an explosion replayed a hundred times—all of the above surrounded by talking heads; or one small war in a distant place with only the most minimal government-supplied visuals. To create more expansive total TV scenarios would have been ruinously expensive without outside help. Even Ted Turner's Cable News Network, set up for any and all twenty-four-hours-a-day media events, would have quickly felt the financial strain of total TV if left purely to its own devices. Just the attempt to re-create the Good War for the miniseries adapted from Herman Wouk's novel *The Winds of War* proved a financial catastrophe for ABC. It was not enough to mobilize an audience. New forms of sponsorship were needed.

Here we have to remember the corporate context within which the possibility for Gulf War–style total television developed. On the one hand, during the eighties media giants like Time-Warner, Murdoch's News Corporation and the Maxwell combine were being stapled together, and under their roofs distinct media forms were blurring into mix-and-match TV/movie/ newspaper/magazine/book/music/theme-park entities. On the other hand, just to put such entities together (as corporations gobbled and were gobbled up, merged and purged their way through the decade) was to incur incalculable billions of dollars of debt. The burden of this debt—and a crumbling ad market by decade's end—gave rise to new pressures to "downsize"these unwieldy, not especially synergistic new entities. Fewer personnel and cheaper production methods were instantly needed to make them more financially palatable to nervous owners (or suddenly anxious potential buyers).

General Electric, Capital Cities and the Tisch family operation, which had come to control respectively NBC, ABC and CBS, also found themselves facing an assault on their audiences and their advertisers from cable television and Murdoch's new fourth network, Fox. The swift erosion of network dominance in the late eighties led money managers within each network to hack away at their prestigious but often unprofitable news fiefdoms. If the Gulf War revealed the media's ability to mount technical operations on an unprecedented scale, it also exposed the need of the financially pressed media giants (and their upstart competitors) for sponsorship on a scale hitherto unimaginable. This is what the Bush Administration seemed to offer in the Gulf War—an outside production company able to organize a well-produced, subsidized total event that could be channeled to the American public at, relatively speaking, bargain-basement prices.

With its million or more uniformed extras, its vast sets and its six-month preproduction schedule filled with logistical miracles (and a few fiascos, too), the Gulf War production involved intense military/media planning on a global scale. It had its own built-in "coming attractions"—the many variations on "Showdown in the Gulf" that teased viewers with a possible January opening on all screens in domestic multiplexes across the nation. It had its dazzling Star Wars–style graphics, theme music and logos, as well as stunningly prime-timed first moments (Disneyesque fireworks over Baghdad).

To succeed as a production company, the Pentagon had to offer the networks five things: first, funding based on a relatively limited financial contribution from the networks themselves. This was accomplished by a State Department/Pentagon financing team that sought out foreign investment much as any Hollywood production team might have—from the Japanese, the Germans, the Saudis and so on—$50 billion, you might say, for "foreign rights," money that insured a break-even point on the government side of the enterprise almost before the first missile was fired; second, the ability to organize round-the-clock, on-location support systems across a vast theater of operations; third, a pre-edited flow of visuals available to all channels; fourth, control over access to the set of the production, thus limiting internetwork competition and consequently network costs (those last two usually fall under the rubric of "censorship"); and finally, the sort of precise scheduling and closure that television craves.

At the Pentagon, much thought had already gone into matters of scheduling and closure—this, out of a post-Vietnam desire to create a Third World battlefield where maximal weaponry and minimal U.S. casualties would guarantee public support. In the eighties, a new wave of "smart" (and not-so-smart but highly destructive) weaponry was brought on-line to complement an already impressive Vietnam-era arsenal. In the Persian Gulf, as a result, the preponderance and superiority of American weaponry—as well as the near nonappearance of the "enemy"—made slaughter on a vast scale, at will and with an eye to television's tight time requirements, achievable.

What President Bush then could promise the nation—and the media—was a war that could be scheduled, and this promise was structured not only into war planning but into the minds of the warmakers. As Bob Woodward reported in his book *The Commanders,* "In the White House, Bush, Quayle, Scowcroft and Sununu gathered in the small private study adjacent to the Oval Office to watch television. When the sounds of bombing could be heard behind the voices of the reporters still in their Baghdad hotel rooms, Bush, visibly relieved, said, 'Just the way it was scheduled.'"

Pressure for closure was built into the war's logo-ized form—"The War in the Gulf, Day X"—and reassurance on this score was forthcoming from the war's first moments. In fact, one striking feature of the war was how often the viewing public was told that it was unfolding "on schedule." Nearly every military news conference included such a reminder, and the schedule being referred to was clearly television's. The public was constantly assured by the war's supporters that it would be clean, manageable, foreseeable, endable—in short, a program.

In the past, the reporting of war had been successfully organized and controlled by governments, and generals had polished their images with the press or even, like Douglas MacArthur, had had publicists do it for them—and, of course, images of war and generalship American-style had been re-created on-screen innumerable times by actors. But never had generals and war planners gone before the public as actors, supported by all the means a "studio" could muster on their behalf, and determined to produce a program that would fill the entire day across the dial for the full time of a "war." What we have to imagine (for we were not shown it) is that behind the dark curtains that screened off the multiple daily press conferences of the various actors, each in his distinctive fashion/camouflage outfit, each wielding his distinctive sitcom quips and put-downs, each giving his distinctive impression of the Victorious General or the In-Control Press Spokesman, lay a globe-spanning network of scriptwriters, makeup artists, fashion consultants, graphic designers, production managers, film editors (otherwise known as "censors") and even a military version of the traditional network Standards and Practices department, with its guidelines for on-air acceptability.

Only military pre-editing of virtually all aspects of the Gulf War made total television's six-week-long ratings hit a possibility. Hence, despite the uneasiness of some journalists on the scene, the TV networks understandably offered no significant protest against the censoring and controlling mechanisms of the Bush Administration—which were largely in their interest. In fact, no well-known media company was willing to join more marginal publications like *The Nation* and New York's *Village Voice* and journalists like *Newsday's* Sydney Schanberg in their legal challenge to Pentagon censorship policies [see Jacqueline E. Sharkey, "The Media's War," (*The Nation*, May 11, 1992)]. In this way, the Gulf War experience, which offered the media giants new possibilities in the production of entertainment, also brought journalism's already tattered post-Watergate, post-Vietnam heroic self-image down to earth.

It's not surprising, then, that reporters in hotel lounges in Dhahran watching the war on TV just like everyone else would see the military's media role mainly as a censorious one, but this was to miss the point. A more useful comparison would be to those TV production companies that, in the early eighties, began creating a new-style children's television program. Usually done in conjunction with toy companies and their ad agencies, these shows in one quick leap eliminated the boundaries between ad and show by making what were essentially animated, program-length catalogues for toys.

In a similar way, the Gulf War production launched a major new form of the program-length commercial. It was as if the whole post-Vietnam era in America had built toward this forty-three-day-long ad, intent on selling both domestic and foreign markets on the renewal of American virtues. If you want to feel good, be U.S. If you want to experience technology and triumph, buy U.S. It even used the simplified visual language of the eighties ad—the upbeat, brightly colored (sales) story, whose happy ending was meant to confound the darkness of the world beyond the screen with the sprightliness of the product. No one looking at the many carefully framed visuals of the Gulf War could doubt the advertorial nature of the show, segmented as it was into sets of mini-ads for various aspects of itself.

What made this program-length ad unique, though, was the length of the program, and the fact that its newness and its commercial form unexpectedly threw into question the nature of normal television advertising. If *this* was The Ad, then what were those? Although CNN, ready-made for total TV, experienced rising ad rates and revenues during the war, for the networks it was another story. Non-CNN advertisers were unsure of how their ads would coexist with "war" in this puzzling new version of entertainment time. Of course, the war they, like so many media experts, military men and journalists, were imagining was a war of body bags. In the end, their failure to grasp the nature of this new media experience and their consequent refusal to support the production helped make total television into a financial fiasco for the big three networks. They found themselves showing a vast commercial while losing revenue from the very advertisers who felt more comfortable inside *Cheers* than inside the cheering framework of a war to destroy Iraq. (According to media critic John MacArthur in his new book, *Second Front: Censorship and Propaganda in the Gulf War,* NBC, which like CBS ran behind ABC in the ratings, claimed losses of $55 million on its war coverage, including $20 million in withdrawn ad revenue. One postwar result at CBS, at least, was a further downsizing of its news department).

This confusion over sponsorship reflected not only total television's primitive state but the likelihood that "war" might not be its ultimate venue. For one thing, the military, with its adversarial attitude toward the media, inhibited the flow of fresh images that might have fed total television's voracious appetite, and so left Monday Night War's color commentators like Anthony Cordesman (ABC) and retired Gen. Michael Dugan (CBS) trapped at halftime with no game to call.

In fact, no greater problem faced the military/media production team than its inability to establish a suitably epic story at the heart of total television. From the initial "Battle in the Gulf" (the 1981 dogfights with Libyan MIGs over the Gulf of Sidra) to the invasions of Grenada and Panama, the Reagan and Bush administrations had engaged in a decade-long experiment in the controlled presentation of American battlefield triumph. This attempt to re-establish a triumphalist American war story via the media and in the wake of Vietnam ended up, in the Persian Gulf, as little more than a passing advertorial. Missing in action in the war's coverage were not so much independent media, which had seldom existed in the history of American warfare (if anything, military censorship and misleading reportage were far more severe in World War II and Korea), but any sense of what form a lasting, empathetic war narrative could take without a military struggle in which to ground itself.

Off-screen, events in the gulf were closer to a mass electrocution than a war, and as a result, on-screen no Iraqi aggressors fell by the hundreds from their charging camels in the sort of battle our film tradition called for. Nor could armies be discovered clashing in their multi-thousands, nor tank battles—billed as potentially the largest since World War II—ranging across desert vistas. In fact, the crucial production number, D-day, renamed "G-day" (for ground war day), turned out to be no day at all. The penultimate event of the post-Vietnam era, in which the Not-Vietnamese were to be crushed in battle, had to be elided, for at the heart of this technically awesome spectacle was an embarrassingly plotless and unwatchable slaughter. The best that could be offered from an enemy who refused to put in an appearance were scenes of bedraggled Iraqis emerging from their dugouts to surrender and shots of Iraqi-commandeered cars, trucks and buses turned to charred rubble on the highway out of Kuwait City by American planes.

In fact, only when reporters were loosed to dash ahead into Kuwait City was there a hint of an on-screen story. If the liberation-of-Paris-style crowds were sparse in population-decimated Kuwait, at least the visuals flowed and journalists had an opportunity to simulate war reporters of the past, down to their safari jackets.

If the Gulf War's lack of a story line accounts, in part, for its remarkable disappearance from American politics and culture, it was not for want of the footage of death. This was, after all, a screen war at the "front" as well as at home. We know, for instance, that cameras shooting through the nightvision gunsights of Apache AH-64 attack helicopters caught graphic scenes of confused and helpless Iraqi soldiers being blown to bits by unseen attackers. But these outtakes would have been appropriate only to a very different production—one geared to a horror film, not a war story.

Given its prodigious vanishing act, perhaps the Gulf War will indeed have little lasting effect on our society. (Its effects on Iraq and the rest of the Middle East are obviously another matter.) Total television, however, could have far more staying power, hinting at possible media and advertising futures we can hardly imagine today. It points toward a world in which, increasingly, everything gets done for the media; in which the more fully meshed media systems of the twenty-first century will need to discover new, more powerful, more all-purpose sponsoring relationships, ones that, at the very least, can raise to a higher power the single-sponsor show *(The Alcoa Hour, General Electric Theater)* of a simpler corporate age. Whichever media giants dominate in the years ahead, the problem of how to pay for such global entertainment shows, what those shows can possibly be and what stories they can be made to tell must be faced. What form total television will take in the future—whether on screen we will see slaughter or some friendlier sport—and who will be its sponsors we can hardly guess.

THE CLARENCE THOMAS HEARINGS[2]

It is an old newsroom axiom that if reporting on a particular event draws protests from both right and left, the journalists on the story have probably done a balanced job. But what if the coverage prompts rebukes not only from the left and right, but from the center as well? What if it arouses the ire of countless generally apolitical people, black and white, female and male? What if it even provokes certain news organizations to attack each

[2]Article by "William Boot," pseudonym of Christopher Hanson, Washington correspondent, *Seattle Post-Intelligencer.* From *Columbia Journalism Review* 30:25–29 Ja/F '92. Copyright © 1992 by *Columbia Journalism Review.* Reprinted with permission.

other's coverage? If all those factors apply, we can only be talking about the Clarence Thomas-Anita Hill sexual harassment dispute, which polarized the country and made for the most bizarre national news story to come our way in years.

Now that Thomas has been confirmed to the Supreme Court, it is time to take stock of the various objections to news coverage that this controversy provoked. First, an assessment of complaints from the right. Many conservatives were convinced that reporters were out to block Thomas by exploiting a news leak. Closely held Senate Judiciary Committee information had been disclosed to *Newsday*'s Timothy Phelps and NPR's [National Public Radio] Nina Totenberg. Their stories about Hill's allegations jolted the country on Sunday, October 6. Coming just two days before the Senate was scheduled to vote on Thomas, the leaks seemed to many to be politically motivated, timed to derail his nomination. The leaks prompted the Senate to delay Thomas's confirmation vote for one week, so the committee—under attack for not having taken Hill's allegation seriously—could probe the charges. For the first time Thomas's nomination seemed to be in real jeopardy.

Conservatives began denouncing the leaks with fierce indignation, demanding a formal investigation (now in progress) and offering to pay a bounty of more than $30,000 to anyone who could identify the leaker. This reaction was, of course, part of a long tradition of selective outrage over leaks (a leak is monstrous if it hurts politically but not nearly so heinous if it helps, and Republicans themselves leak like crazy when it suits them). But what was the substance of their case against this particular leak? For one thing, they argued that reporting it was unethical, because it would damage Hill, who wanted to keep her allegations confidential. "This is going to be one of the saddest chapters in American journalism," Senator Alan Simpson predicted during an October 7 ABC *Nightline* confrontation with Totenberg. Casting himself as a protector of women, he said that disclosing Hill's name was like disclosing the name of a rape victim: "You've blown the cover of a person on a sexual harassment charge . . . you will have destroyed this woman." Of course, it was Simpson and his allies who immediately set about trying to destroy her. Judiciary Committee Republicans accused her of concocting her story and of committing perjury and eventually branded her mentally unstable.

There is no question that journalists trespassed on Hill's privacy in exploiting the leak. Senate staffers had approached her, having heard that she had been harassed, and Hill had provided details on condition that they not be made public. But then someone leaked her affidavit to reporters, who leaped on the story. Thus, against her will, Hill was placed in the spotlight. On balance, this intrusion seems justified, considering that most of the senators preparing to vote on Thomas were not even aware of the allegations against him, and should have been. (Judiciary Committee members say they kept their knowledge of Hill's allegations under wraps to protect the privacy of the nominee and his accuser.)

Thomas's defenders also suggested that reporters who exploited the leak were, in effect, assassinating the federal judge's character on behalf of the Democrats. This argument confuses two issues—the motivation for the leak and the question of whether the allegations were true. The leakers may well have been Democrats out to get Thomas because he is a conservative (I'd be surprised to learn they were anything else). Even so, it is still possible that Thomas was guilty of sexual harassment. This surely was a serious matter that had to be explored by the media. Since the Judiciary Committee had opted not to explore it, reporting the leak was necessary to force the Senate into action. Reporters' responsibility is to try to get to the bottom of things, not cover them up, even if some news subjects suffer as a result. (It does seem that the possible motivations of leakers should be addressed in a story like this. What both the Phelps and Totenberg pieces lacked was a section that, without giving away the leakers' identities, could have suggested what might have prompted this disclosure at the time it occurred—i.e., only after Thomas's foes had exhausted their other anti-Thomas ammunition.)

Another, more considered, objection to the leak reporting comes from Brent Baker of the conservative Media Research Center. Baker argues that Phelps and Totenberg reported their leaks too hastily, recklessly jeopardizing Thomas's reputation before they had done enough reporting to justify their stories. He noted in an interview that Hill's allegation was far different from a claim that nominee X was guilty of something that definitely could be proven, such as stock fraud. Hill's allegation was an instance of her-word-against-his (as is generally the case in sexual harassment cases); there were no witnesses and real corroboration was impossible. Baker contends that, given those limitations and the inevitable damage to Thomas's reputation that disclosure would cause, Phelps and Totenberg should have held their stories until they had established, among other things, that there had been some *pattern* of misbehavior, with other women claiming he had been guilty of sexual misconduct with them. (*Charlotte Observer* editor Angela Wright eventually contacted the Judiciary Committee to allege that Thomas had put sexual pressure on her when she worked for him at the EEOC.)

Baker makes a strong case, but he does not give sufficient weight to the high-pressure situation in which Phelps and Totenberg found themselves. The Senate vote was just a couple of days away that Sunday, and if the story had not gotten out immediately there might never have been a Senate investigation. Given the time constraints, the two reports were not irresponsible. They cited "corroboration" from a friend of Hill's, who said Hill had complained of being sexually harassed at the time of the alleged conduct in the early '80s. The Totenberg piece carried Thomas's denial of the allegations. Phelps, unfortunately, could not reach him for comment, but he did include quotes from employee Phyllis Berry-Myers, who had worked for Thomas and who said it was inconceivable that he could be guilty of harassment.

Leaks aside, conservative groups like Baker's complain of a pervasive liberal bias in coverage. Even the *Wall Street Journal* editorial board got into the act, accusing *The Washington Post* and *The New York Times* of taking a "politically correct" pro-Hill approach to the issue (October 17 lead editorial). Conservative critics are able to cite some specific instances of slanted reporting (see below), but overall it does not appear that liberal bias was much of a factor during the Hill-Thomas hearings. On the contrary: a report by the Center for Media and Public Affairs in Washington concluded that Thomas got much better press than Hill during the hearings. This study of some 220 network news broadcasts and newspaper articles found that, after the hearings began, nearly four out of five individuals quoted in news accounts backed Thomas. (Just prior to the hearings, a majority had been critical of him.) As to Hill, "more than three out of four [sources] expressed doubt or outright hostility towards her allegations." These data hardly suggest pervasive liberal bias. Instead, they suggest that pro-Thomas forces dominated the debate during the hearings on Hill's allegations of sexual harassment and that the media rather passively reflected this, just as they reflected the domination of pro-Hill advocates in the days prior to those hearings.

As to specifics of bias, consider these excerpts from the October 21 edition of *Time*, cited in the conservative newsletter *Media Watch*. *Time* associate editor Jill Smolowe wrote: "Given the detail and consistency of her testimony, it was almost inconceivable that Hill, rather than describing her own experiences, was fabricating the portrait of a sexual-harassment victim. . . ." In fact, it is not "almost inconceivable" that she was fabricating—the polls indicated that millions of Americans found the idea quite conceivable. In the same edition, senior editor Nancy Gibbs declared:

Harriet Tubman and Sojourner Truth were slaves by birth, freedom fighters by temperament. Rosa Parks was a tired seamstress who shoved history forward by refusing to give up her seat on the bus. . . . The latest to claim her place in line is Anita Hill, a private, professional woman unwilling to relinquish her dignity without a fight.

In fact, Hill is another Rosa Parks only if one assumes she is telling the truth.

Elsewhere, of course, one could find pro-Thomas biases. *The New Republic*'s Fred Barnes asserted without evidence on the October 12 *McLaughlin Group* broadcast that Hill was spinning "a monstrous lie," and Morton Kondracke, also of *TNR*, bolstered the theory, saying Hill might be compared to Tawana Brawley. John McLaughlin (himself no stranger to sex harassment allegations) compared Hill to Janet Cooke.

For some less ideologically driven critics, a major complaint centered on sensationalism of this story. Political scientist Norman Ornstein, a barometer of centrist conventional wisdom, said in an interview that television coverage revealed warped news priorities at NBC, CBS, and ABC. They ran hours of Hill-Thomas testimony, whereas they had not provided live coverage of his pre-Hill confirmation hearings, at which big issues like abortion were on the table. This showed that ratings drove their news decisions and that personal scandal wins out every time over drier but equally important issues.

This is true, up to a point. Commercial networks do pander shamelessly. But as Ornstein acknowledged in a second interview, Hill-Thomas was, by almost any measure, a bigger story and deserved more coverage than the first round of Thomas hearings (where the nominee spent hours ducking the abortion issue and revealing as little about himself as possible). Once Hill's allegations became public, much more drama was to be had: there was a substantive issue (sexual harassment), and there were multiple conflicts (one man vs. one woman, men vs. women, black men vs. black women, women vs. Congress, Congress vs. the White

House). And, of course, there was sex. Judiciary Committee chairman Joseph Biden described the high megatonnage of the story: "I know of no system of government where, when you add the kerosene of sex, the heated flame of race, and the incendiary nature of television lights, you are not going to have an explosion" (quoted on an *ABC Town Meeting*, October 16.)

Other objectors offered a kind of prude's critique, complaining that it was a travesty to bring all that graphic talk about Thomas's alleged references to sex with animals, and porn star Long Dong Silver, and pubic hairs on Coke cans into our living rooms, where children and old ladies could be watching. According to an ABC News poll released after the hearings, news media were rated lower for their Hill-Thomas performance than were the Democrats, the Republicans, Congress, or George Bush. One has to assume that the low rating was due in part to the graphic subject matter.

Of course, even those who voiced disgust kept watching. They could not do without the details. The story could not be told adequately without them. In fact, some TV journalists issued warnings to parents that simultaneously served as advertisements for the juicy material to come. Dan Rather, at the start of the Saturday, October 12 hearings, said earnestly: "Now we want to *strongly* caution parents . . . there may once again be *extremely graphic testimony* that you may not want your children to watch. You may want to think about that." A few moments later, correspondent Bob Schieffer voiced awe at a case so unprecedented that it had forced the anchor of CBS News to say such a thing:

SCHIEFFER (intense, portentous delivery): Let me just go back to the words you used at the start of this broadcast. We want to warn parents that what they may hear might be offensive to their children. Have you *ever* begun a broadcast of a Senate hearing with those kind of words?
RATHER: Never
SCHIEFFER: It seems to me that that illustrates and underlines just how *very different* this is. . . .

Come now, wasn't this laying it on a bit thick?

Enough of the prudes—on to the feminists, who had quite different objections. One was that the news media, especially TV, were manipulated by the Republicans and used as tools to demolish Hill. Judith Lichtman of the Women's Legal Defense Fund argues, for example, that, during the hearings, journalists failed to draw the attention of viewers to Republican strategies and to the fumbling of committee Democrats. She contends that the networks and newspapers should have brought in experts to challenge questionable claims like the allegation that Hill had committed perjury, the insinuation that Hill might be "delusional," and Thomas's striking claim that he was the victim of "a high-tech lynching for uppity blacks." Instead, Lichtman says, most reporters were mere conduits: "The media portrayed what was presented to them—they therefore were manipulated. . . . We were let down by the media."

Lichtman is correct that reporters had seemingly little impact on public perceptions during the hearings. She is a bit off the mark as to why. Networks and newspapers actually did make some effort to provide the sort of commentary she says was lacking (as well as counter-opinion from conservatives). But, for reasons we'll get to shortly, this news analysis does not appear to have mattered much.

Here are some examples of the critical commentary. NBC's Robert Bazell, on the October 13 *Nightly News,* interviewed New York psychiatrist Robert Spitzer, who voiced extreme skepticism about the assertion that Hill was living in a fantasy world. Black commentator Bob Herbert on NBC's *Sunday Today* (October 13) sharply questioned Thomas's claim to be a victim of racism. In a series of live network interviews, sexual harassment experts like University of Michigan law professor Catharine MacKinnon disputed a Republican claim that no genuine harassment victim would have followed Thomas to a new job, as Hill did in 1983. (Hill went with Thomas from the Department of Education to the Equal Employment Opportunity Commission.) Reporters also tried to give audiences an idea of Republican strategy and Democratic timidity. "One had the impression that . . . Orrin Hatch sort of played the part of Mike Tyson," Dan Rather told CBS viewers October 11. "Before Senator Biden could sort of get off his stool, Hatch was at him, all over him, and decked him." ABC's Tim O'Brien (*World News Sunday,* October 13) reported that Biden had acquiesced to Republicans, giving Thomas the big P.R. boost of live prime-time exposure.

As the opinion polls suggest, however, the impact of all this critical reporting was marginal. Why? The main reason, I suspect, is that this was a riveting live television event. Millions were watching and drawing their own conclusions. They did not need reporters to provide a news filter, so viewers may have listened even less closely than usual to commentary and analysis.

Live TV was only part of the press's "control" problem. In some cases, we lost control over some of our own debilitating impulses, which helped to undermine whatever small influence critical commentary might otherwise have had. For instance, there was the "Babble Factor": much of the intelligent news analysis (liberal, moderate, and conservative) was simply drowned out by the compulsive babbling and hyperbole that this event seemed to arouse in journalists. On October 11, Peter Jennings said of the Judiciary Committee, which has its share of dim bulbs: "One of the things we of course might remind people as they watch these proceedings . . . is that these senators are all profoundly intelligent men on this committee. In many cases they're all lawyers." Over on CBS, Dan Rather was groping for simple solutions. "If the FBI can't determine who's lying between the two, let's have some homicide detective out from Phoenix or New York City to spend a few days on this," he blurted on October 12. NBC's Brokaw said on October 11 that it would be bad if the hearings were to last several days because "it's in the national interest to have this all done as quickly and efficiently and completely as possible." As if doing it quickly were compatible with doing it efficiently and completely! (In order to meet the tight Senate-imposed timetable, the committee decided not to call any expert witnesses at all—making a thorough investigation virtually impossible.)

Then, for a few minutes on October 15, just before the Senate vote on Thomas, NBC seemed to lose complete control of its critical faculties. The network jumped from Capitol Hill coverage to Pinpoint, Georgia, where Thomas's mother could be seen live, rocking back and forth and praying in a neighbor's kitchen ("They're trying to keep him from helping us, Lord, but I ask you, Jesus, to please give it to him!" etc.) The sequence was captioned "NBC News Exclusive." The network seemed to be boasting, but why was difficult to fathom.

Another way in which journalists got side-tracked might be called the "Perry Mason Factor." Refusing to heed warnings from calmer heads, like ABC correspondent Hal Bruno, an astonishing number of journalists accepted a Republican comparison between the hearings and a trial. Republicans (and some Democrats, including the feckless Biden, at times) advanced the trial metaphor, emphasizing that Thomas must be judged by the standard of innocent until proven guilty, even though other nominees have been rejected on grounds of reasonable doubt and no candidate has a *right* to a seat on the Supreme Court. Reporters took the bait and reinforced a presumption-of-innocence message. "A political trial [is] effectively what we have going on here today. . . . There is a kind of trial aspect to all of this after all," said Brokaw during coverage of the October 11 hearings. "We have four institutions and people on trial . . . in a nonlegal proceeding," said Bryant Gumbel on the same broadcast. "I guess in a sense it is a trial in a way [and] we're seeing the defense lay out its strategy here," said Bob Schieffer over on CBS on October 12; "It is a trial in a way," agreed his boss, Dan Rather. And so on. By the eve of the confirmation vote, over half the public agreed that Thomas should get the benefit of the doubt, according to a CBS–*New York Times* poll. Senate Republican leader Bob Dole said polls like that were what assured Thomas's confirmation.

Finally, there was the "Shovel Factor." Reporters (including me) failed to dig hard enough on their own during the Senate's consideration of Thomas. Why weren't the sexual harassment allegations against Thomas disclosed earlier? After all, Phelps of *Newsday* says reporters were hearing about the allegations as long ago as last July. Why wasn't more done to investigate Thomas's alleged taste for pornography, an allegation that became very pertinent in sizing up Hill's veracity? Why didn't reporters explain why Angela Wright, who complained that Thomas had sexually pressured her, was never called as a witness?

Before Hill's accusations became public, why wasn't more done to explore allegations that Thomas had breached conflict of interest standards? In one case, he ruled in favor of Ralston Purina, rather than recusing himself, even though his mentor and patron, Senator John Danforth, had a big interest in the company. In another case, Thomas was accused of delaying release of one of his controversial appeals court decisions, possibly to bolster his confirmation prospects. (Thomas denies any delay.) I was able to find fewer than ten stories devoted to the Ralston Purina issue and only a few focusing on the delayed ruling controversy. Meanwhile, as the left-leaning Fairness and Accuracy in Reporting group points out, news organizations ran dozens of articles about Thomas's climb from rags to riches—the Horatio Alger theme that the administration played up to divert attention from the nominee's meager judicial experience. Reporters had, once again, bought the Republican sales pitch.

Pro-Thomas salesmen continued to pitch successfully even after the nominee was confirmed, with Justice Thomas actively participating (which is highly unusual conduct in that Supreme Court members have traditionally been media-shy). Thomas cooperated in the ultimate puff piece, a seven-page, November 11 *People* magazine cover article, "How We Survived," told in the first person by his wife, Virginia. In it, she asserts that Hill "was probably in love with my husband" and that her charges "were politically motivated." She makes a point of describing the importance of home prayer sessions to the family. In a photograph illustrating the article, the two pose on a sofa, reading a Bible together.

Why are the Thomases continuing a P.R. offensive? Perhaps as a kind of preemptive strike. As Phelps pointed out in a recent panel discussion, reporters are still on the case, investigating whether there is solid evidence to back up allegations that Thomas committed perjury during the hearings. "We hear that people are still digging, trying to impugn his integrity," Virginia Thomas said in *People*. "But it's over." That may be so. But if new derogatory stories about the judge are broken in the months ahead, I would not be too surprised if we hear even more about the Thomas family's devotional habits—stopping short, one can only hope, of another urgent TV prayer bulletin from Pinpoint, Georgia.

YOU HAD TO BE THERE[3]

During the days of rioting that followed the verdict in the trial of the police officers who beat Rodney King, I received telephone calls from friends and family in other parts of the country. After first asking if I was safe, they asked what was going on here in Los Angeles. I told them all I knew was what I saw on television—that I didn't know any more than they did. But as the conversations progressed, it quickly became apparent that what I was seeing on local television differed quite a bit from what they were seeing on ABC, NBC, CBS, and CNN.

Repeatedly from them and from callers to talk shows on CNN and C-Span, I heard comments that made it clear that the national networks were playing catch-up, giving viewers reports and

[3]Article by Charles Oliver, from *Reason* 24:35–38 Ag/S '92. Copyright © 1992 by the Reason Foundation. Reprinted with permission.

analysis that had little to do with what was actually occurring at the time in Los Angeles. On Wednesday and Thursday, after the riots had begun, the networks were still covering the trial, and callers were still ignorant of its particulars—from the makeup of the jury to the arguments of the defense and prosecution.

Once the networks finally turned to the riots themselves, they gave viewers little geographical or historical context. They didn't explain about ethnic relations within Los Angeles, about earlier cases with racial overtones, or about the role gangs play in the everyday violence that marks life in South-Central L.A. The networks' coverage was often overly simplistic and sometimes out-and-out wrong.

"What were your professional actions in the approval of an all-white jury who may have been culturally biased?"—Question for Rodney King's attorney, Steve Lerman, from a caller from Baton Rouge, Louisiana, on *Larry King Live*

Rodney King's attorney had no say in the conduct of what networks called "the Rodney King trial"—a criminal prosecution in which King did not even appear as a witness. Larry King reminded his viewers that Lerman "had nothing to do with this trial." Other network representatives were not so fastidious about the facts of the case.

Except for Court TV viewers, most people outside Los Angeles didn't follow the trial. After turning the King beating into a national story, the major networks dropped it. So on Wednesday and Thursday night, as Angelenos were watching their city go up in flames on local television, the networks were trying to explain to viewers in the rest of the country how the four men who beat Rodney King had gotten off.

During that time, I repeatedly heard the jury referred to as "all white" both by national network anchors and reporters and by average people from around the country. The truth is that the jury included one Latino and one Asian. The four blacks in the jury pool were dismissed because their answers to jury questionnaires showed that they seemed to have prejudged the officers and could not render an unbiased decision.

This isn't nitpicking. Having followed the trial on local television, I was surprised by the verdict but not shocked. I had seen the prosecutors try to argue that Rodney King had *never* acted in what could be perceived as a threatening manner on the night of his arrest, a point that even their own witnesses wouldn't back them up on.

The defense managed to focus much of the trial on those initial moments when Rodney King stepped out of the car and seemed to lunge at the officers, rather than that last minute when King was flailing about on the ground as the policemen continued to beat him. Even the two California Highway Patrol officers who testified against the four policemen said that Rodney King's initial actions frightened them.

I had watched as defense attorneys marched the jury through the infamous videotape again and again, arguing that it was impossible to tell if the policemen had deliberately struck King in the head (which would have been a violation of department policy) and that King's attempts to dodge the blows could be interpreted by frightened police officers as aggressive behavior. Yet none of the network reports that I saw mentioned that the law required the jurors to take into account the mental state of the four officers when rendering their verdict.

And most important, I had seen how the defense attorneys played on the tremendous fear that suburbanites of all colors have of crime. The change of venue from Los Angeles to Simi Valley was probably the turning point in the trial. Not because Simi Valley is "all white," as people kept saying, but because it is populated by people of all races who fled the city because of violent crime. Indeed, remarks made by jurors after the trial showed that they were more concerned about not handcuffing the police than about giving justice to Rodney King.

Further, eight of the 12 had served in the military. I didn't hear one network reporter mention this fact. But it's reasonable to assume that people with a military background would be sympathetic to police officers who claimed that they were just following department regulations.

The networks also overlooked the fact that the defense made what was in hindsight a brilliant gamble. It refused to allow the jury to consider lesser charges against the four policemen. They would have to vote on the most serious felony charges. The men and women on that jury might well have found the four guilty of offenses that carried a short sentence, but there was no way they would give eight years of hard time to four members of, in one defense attorney's words, "the thin blue line" that separates law-abiding people from the violence of the big city.

The networks did mention that the defense got lucky when

the trial was moved to Simi Valley, but they didn't mention that Oakland had also been under consideration as the venue. While the prosecution had originally argued that if the trial were moved it should be to a venue that resembles Los Angeles demographically (such as Oakland), it did not oppose the decision to move the trial to Simi Valley.

"I think these riots that we've been experiencing the last couple of days might well be called the Willie Horton Memorial Riots, reflecting the ugly racism that was fostered by President Bush's campaign four years ago."— Erwin Knoll, of *The Progressive* magazine, on the *MacNeil/Lehrer Newshour*

One of the ideas voiced frequently by left-wing pundits is that the beating was motivated simply by racism. If one only saw the videotape of a bunch of white police officers beating a black man, it would be easy to come to the conclusion that the police were racists. And the remarks made over the police radio by defendant Laurence Powell, referring to an earlier case involving blacks as a "gorillas in the mist" situation, certainly raises suspicions about his racial prejudices.

But again, those of us here in Los Angeles saw a more complex picture. Profiles of Stacey Koon, the senior officer on trial, revealed that only a few months before the beating, he had leaped to give mouth-to-mouth resuscitation to a dying "black transvestite prostitute with open sores around his mouth" as other police officers looked on in shock and horror.

Nor do the police limit abuse to black suspects. After the King beating, a commission headed by Warren Christopher investigated police brutality within the LAPD. The commission found the police department regularly treats innocent people with incivility and often abuses them. While blacks and Latinos suffer the brunt of this abuse, whites are treated badly as well. The Operation Rescue protesters who were brutalized by Los Angeles policemen two years ago will testify to that. Even after adjusting for the large size of the city's population, Los Angeles leads all other major U.S. cities in attacks by police dogs and in awards in police-brutality suits.

The problem, the commission found, stems primarily from the police department's unwillingness to investigate and punish its own (the department simply sat on most excessive-force complaints); from the lack of civilian oversight of the department;

and from the paramilitary attitude that has been promulgated within the department for several decades.

The LAPD takes the "war on crime" metaphor quite seriously. As other big-city police departments have turned to community-based policing and an increased emphasis on foot patrols, the LAPD has emphasized the swift use of force as a deterrent to crime. The people the department arrests are treated not as potentially innocent persons or citizens with rights; they are the enemy.

The national networks barely noticed the release of the Christopher Commission report, and by the time of the riots they seemed to have forgotten about it.

"Increasingly, people are saying that all of the violence had very little to do with Rodney King. Instead, it was the desperate call of a community fighting for change."—ABC reporter Tom Foreman

The idea that the riots were an unfortunate expression of black America's rage against its mistreatment by white America's political system was voiced by a number of reporters and weekend talk-show pundits. But the pictures from Los Angeles told a different story.

Certainly, blacks were upset with the trial verdict. Only a relative few, however, took part in the looting. Street gangs were the shock troops of the riots. They were the ones who pulled Reginald Denny from the cab of his truck and beat and stomped him. Gang members committed most of the violence and the arson. Their victims were quite often black. Buildings that would have been spared during the more truly political Watts riots of 1965 were attacked. Libraries, the offices of black politicians, and the headquarters of community-action groups all went up in smoke.

And putting signs in the windows telling people that shops were black owned didn't spare the owners. The saddest part of the riot may have been watching black shop owners return to their burned out stores and ask reporters what was going to happen to them and to the people they employed. One wonders whether Ted Koppel had seen these pictures when he didn't challenge a gang member who told him, "We're renovating our neighborhood."

Following the gang members, scavengers moved in to loot the remains of stores. The pictures didn't show anger; they showed people—sometimes whole families—gleefully grabbing "free" goods. And these people weren't all black. About a third of those arrested were Latino; a substantial number were white.

That's only to be expected. The riots quickly spread out of areas populated by minorities into neighborhoods dominated by whites. And as the riots spread, the participants mirrored the populations of the new neighborhoods.

Part of the problem is that the networks didn't do a very good job of showing people what was happening where on the sprawling L.A. map. Some people I talked to thought the riots were occurring in Watts. Others thought the entire city was ablaze. Neither of those impressions was true.

The networks also didn't do a very good job of explaining the interethnic group violence that occurred during the riot. I'm sure that most Americans understood, or thought they understood, the black-on-white violence that occurred early on. But the black-against-Korean violence must have perplexed most TV viewers.

Here in Los Angeles, however, we are only too aware of the tensions that exist between Korean immigrants and blacks. Many of the shops in black neighborhoods are run by Koreans. Many blacks complain that the Koreans charge too much for the stuff they sell and treat their customers without respect. Some even believe that Koreans get special loans from the government to go into black neighborhoods and start businesses to keep blacks from owning their own businesses.

Koreans, on the other hand, complain of their losses from shoplifters and armed robbery, crimes in which blacks are usually the perpetrators. Several months ago, Korean shop owner Soon Ja Du shot in the back and killed Latasha Harlins, a 14-year-old black girl who had attacked her. Blacks in Los Angeles were outraged when the Korean woman received no jail time for the crime.

So it wasn't surprising when the violence took on an anti-Korean tone. Apparently, the very first business looted was a liquor store targeted because the owners were Korean. And looters soon marched out of South-Central L.A. to Koreatown.

Television reported that Koreans were special targets for violence, but much of the audience was probably left wondering why. And when reporters did try to explore the "Korean angle," they left out inconvenient facts—for example, that many Koreans had purchased or leased their stores from black owners who had moved into more profitable businesses or that 30 percent or more

of looted stores were owned by Latinos. On this story, as on so
many other aspects of the riot, the networks left viewers with only
a partial picture.

What caused the L.A. riots is a question that will be asked for
a long time. But we can't figure out the answer unless we know
what happened. And for that, Americans will have to depend on
something other than national television.

NAMING NAMES[4]

At first, she was simply The Accuser, The Victim, The Woman in the Palm Beach rape case. But when a supermarket
tabloid—and then NBC, The New York Times and several other
newspapers—disclosed her name and details of her personal life
last week, she assumed a unique and precarious spot in the annals
of modern celebrityhood—exposed, yet still hidden. Millions of
people have now seen the grainy black-and-white picture with the
Mona Lisa smile. They've shared her secrets: her drinking habits,
her high-school grades, her unwed-motherhood, even her 17
traffic tickets. But to everyone else, she is still a tantalizing
cipher—silent and faceless, trapped by her self-imposed exile,
perhaps in the sanctuary of her stepfather's house.

The truth about that March night is known only to the two
people who were there, the woman and the man she has accused of
rape, William Kennedy Smith. As of last week, Palm Beach officials
had yet to bring charges; their slowness raised new questions about
the thoroughness of the investigation. Whatever the eventual outcome, the Kennedy case has already focused public attention on a
mounting controversy over privacy in rape cases. It is a deeply
emotional issue that divides journalists, law-enforcement officials,
feminists and rape victims themselves. Says University of Texas
sociologist E. Mark Warr: "Ultimately what you have here is a
conflict between two worthy goals—protecting personal privacy
and changing social attitudes."

Rape is the most intimate of crimes; it is the dark terror in a
woman's heart as she crosses an empty parking lot. It is also the

[4]Article by Barbara Kantrowitz, from *Newsweek* 117:26–29+ Ap 29 '91. Copyright © 1991 Newsweek, Inc. Reprinted with permission.

only violent crime that tarnishes the victim as well as the criminal. "There is a historical tradition that victims are viewed as damaged goods," says Mary Koss, a University of Arizona psychologist. "Rape first became a crime to protect the property rights of the father whose daughter had been raped." And there is still a widespread belief that the victims may have asked for it. "If a man is mugged, they don't talk about what he was wearing," says Mitzi Vorachek of the Houston Area Women's Center. Women say they are made to feel guilty until proven innocent, as though they have somehow encouraged their attackers by looking attractive—or perhaps by just being female.

Those who oppose naming names say that honoring a victim's privacy avoids the potential stigma of public exposure. With only a few exceptions, news organizations have kept names secret—a position that has wide public support. A NEWSWEEK Poll found that 77 percent of those surveyed think the media should not disclose rape victims' names. And 86 percent believe that disclosure would discourage women from reporting the crimes. But even before the Palm Beach case, there was a growing movement to push aside the shroud of secrecy as a way of removing the stigma of rape. Last year, when The Des Moines Register published the story of a rape victim with her consent, the paper earned professional praise (and, earlier this month, a Pulitzer Prize) for bringing the subject out into the open. A few other news organizations saw the Register series as a catalyst for rethinking their own policies, and rape was discussed at editors' conventions. The massive publicity surrounding the Central Park jogger trial tempted some news executives to break with tradition. But in the end only a couple of small newspapers published her name. Mainstream newspapers and television stations maintained her anonymity.

The Palm Beach story elevated the issue to the front page. In the last few weeks, the newsstand allure of the Kennedy name and the decadent upper-crust backdrop have sharpened the public appetite for information on the case. The first American paper to disclose the woman's name, the racy tabloid the Globe, explained its decision by referring to earlier reports in sensational British papers like the Sunday Mirror. Then editors of establishment news organizations (including The Des Moines Register) started playing follow-the-leader, even though the leader was a scandal sheet from a supermarket checkout rack. NBC began its report with a story on the Globe, and the Times said it was weighing in because of NBC. This prompted one rape victim, University of Southern California law professor Susan Estrich, to compare the media to toddlers misbehaving because their sandbox buddies had done so. NBC News president Michael G. Gartner said his decision was based in part on the greater good of removing rape's stigma. The short-term consequences will be "extraordinarily difficult for this generation," he conceded, "but it may perhaps help their daughters and granddaughters."

Most news organizations, including NEWSWEEK, decided to withhold the woman's identity. At WBZ-TV, NBC's Boston affiliate, station officials blotted the report out of the network news, in keeping with its "longstanding policy not to use the names of rape victims and to protect them from any unnecessary publicity," explained spokesperson Kim Harbin. But Boston viewers of NBC heard the whole story the next morning on the "Today" show, which is broadcast live and can't be edited.

Women's groups are split on the wisdom of invading a victim's privacy. Some agree that secrecy adds to the shame. "It would probably be better to identify the victim regularly in all cases," says Elizabeth Fox-Genovese, director of the Women's Studies Program at Emory University in Atlanta. "What we're talking about is a crime of violence," just like murder. Some say if the accused rapist is identified (as Smith was, almost from the start), then, in fairness, the victim should be named as well.

Other feminists think disclosure has a chilling effect. "What is happening to this alleged victim is a feminist nightmare," says Los Angeles attorney Gloria Allred. "It is what we feared would happen if names were disclosed. It's the survivor being placed on trial . . . I think it's enough to put fear in the hearts of other rape survivors, to make them think about proceeding with charges if their names will end up in the newspapers." There is justification for her concern. A recent study by the Senate Judiciary Committee found that fewer than one in 10 rapes is reported to the police. A committee aide predicted that if victims were routinely identified, that percentage would drop to one in 200.

Law-enforcement officials say the Palm Beach case may have already had repercussions. A key witness in an Oakland, Calif., trial threatens that if her name or picture is published, she will drop charges against a man she alleges had sex with her without telling her he was HIV-positive. The man, William Lucas Barker, is an ex-convict who police said had vowed to "take all the women I can with me before I die." Though Barker is thought to have infected other women, the 22-year-old witness is the only one who has agreed to testify. But now she's having second thoughts. "She doesn't want her mother or friends to know," says Lt. Craig Stewart of the Oakland police. If her identity becomes public, "she'll drop the whole thing and he will walk out and do it again."

People who oppose printing names say that a victim's emotional state is fragile for months, even years, after the attack. Experts say that 60 percent of rape victims experience post-traumatic stress syndrome, the highest percentage of any crime victims. A Baltimore study found that rape victims suffered more nervous breakdowns than victims of any other crime; 20 percent tried to commit suicide. Forced public exposure can make a woman feel violated a second time. "You're re-creating the trauma of the rape," says Veronica Ryback, director of the Rape Crisis Center at Boston's Beth Israel Hospital. "You're taking away that person's control of the situation. That reincites the feelings of helplessness and powerlessness that essentially mirror how she felt during the rape."

Car Crash

In one of the most notorious rape cases of the past decade, a woman was assaulted by four men at a New Bedford, Mass., bar called Big Dan's. The movie "The Accused" was loosely based on the 1983 attack. A local talk-show host disclosed the victim's name. Although that was the only public disclosure, the consequences for her were disastrous, says Debra Robbin, executive director of the New Bedford Women's Center. The victim moved to Florida, where she died in a car crash that friends believe was actually a suicide. "She felt very maligned, very discredited and very unprotected," says Robbin. "It greatly increased the stress trauma on her and her family."

As a matter of law, there isn't much protection for rape victims outside the courtroom. Rarely can the defense disclose some potentially damaging details of a victim's life. Newspapers and television operate without such restrictions; only Florida, South Carolina and Georgia have laws preventing the media from disclosing victims' names. "There is this awful almost compulsion . . . to discredit the victim," says Fredrica Gray, executive director of Connecticut's Permanent Commission on the Status of Women and a rape victim herself. "That's why victims don't come forward. That's why it's a crime of silence."

Bedroom Window

Complaints about The New York Times profile of the Palm Beach woman focused on the tone of the piece as well as the disclosure of her name. The story discussed the accuser's "wild streak" in high school, her mother's divorce and remarriage, and her barhopping in Palm Beach. A reporter even peeked into the window of her daughter's bedroom to discover that one of the volumes on the bookshelf was "Two-Minute Bible Stories." Such Peeping Tomism is generally considered the province of more freewheeling publications. Even National Enquirer editor Iain Calder chose not to publish the name. "If she had been a former Nazi prison guard or a happy hooker, I could see it," he says. "This was just gossip."

Some critics suggest that if the Palm Beach woman's background had been a little less colorful, she might have been spared such tawdry scrutiny. The Central Park jogger—who had degrees from Wellesley and Yale and a job in investment banking—was consistently portrayed as beyond reproach. In contrast, the Palm Beach woman is perceived as "some sort of *arriviste*," says Martha Howell, director of the Institute for Research on Women and Gender at Columbia University. "It's possible to imagine she's using her sexuality for social advancement."

The nature of the attack also plays a role in how the victim is perceived. The Central Park jogger was assaulted by a gang of strangers; the Palm Beach woman willingly went back to the Kennedy compound after midnight. Victims of "acquaintance rape" are often viewed less sympathetically than victims of stranger rape, although their psychic wounds are just as profound. "The victim in this case is viewed as the victimizer," says Katha Pollitt, a New York feminist writer. "A lot of people think that if you go back to a man's house after meeting in a bar, you're on your own."

Campus Customs

Colleges have taken the lead in countering that misperception. "Ten years ago people wouldn't have thought of turning in an assailant they knew," says University of Maryland associate professor Shirley Damrosch, who has studied rape. "But on university campuses, there's a new consciousness that this is a crime and the assailant should not escape unscathed." Schools around the country now routinely include discussions of acquaintance rape in their orientation sessions and have set up special procedures for helping victims.

In both acquaintance and stranger rape, psychiatrists say confidentiality is a key to recovery. Dr. Nada Stotland, chairman of the American Psychiatric Association's committee on women, compares disclosure to organ donations."We have the highest regard for people who donate organs," she says. "Yet we have the most absolute rules against forcing anyone to do it . . . We shouldn't be coercing anyone to make their identity public." Because of the stigma of rape, forced disclosure is comparable to the recent practice of "outing" closet homosexuals by gay activists. "Both are things nobody should have to hide," says Carol Sternhell, director of women's studies at New York University. "But you can't just drag somebody out."

Rape victims who choose to go public—often with the help of counseling—say openness helps their healing process. Kim McSherry of Houston was raped last year in her apartment. When her assailant returned to her home and started leaving messages on her window ("You snitched, but I still love you"), she fought back by plastering thousands of posters with a police composite around her neighborhood. Within 24 hours the 22-year-old man was arrested. "You have to report the crime and overcome the trauma and the unbelievable depravity that comes with the crime," McSherry says. "It makes you feel like a worm. It's so important to stand up and say, 'I'm not a worm. I'm a human being with integrity and I will fight back'."

Victim's Choice

In some cases, victims who "come out" of their own volition turn into activists. The woman in The Des Moines Register series, Nancy Ziegenmeyer, has become an advocate for rape victims' rights. She believes that going public should always be the victim's choice, not the media's. She is currently lobbying in the Iowa Legislature for a bill that would prevent police from releasing names of alleged victims until formal charges are filed. "All it is," says Ziegenmeyer, "is a little bit of time [for the victim] to tell her husband, her family and to get the help she desperately needs." Time helps, Ziegenmeyer says, but recovery is a slow, continuing process and hers is not yet complete. She was attacked in 1988 while sitting in her car outside a Des Moines community college where she was cramming for a real-estate license exam. She told her story after reading a column by Register editor Geneva Overholser encouraging rape victims to speak out. "I have gotten over the physical trauma that Bobby Lee Smith did to me," she says. "But I live everyday with the emotional trauma."

Women willing to speak out, like Ziegenmeyer, remain the exception. "It takes some courage to change social attitudes," says Warr, the University of Texas sociologist. "It will take the courage of some women who have been raped to reduce the social stigma of that crime." Victims can become survivors—and it's more than just a change in terminology. "It can be a very empowering and liberating experience," says Judith Herman of the Victim of Violence Program at Cambridge Hospital in Massachusetts. "We see survivors drafting legislation, volunteering at the rape-crisis centers, doing public speaking."

After her story appeared in the Register, Ziegenmeyer became a beacon for other women. "I received letters from women who had been raped 30, 40 years ago and had never told anyone," she says. One woman wrote her once, and then, months later, wrote again. The second time, she found the courage to sign her name.

The Plugged-In Voter[5]

Minutes after the last presidential debate, when it was clear that he had let the news media run him out of a campaign he could have taken much further, Ross Perot taunted the mob of assembled reporters: "You hate the fact that the American people put me on the ballot."

It was an amazing accusation, one no other presidential candidate had ever made. It was all the more remarkable for being true. Reporters did, in fact, hate Perot's candidacy, a stinging rebuke to them and their impact on politics.

If Perot ended up achieving almost none of his political goals in 1992, he did leave one of the country's most powerful

[5]Article by Jon Katz, first appeared in *Rolling Stone*. 115–117 D 10–24 '92. Copyright © 1992 by Jon Katz. Reprinted by permission of Brandt & Brandt Literary Agents, Inc.

institutions—the national press—nearly in ruins. Everything he promised to do to politics he did to the media, breaking open the decades-old monopoly they have had over presidential politics.

By using new phone technology and talk shows to answer voters' questions directly, Perot returned individuals to the center of the campaign and gave millions of citizens the sense that they were once again participating. By ignoring the Washington press corps for the likes of *Larry King Live* and *Donahue,* Perot legitimized the commercial and cable talk shows, leading the other candidates and tens of millions of viewers away from conventional media outlets. Insofar as the campaign rose above name-calling to invoke higher ideals and substantive themes at all, talk shows and their more flexible and personal formats were responsible.

By airing primitively produced half-hour spots that outdrew prime-time network entertainment programs, Perot undercut the notion that slick and nasty advertising was the most effective way to reach the electorate. And by clinging to the economic issues he cared about, refusing the media's demands that candidates prove they've done their homework by spouting statistics on every subject, Perot showed that presidential contenders could and should set their own agendas, define broader visions and focus on issues they feel are critical.

Perot paid dearly for his gall. The press attacked him continuously from the moment it was clear how he intended to run his campaign. That Perot is arrogant, egotistical and obnoxious was always clear. But he was cast as a dangerous and troubled man as well, a monomaniac, a paranoid and a liar. That we still don't know which Perot was real—the Caligula of the early and late campaign or the sensible, homespun CEO of the debates—shows how frantic and unnerved journalists were by his renegade candidacy.

When they helped force Perot from the race in July, many reporters felt almost gleefully affirmed. They were important after all, and candidates who didn't deal with them would be sorry. But they were wrong. They'll be seeing his face in their dreams for years to come.

By the last few weeks of the campaign, as he liberated politics from journalists, Perot's revolutionary tactics had made clear the dimensions of the new media age and how it would change news: what news is, who asks questions about it, who delivers it and how. It also gave us an inkling as to how the media—and their many consumers—will reconfigure themselves as new information technologies emerge and as viewers and readers continue to wrest control of the news.

In the new, emerging information world, mainstream journalism is floundering. Still struggling to recover from the Persian Gulf War (from which it was largely banned) and the Anita Hill hearings, it reeled from story to story all year: amazed at the economic anger displayed in New Hampshire and other primary states, shocked by Pat Buchanan, struck dumb by Perot, completely taken by surprise by the collapse of the legendary GOP campaign machine.

On every issue, nipping at every journalistic heel was the New News. Old Newspeople were debased and humiliated, forced through gritted teeth to point to talk shows—*talk shows*—as turning points in the campaign: when Perot declared on *Larry King*, when George Bush took questions from befuddled Rose Garden tourists hurriedly rounded up by *CBS This Morning* producers, when Bill Clinton told Donahue to get off his back about Gennifer Flowers and the audience roared, when he played the saxophone on *Arsenio Hall* and appeared on MTV and energized young voters.

The year began with Jerry Brown giving out his 800 number and challenging voters to take back their politics. By the campaign's close, viewers couldn't zap for two channels without running across a current or potential president. During the last week of the election, Bush—who'd once clucked in astonishment at the "weird" media—made the morning network rounds, as did Clinton. And Bush, Clinton and Perot closed their campaigns with back-to-back appearances on *Larry King*. The weird media had taken over.

The collision of these old and new media cultures—more and more separated from each other along age, racial, cultural and class lines—was most vividly on display during the second presidential debate, in Richmond, Virginia, a hypnotic confrontation between the two cultures, the young and the old, the enfranchised and the ascending, those who get it and those who don't. It was telling that the only debates that really worked—Richmond and the one between Gore and Quayle—barely used journalists at all.

In a hundred years the Richmond debate will be seen as synonymous with an epochal change in news. Journalists and politicians couldn't and wouldn't heed the message. Just a few days later, in the final debate, the lethal old format returned, with journalists once again blocking any dialogue between the public and the candidates, setting their clunky traps, invoking their hoary record checking.

All year journalists and media writers railed at Perot and at the New News and tried to belittle, explain or rename it: talkshow journalism, strange bedfellows, cable politics and, more often than anything else, trash. Donahue was too sensational, King a patsy. The idea was that the republic's governing process was not in responsible or adult hands.

Journalists could not accept the fact that King had become more popular and influential than they are and demanded that he alter his style to become as out of touch as they are. In the media, it's not only okay for tough guys to finish last, it proves they're taking the high road.

What the press seemed to miss all along was that the emergence of the New News didn't signal the demise of interest in politics amid a TV-numbed culture. Far from it. News is literally being reborn, in new forms with fresher voices, which in turn are breaking the closed circle of journalists, politicians and think-tank drones and flooding the process with humans. These are the people who've always been told it's their system; only now can they actually participate.

In 1992 viewers could watch and read the Old News if they wanted, catching sum-ups on fixed-time newscasts with anchors, pollsters and Washington analysts. Or they could meet and call the candidates on the newly politicized talk shows, where they could see, hear, evaluate and even talk to them for hours. They could watch CNN or C-Span, both on the air with more political coverage for longer periods of time than has ever been available in the history of broadcasting. Or they could watch MTV News' daily profiles and summaries of the campaign.

Comedy Central aired its own live coverage of both conventions alongside the sober networks, with comedian Al Franken anchoring and Roy Blount Jr. lounging folksily in front of a wall of TV monitors. Norman Ornstein parodied network pollsters who overwhelm viewers with numbers and graphs, at one point pondering a "poll" of men who thought they might have had abortions but were undecided. In a spoof of both conventions' smarmy candidate-profile films, Franken's son recalled how the family had really come together after his father backed over him in their car.

But Comedy Central could get serious, too. Franken sensed— and said—that the ugly tone of Pat Buchanan's speech was a mistake for the Republicans, that it would backfire. It wasn't until days or even weeks later that the traditional pundits called the speech the beginning of the end for the Bush campaign. It was disorienting to watch a comedy broadcast that almost incidentally told more truth and offered more insight than most networks and newspapers and at the same time was so much more comfortable to watch.

Far from trivializing or diminishing the race, these new ways of covering it seemed to energize presidential politics. Election officials across the country reported a surge in voter registration for the first time in two decades. The biggest single spark, according to the new registrants, was Perot, whose antimedia campaign of direct conversations, direct appeals and purchased air time seemed to reengage millions, even those who had no plans to vote for him. MTV, with its Choose or Lose coverage, and Rock the Vote were also credited with registering close to a million young voters.

The very media that we have been warned for years were rotting the brains of kids and distracting everybody else from the serious business of the country—TV in general and the talk shows, tabloid telecasts, cable music and comedy channels, rock and rap—were in fact opening doors that let them in. But it became clear by the fall that this was a reality the Old News could never reconcile with its own self-righteous notions.

For all that the New News overwhelmed the old in 1992 and dominated the campaign, it offered only a taste—and a primitive one at that—of what is to come. Just as cable freed politics, viewers and TV itself from a few powerful networks, new lightning-fast satellite transmission-and-receiving technology and the hundreds of new channels that will shortly be beaming into the country's millions of TV sets will take us another giant step forward.

The coming changes have two fundamental things in common. By duplicating or eliminating the function of a reporter, they will threaten to make reporters obsolete. Even more importantly, they will speed the process by which viewers have taken control from broadcasters of what appears on their TV screens.

High-powered broadcasting satellites, a million times more powerful than the one that beamed pictures to the eighty-five-foot-in-diameter dish during the Tokyo Olympics in 1964, can now send infinitely more signals to window-mounted dishes the size of a cake. New video-compression technology will permit a single satellite channel to carry scores of separate programs.

Higher picture definition will bring movie-quality clarity to flat-panel, wall-mounted TV screens.

Interactive TV will allow viewers to send messages to friends or people with similar musical or political tastes anywhere in the country, to order from vast movie libraries, to play video games, to order products from stores that now use catalogs or to select and edit the parts of news programs they're interested in.

The entity the news media most dread—the seven Baby Bells—is now poised to enter the $25-billion-to-$40-billion-a-year information business. Bell Atlantic will soon offer an electronic video-rental store, enabling customers to dial up movies or TV programs over the phone. Pacific Bell plans to sell new information services next year, giving customers better directory assistance, access to university libraries and news, sports scores and weather. Other Baby Bells are moving to market additional services. Users will scan electronic Yellow Pages, which newspaper executives rightly fear will displace classified advertising. Users will make travel reservations, shop at home, play the stock market and probably offer their own cable TV programs in a few years.

These new phone, screen and satellite technologies make Ross Perot's mad vision of an electronic town hall inevitable. Perot was on the mark when he said his notion makes reporters crazy by making the White House press conference obsolete.

Reporters are also being shoved aside by a relatively low-tech opponent: video-driven, reality-based TV. How can a police reporter describe a murder when viewers can see one on *Cops*? What some producers call "unfiltered" programming, *Cops* is one of a whole generation of reality broadcasts—*Rescue 911, Code 3, Top Cops, Unsolved Mysteries, America's Most Wanted, Sightings, I Witness Video*—which prove nothing is more gripping than a real story. None of the broadcasts use what used to be called reporters.

This fall Time Warner unveiled New York 1 News, New York City's first twenty-four-hour local news channel. Local cable news operations already exist in Washington, D.C., California and New England, but the debut of New York 1 in the nation's largest TV market has gotten the attention of the thousands of journalists who live there, providing a showcase of the world to come. New York 1 News, and other cable channels expected to follow, will broadcast live high-school football games and City Hall tax hearings and Board of Education condom fights and four-alarm fires—things we used to need reporters to learn about.

In the United States anyone with a pen or a pencil, a notebook, a still camera or a videocam—there are tens of millions—is a reporter. Some of them, like the amateur journalist who shot the police beating of Rodney King, will break the biggest stories in the country. They will provide the manpower, the audience and the voice for the next step in the evolution of information: the People's News.

The inevitable successor to the old and new kinds of transmitting stories, the People's News will make journalists out of all of us and plug us back into the political system in ways that would have had the radicals who founded the nation's media dancing in their cobbled streets.

The People's News is, in fact, already on the air, although most journalists have never heard of it. It is CamNet, a nine-month-old cable network that airs documentaries and features shot on Hi-8mm video cameras by amateurs, artists, activists. Like Ted Turner's belittled vision of CNN a decade ago, CamNet is the brilliant vision for the next decade and beyond. Founded in a back room of a Venice Beach, California, home by two former PBS producers, CamNet has no corporate backing or market research. Just twenty picture makers scattered around the country.

CamNet is so far available in only eight cities, including Los Angeles, Denver, Baltimore and Philadelphia. But it or something like it is coming soon to a TV set near you. It's the inevitable next stop in the liberation of television from network owners and broadcasters and its evolution as a medium that can interact with millions of people and return TV to individual Americans, a process Clinton, Perot and Brown legitimized.

CamNet's pieces are eclectic, odd, funny, haunting, spontaneous and strikingly apart from slick commercial-TV production values. CamNet stories include condom stores in L.A., skinheads taunting Mexicans along the border, the Richard M. Nixon museum, a Washington, D.C., march against police brutality.

"You really can get lost in this place," a CamNet correspondent reported during the Democratic Convention in Madison Square Garden. "You get hungry, you get thirsty, and the food here is really awful. And that very much symbolizes how hungry Americans are for some real food." CamNet returns individual, idiosyncratic, untutored voices to broadcasting, where the whole culture of TV journalism—pollsters, blow-dried reporters and anchors, advocates, spokespeople and lobbyists—is structured to keep them off. The People's News will show us in the mirror, not just them.

There may be lots of good reasons why reporters need to survive and why the current structure of journalism ought to be preserved. But if they do exist, the media need to start articulating them.

So far the media, like the White House during 1992, show few signs of seeing themselves in crisis. The New News is largely still pooh-poohed as unnerving, slightly dangerous and frivolous mush. Newspapers still run black-and-white pictures of events the rest of us saw twenty-four hours earlier in color, and white, middle-aged men in suits still sit behind evening-news anchor desks and say nothing much in grave and mellifluous voices.

Time does finally seem to be getting short. Perot's bloody loss did not reaffirm the media's importance or service to the republic. Quite the opposite. Like Marley's Ghost, his campaign brought with it visions of the future nobody wants to see.

The blunt reality is this: In a world where everybody is a journalist, then nobody really is. Journalists derived their power and special place in the country from the fact that they got to see history and relay it to us. If we're all seeing history as it unfolds and taking the pictures ourselves, then journalists seem increasingly, and sadly, doomed to follow the lumbering, awkward and poorly adapted institutions they work for into the country's history. The 1992 campaign and the technological revolution that is charging along on its heels suggest the death of the reporter is just a few channels away.

GAVEL-TO-GAVEL COVERAGE[6]

Anyone interested in either the judicial branch of our Government or the mass media had a busy few months last fall. If your list of major interests also includes—and whose doesn't?—sexual politics, you are probably suffering, as I am, from post-major-media-event trauma syndrome.

In the wake of the Clarence Thomas confirmation hearings and the William Kennedy Smith rape trial, the couch potatoes of

[6]Article by Elayne Rapping, from *The Progressive* 56:34–37 Mr '92. Copyright © 1992 by *The Progressive*. Reprinted with permission.

the nation are certainly due for their very own Twelve Step Program and some prominent space on the "Recovery" shelves of neighborhood bookstores.

From its birth, television has played a central role in presenting, framing, and highlighting public events, in re-presenting them to us as larger-than-life spectacles, or in rerunning key scenes and episodes until they become part of our conscious and unconscious experience, like bad dreams which seem to haunt us long after we awaken.

As early as 1952, when Dwight Eisenhower, with the expert help of a pricey Madison Avenue ad agency, stole the Presidency from the bookish, uncharismatic Adlai Stevenson, the ability of home television, in alliance with the networks and corporate sponsors, to package and spectacularize public life was clear.

John F. Kennedy, the most media-savvy of presidents (until the inimitable Ronald Reagan), virtually planned the space program as a Cold War media event; there was no scientific reason to man the space flights. But anyone who has ever watched MTV—whose famous logo features a clip of the first-man-on-the-moon walk—knows the importance, symbolically and culturally, of that decision. For the MTV generation, born and raised with television, history does indeed begin with the videocamera and the ominous "We interrupt our regularly scheduled programming to bring you this special report. . . ."

Nonetheless, cable television, with its capacity to allow for "narrowcasting"—that is, entire channels, operating twenty-four hours a day, focusing, "narrowly," on a single type of content—has significantly changed the relationship between media and public life and altered the terms of the perennial discussion about "television effects." Until Cable News Network, the twenty-four-hour-a-day all-news network, came along, we had pretty much stabilized the TV/public-life equation.

Certain events—most dating back to the 1950s—were understood to warrant full coverage. The networks have always covered Presidential nominating conventions, elections, and Presidential press conferences, wars, national tragedies (Kennedy's assassination was the ironic first there), national catastrophes, or potential catastrophes (such as the Watergate or Iran/contra hearings), and certain natural disasters. And that's pretty much the list.

Most people don't question the legitimacy of this regimen. Television came on the scene, after all, as a rational response to the felt need for a central system of communication for a nation increasingly fragmented, dispersed, out of touch with its leaders and institutions and falling away from the traditional values and beliefs that had unified it in earlier days.

Now it is becoming questionable whether these "major media events" still have the compelling emotional power, the dramatic effect, they once did. Since Watergate, we have grown disillusioned with public figures and their mock mea-culpa hearings. Since Vietnam, the media themselves have become so slick at sanitizing political events that may be disturbing—I am thinking, of course, of the Gulf war—that even when we do pay attention, we are being pacified rather than aroused.

Suddenly, though, with the rise of narrowcasting, we have something new to worry about. Certain events that previously were not deemed important enough for full coverage—most especially, criminal trials—are now given gavel-to-gavel attention, opened up for all the world to see and hear. And people are watching and talking like crazy.

So begins the new round of the old debate: "Is television sensationalizing public life?" Is it making us into a nation of peeping toms? A society of tabloid-sleaze consumers? Filling our heads with ever more bizarre and disgusting garbage? Melting our brains and tainting our souls? Is it seemly for a nation to participate in public events—especially serious ones like the confirmation hearings of a Supreme Court justice—in which such embarrassing and tasteless subjects as penis size and pubic hair are discussed? (Why penises should be more disturbing to the fragile national psyche than Scud missiles is unclear, but I'm sure someone will explain it to me.)

If the Thomas hearings were all that is at issue, the debate would not be particularly important. Or, at least, it would take a different shape. No one could predict the Thomas debacle, after all. And it's unlikely that the networks or the Government will seriously consider banning media from such important proceedings as Supreme Court confirmation hearings.

But narrowcasting has brought with it coverage of far less nationally significant, though equally sensational, trials, making many people nervous indeed. No less prominent a straight arrow than George Bush has worried, publicly, "about so much filth and indecent material coming in through the airwaves and through these trials into people's homes." In Bush's lofty, paternalistic opinion, "the American people have a right to be protected against some of these excesses . . . an overriding right to have these matters settled behind closed doors."

Of course, Bush's views, if taken seriously, would pretty much do away with the First Amendment, and yet he is not alone in feeling uneasy about the social consequences of allowing the American people to get a good look at what goes on in the courtrooms of America. He is suggesting, and he has much company among those who worry about the disintegrating moral fiber of the nation, that the influx of boundless information about areas of life previously shrouded in darkness should be curbed in the interest of the greater public welfare.

As with most right-wing hand-wringing over moral corruption resulting from free expression, this anguish is hypocritical. What worries Bush and his friends is the obvious fact that—so far—the judiciary is the only branch of government which has not been thoroughly discredited. And that is because it is the only branch that has not yet been brought under scrutiny by television.

The executive and legislative branches—especially since Watergate—are so much distrusted, disbelieved, and disrespected that it is hard to get young people to vote, much less participate in political activities. And most kids today—like their idol Bart Simpson—do not believe anything they hear from their elders, especially those in positions of power and authority.

To blame the media for this breakdown in the legitimacy of our institutions is just an up-to-the-minute version of killing the messenger. It is our leaders themselves, whose conduct cannot stand up to scrutiny and exposure, who are responsible for the crisis of authority. The state of the nation is surely lamentable. But it is all to the good that we are allowed to see it for what it is.

We not only have the right to watch legal proceedings; we cannot participate as members of a functioning democracy without doing so. Thomas Jefferson, who believed trials should be public events, said as much in the early, more idealistic days of this nation. And he would, most certainly, have approved of cameras in the courtroom. Why shield the lawyers and judges from the scrutiny they deserve? Why let such anachronistic paragons as Ben Matlock and Perry Mason stand in for the less virtuous real thing in this key area of public life?

Jefferson might be shocked at the content of the trials we are now watching with so much fascination. But that would be because he—an aristocratic white male of the eighteenth century—was ignorant of and insensitive to matters of race, class, and gender. In that respect, we have progressed far beyond the Founding Fathers. In fact, it is quite obvious that the real reason the right is so uptight about sex in the courtroom is that male privilege is being challenged when men are put on trial for taking sexual license. In the courtroom and everywhere else, the assumption that women will quietly and smilingly acquiesce to male sexual aggression is under siege.

Having cut through the posturing and hypocrisy that informs the debate about cameras and courts, we are nonetheless left with some real problems about media coverage. The commercial media, both print and electronic, are not untainted by the interests of money, power, and the privileges of race, gender, and class. To read the press, even—especially—*The New York Times,* or to watch the news on NBC, ABC, CBS, and the more thorough but still highly biased CNN is to get a slanted picture and analysis.

The reason is selectivity. The editors and producers make important decisions about what to print, what to televise. They choose commentators who "analyze" events from a particular slant. They worry about sponsors and other important friends in high places. They worry (as the hullabaloo over Oliver Stone's movie *JFK* makes clear) about anything that seems to go too far in making our institutions and leaders seem too corrupt and untrustworthy. And they are themselves members of privileged categories, whose own real attitudes and values tend to be much closer to those of the powerful and successful than to those who challenge authority.

This is a well-known situation, at least to progressives. But it became dramatically clear to me during the rape trial of William Kennedy Smith, because I actually had something positive to compare it to. I had Court TV, a veritable godsend for inquiring minds who actually want to know about serious judicial matters, who are concerned about the many political issues now being raised and settled through the judicial process in civil and criminal courts throughout the nation.

Court TV runs twenty-four-hour-a-day coverage and commentary on current trials. It is, so far anyway, only marginally commercial. Small, politically negligible sponsors, selling such items as classical music cassettes and *The Doctors' Book of Home Remedies,* now advertise, and one can watch for an entire morning without a single commercial interruption.

Its choice of trials is predictably sensational, of course. But, again, that is not a bad thing. Cases of sexual harassment, obscenity and the First Amendment, the right of white supremacists to burn crosses on neighbors' lawns, of religious fanatics to block abortion-clinic entrances, the use of an insanity defense by sex offenders who were themselves sexually abused: All these have come up in trials I have watched with fascination in the few months since I subscribed, and all raise pressing current political and social issues.

Unlike the networks or CNN, Court TV uses the services of a great variety of legal experts, including feminists, First Amendment specialists, defenders of alleged rapists, and so on, many of whom are women and blacks. Even CNN will stick with the predictable and biased; F. Lee Bailey and Alan Dershowitz, rich and famous white male friends to the rich and famous white male defendants everywhere, have a virtual monopoly on legal expertise, according to the mainstream media. But Court TV offers a variety of opinions and voices, with debates among them concerning specific strategies as well as larger legal issues.

During the Thomas hearings, for example, Court TV ran educational programs about sexual harassment. During the Smith trial, it aired a similar educational program on the consent defense in date-rape trials. I recently watched another on constitutional law and racial justice. And, instead of one or two tried-and-true apologists for the status quo such as we get from the other media, I heard from scores of individuals with differing opinions about and experiences of issues raised by key trials, as well as general ferment in the profession.

Court TV has no political agenda beyond a commitment to and respect for the legal system as it exists and functions. Insofar as it has no critical perspective but simply exists to reveal and explain the workings of the judiciary, it gives an unusually transparent image of the legal system—or as transparent as any mediated representation can be. What is wrong with the system is evident to those with critical faculties. Its limits are obvious. Its tendency, for better or worse, to reflect the political assumptions of the larger society is clear.

The "for the better" part comes through most noticeably in the way "objective"—that is, nonpolitical—discussions of what strategies would work in certain situations take on political coloring as the law changes under pressure from progressive forces.

For example, the implicit feminist assumptions about sexual behavior which every "expert" was forced to make in explaining how she or he would have prosecuted Smith were apparent. Once sexual harassment or date rape become legal concepts, every lawyer must be educated to accept and deal with the feminist assumptions such changes in the law reflect. And to hear discussions in which white male attorneys, for strictly practical reasons of winning a case, put forth arguments about women's rights and men's responsibilities is more than refreshing; it is consciousness-raising.

Mainstream media, in such discussions, always label guests politically in an effort to alert audiences that they are listening to "biased" views. On Court TV, things are far less managed. Participants are speaking professionally, not politically, and without obvious political agendas, so political views get through the crevices unannounced and uninflected.

The "for the worse" part is apparent in the many instances in which the failure of the system to incorporate progressive values and ideas results in juries and judges behaving in ways that are necessarily reactionary. The fact that defense attorneys can so easily choose jurors with no knowledge of the political discussions surrounding sex crimes; that judges can, in good conscience, bar testimony from experts on rape trauma, sexual harassment, sexual violence, and so on, means such cases will be judged on objectively sexist criteria and data.

Watching the tedious—and therefore ignored by the other media—jury-selection proceedings for the Smith trial, which lasted weeks, was as enlightening a political event as I have seen. It showed, without doubt, what Star Jones, a black woman prosecutor, rightly observed on Court TV: that the case was decided long before the trial began; that the decision turned not on "evidence" but on the "attitudes toward women" which the carefully selected jurors brought with them. This, combined with the equally biased (although legally impeccable) judge's rulings to exclude prosecution witnesses who could discuss rape trauma or testify to the defendant's previous sexual aggressions, made the acquittal inevitable—and inherently unjust.

In a society such as ours in which power, money, and privilege are unevenly distributed, in which these inequalities are reflected in the workings of every institution—the family, the press, the courtroom, the Congress, and so on—the best we can hope for is unfettered, relatively undoctored access to the ways in which these institutions, in their public proceedings, mete out truth and

justice. Court TV—so far—offers more of that access than anything else around, except the unwieldy *Congressional Record* and,
possibly, C-Span.

No, it is not perfect. No, it is not free of its own milder versions of commercial and institutional distortions. But in an age
when visual media are being attacked as *more* damaging to the
public welfare than the equally biased print media, it is important
to counter those arguments with demands for more, not less,
access and exposure. For the more unedited access we have to
public events, the more points of view and differing opinions we
are allowed to hear, the more qualified and armed we will be to
judge and act on matters of social and political concern.

To support this position, let me give just a few examples of
coverage of the Smith trial from Court TV as compared to that of
The New York Times and NBC News. In direct contradiction to
common-sense notions about visual sensationalism, it was *The New
York Times* that most outrageously distorted and sensationalized
the entire event, with NBC a close second.

It was, after all, *The Times* and NBC that named the alleged
victim; it was *The Times* that brought up her past (supposed) sexual promiscuity and emotional instability. All of which—it was clear
if you watched the entire proceedings rather than clips and
bleeps—was nonsense. She was absolutely coherent and rational.
Even the *defense's* witnesses to her character, including a bar-
tender brought on to discredit her by association, ended up describing her as "shy," a woman who rarely went out, who was
obsessively concerned with her small child, who dressed "casually,
a little sloppy maybe, like a student," and who was not known to
come on to men, drink excessively, or use drugs.

This was to be expected, I suppose. What was truly shocking,
however, was the media's—especially *The Times's*—trashing of
prosecutor Moira Lasch. If the accuser was supposed to be an
unstable slut, Lasch—you just can't win with these guys—was
equally vilified for being an uptight, sexually inexperienced prude
who "never smiled" (as in "Smile, Honey") and who, because of
"her own limited experience in these matters" (meaning the sexual
mores of the hip singles-bar scene) ineptly "spun a primitive feminist tale." Such distortion could only be effective, or acceptable, to
a public without means to check its accuracy. Only those who saw
otherwise knew for certain how outrageously biased *The Times* was.

The garish, out-of-context use of clips and sound bites by
television similarly distorted reality. For example, mainstream

coverage gave a very distorted version of the trial in which the state's case and Lasch's performance were presented as far weaker than they were. It also obscured the fact that the courtroom itself was a model of decorum, that only the networks and newspapers created the impression of a sensational circus. Judge Lupo ran so tight a ship that a *Newsweek* reporter was expelled for "smirking" during medical testimony and defense attorney Roy Black was stopped from hugging Smith upon hearing the verdict.

Court TV allowed all this to be seen and grasped. The other media flagrantly manipulated the voluminous footage and chose commentators about as qualified to speak on date rape as Clarence Thomas is to rule on women's rights.

Luddites among us may rant and rave about the evils of television, but they are off the mark. Television is, potentially, a miraculous invention. If it is abused today, it is no more abused than any other powerful force. If it is to be better used, it will only be because we, as citizens, learn to use it better, privately and collectively, and demand that those in power make that more and more possible.

For the time being, that might mean demanding that city councils, which regulate and license local cable franchises, provide space on the airwaves—a scarce natural resource—for more and more such services as C-Span and Court TV, even if it means dumping some of what passes for "public-service programming" on the networks.

COVERING THE COPS[7]

Perhaps the most mythologized figure of modern journalism is the urban police reporter, that tough-talking, street-savvy wise-ass who matched cops drink for drink and wisecrack for wisecrack, and who got rewrite from Sweetheart.

But that reporter looked a lot better *in The Front Page* than *on* it. Coming, most likely, from a working class background, he identified with and protected the men he covered, becoming their

[7]Article by Jon Katz, first appeared in *Columbia Journalism Review.* 31:25–30 Ja/F '93. Copyright © 1993 by Jon Katz. Reprinted by permission of Brandt & Brandt Literary Agents, Inc.

ideological comrade-in-arms rather than watchdog or chronicler. Rarely did he report on police racism, brutality, and corruption and therefore, for middle-class America, such evils hardly existed. These days, the stereotypical police reporter has virtually vanished from the country's newsrooms, while the police are often shown to be corrupt, brutal, and bigoted.

Today's upper middle-class, college-educated journalists have little in common with the police, and are frequently to the left of them politically. Brutal police response to antiwar demonstrations and the civil rights movement shook idealized notions of law enforcement. Officer Murphy, twirling his baton and occasionally cuffing an errant rascal for the lad's own good, was replaced by Bull Connor—or, more recently, his heirs on the LAPD. Meanwhile, police seem increasingly isolated, abandoned by journalists and everyone else as they try to deal with horrifying levels of social decay, hatred, and bloodshed. They seem to have turned inward, talking to and trusting no one but their lawyers and each other.

Against this backdrop comes *Cops*, perhaps the inevitable television appropriation of the police reporter's role. Syndicated nationwide by Fox television, *Cops* is one of the most successful of the gritty new telecasts that offer Americans more reality than they ever imagined possible. Taped by crews carrying mobile shoulder-held video cameras, shows like *Cops* are what producers call "unfiltered" television—a new wave of reality-based entertainment with serious implications for a news media already reeling from the invasion of talk shows, tabloid telecasts, newsmagazines, and cable-casts.

No reporter or producer narrates *Cops;* no equivalent of the journalist offers a detached perspective. The cameras ride with the police in their patrol cars, following the officers and picking up the sounds of jangling keys and handcuffs, squawking radios and creaking leather as they arrest drunk drivers, rush into vicious bar brawls, quell domestic disputes, chase burglars onto rooftops, arrive at murder and accident scenes, pursue kids in stolen cars at hair-raising speeds, and get punched, kicked, run over, spat upon, stabbed, and sometimes shot at by the people they confront. Those old-time police reporters would keel over in shock.

Some departments—in Los Angeles and New York City, for example—have declined to allow *Cops* cameras in their police cars, citing legal concerns or fears for the safety of camera crews.

Many, including those in Kansas City, Hoboken, San Diego, Pittsburgh, Houston, and Boston, have agreed to be subjects for the broadcast. Needless to say, the officers selected by their departments to participate are articulate, meticulously professional, sometimes even laughably solicitous. On *Cops*, the police thank drunk drivers profusely for cooperating and hand out quarters to teenagers caught driving without licenses so they can call Mom and Dad to come pick them up.

But the officers on *Cops* are nonetheless revealing, often poignantly so. They almost pleadingly make their case to a public they know is skeptical. An officer in New Jersey wonders how the wailing grandchildren of the woman he has just arrested will feel about the police who searched their grandmother's apartment and arrested her on drug charges. A California policeman frets about court rulings that allow lawsuits against individual police officers as well as the municipalities they work for, endangering everything he owns. An officer in Kansas City talks about how serious the consequences of a policeman's mistake may be—far more serious than mistakes made by other American workers.

What is striking about these sometimes-eloquent voices is that they rarely are heard in the conventional press.

The cameras recording *Cops* probably would not catch a Rodney King-style beating. The officers would know better than to behave like that; even if they didn't, it's unclear whether the broadcast's producers would show it, since the program depends on the voluntary cooperation of the police. As with the old police reporters, the police point of view is what the audience sees and hears.

But *Cops* can be riveting, as it is when the camera moves into a woman's house minutes after she's been murdered and lies in a pool of blood, or when it looks over an officer's shoulder as he or she prowls through a pitch-black attic in search of a man they've been told has a gun. In one episode, officers rush to surround a woman who, a caller to 911 has said, is carrying an Uzi submachine gun. As the officers frantically scream for her to put her hands up, a machine gun protrudes visibly from her rear pocket. It turns out to be a realistic-looking plastic toy. The viewer can't help but wonder what would have happened to the woman—and the officers—if she had reached suddenly for her pocket or had not understood English or had been drunk or high on drugs.

The media have made it clear that members of minority

groups fear and resent the way they're treated by some officers, especially whites from other communities. What *Cops* reminds us is how dangerous, terrifying, and complex a police officer's job is, and how unseemly it is for journalists sitting in safe and comfortable newsrooms to make self-righteous snap judgments about police work.

As angry young men screamed "assassins" at police in Washington Heights yesterday, the sisters of a man killed by a police officer wailed and fainted in the hallway where their brother's blood still stains the walls. "Oh God, Oh God," the sisters of Jose Garcia, 24, yelled in Spanish as they collapsed in the hallway at 505 W. 162nd St., their voices echoing in the room overcrowded with screaming spectators.—New York Newsday, July 6, 1992

In Los Angeles, New York City, Miami, Detroit, and scores of other cities and towns, police behavior has led to bitter condemnations and sometimes to rioting, destruction, and killing. Typically, the officer confronts a young male in an urban neighborhood, is or feels threatened, and wounds or kills the young man. If the officer is white and the youth black or Hispanic, the community and the media—sometimes both—explode.

The shooting of Jose "Kiko" Garcia in New York City's teeming Washington Heights last summer is a case in point, not only embodying the tensions between minority groups and the police, but also posing serious questions about how the media cover them.

According to the police, on the night of July 3 plainclothes detective Michael O'Keefe and two other officers spotted Jose Garcia on a crowded street and thought they saw a gun in his pocket. O'Keefe became separated from his partners and confronted Garcia alone. Within minutes, O'Keefe was shrieking for help on his police radio; by the time other officers arrived, Garcia lay dead.

For days, local newspapers, but especially local television, aired account after account suggesting that Garcia had been killed for no reason. A deputy mayor was widely quoted as saying that Garcia had no arrest record and never carried a gun, and that O'Keefe had been "abusing people for a long time. There was no reason to kill Kiko." The Garcia family's lawyer said pretty much the same thing.

On the night of the shooting, an unidentified man told

WNBC-TV that O'Keefe had beaten Garcia "until he couldn't stand up, and then just pulled out a gun and killed him. No reason." The reporter, shaking his head sympathetically, never questioned his account in any way.

Other eyewitnesses told reporters that O'Keefe beat and kicked Garcia through the inner hallways and lobby of the apartment building into which he had pursued him, then shot him three times as he lay helpless on the floor. Several people said they saw O'Keefe using his radio to beat Garcia and heard Garcia screaming "Mommy" and "Why are you doing this to me?" in Spanish. "He's laying on his face in blood, and then the cop takes out his gun," one supposed eyewitness told *New York Newsday.* "I ran back to my apartment, and then I heard the shots." Some neighbors claimed that O'Keefe was not only a brutal cop, but that he had a reputation for stealing from drug dealers.

Not surprisingly, the shooting and its subsequent coverage sparked several days of disorder, looting, and destruction. O'Keefe was burned in effigy, and Washington Heights residents threw trash cans, bottles, and rocks at officers, smashed windows, and burned police cars.

Two months later, a Manhattan grand jury cleared Officer O'Keefe of any wrongdoing in the shooting of Garcia, who, it turned out, did have a criminal record involving drugs. The shooting occurred in a building sometimes used by drug dealers. Garcia did have a gun, said the grand jury, and O'Keefe was justified in feeling that his life was in danger during the violent struggle between the two men. Pathologists found cocaine in Garcia's system at the time of his death. There were no bruises or marks on Garcia's body to suggest a beating, nor were there any signs that O'Keefe's radio had been used to beat Garcia.

The audio tapes of a panicked O'Keefe shouting for help were shockingly at odds with accounts that had O'Keefe mercilessly beating Garcia. Moreover, the grand jury found, those eyewitness accounts would have been impossible given lighting, sight lines, and the witnesses' supposed locations. Other witnesses wouldn't testify, recanted their original testimony, or disappeared. Nor did the grand jury find any evidence to support charges that O'Keefe was brutal or corrupt.

The most detailed media account of O'Keefe's version of events did not appear until two months after he had been exonerated by the grand jury. In a November 2, 1992, interview in *New York* magazine, O'Keefe described being cut off from his partners in a brutal battle with Garcia that saw the two men fighting desperately for Garcia's gun, O'Keefe screaming for help over his radio as Garcia pointed the barrel of his gun into the officer's face. "I thought I was going to die," O'Keefe told the magazine. The officer said he grabbed Garcia's wrist, drew his gun, and fired a shot at point-blank range into Garcia's stomach.

Two days after the shooting, in an effort to calm the Washington Heights community (the Democratic National Convention was only a week away), Mayor David Dinkins visited Garcia's family, enraging many of the city's police officers. The mayor's call for an all-civilian review board enraged them further: in September, more than 10,000 cops and supporters demonstrated at city hall in protest. Some of the officers and their off-duty supporters staged, in effect, their own riot, storming police barricades, blocking the Brooklyn Bridge, shoving reporters and photographers. Some were overheard shouting racial slurs.

The protest touched off another wave of condemnation of the police from politicians, community critics, and journalists. THUGS IN BLUE was one tabloid headline. Columnists and editorial writers cited the cops' behavior as yet another example of why minority groups were right to distrust and fear the police. "All those years when we gave police the benefit of the doubt seemed extraordinarily naive in retrospect," wrote Anna Quindlen in *The New York Times*.

The media's outrage was certainly appropriate. But no New York City news organization acknowledged that it would also have been appropriate to point out the errors of its coverage of the Garcia shooting, apologize to O'Keefe, or explain to readers and viewers why much of their reporting had been false and misleading.

Everything about the shooting—the time of year, the place it occurred, the ethnicity of the officer and of the person he shot—cried out for journalistic restraint. Reporters know that eyewitnesses at crime scenes are often unreliable, excitable advocates for one side or another, sometimes so anxious to be on television that their accounts become more melodramatic than what they actually saw. Reporters also know that some politicians exploit police-community tensions. Besides, police brutality lawsuits can involve enormous amounts of money—some damage settlements have reached into the millions—so that principals and attorneys often have financial stakes in eyewitness accounts and in the outcome of investigations.

Add the threat of violence and civil disorder and there are lots of reasons for reporters and editors to be extraordinarily cautious about explosive eyewitness accounts of police-community confrontations offered in the heat of the moment. New York's media, prodded by the city's first black mayor, had helped to squelch rumors and maintain calm in the wake of the L.A. riots last spring. But there seems to be less restraint or caution when police shootings are involved.

"So what were the Washington Heights riots all about?" *The New York Times* disingenuously wondered in an editorial following the grand jury report. The editorial cited a number of factors that might have led to the unrest—drug gangs trying to force a police retreat, past complaints of police brutality. Coverage of the shooting was not on the list.

Among the questions the press faces in dealing with its coverage of the police is whether or not the overwhelming focus on brutality and racism obscures fundamental issues about urban policing:

• Has violence in some urban neighborhoods escalated beyond the ability of police departments to cope with it? In Newark, young—sometimes pre-adolescent—thieves in stolen cars ram police cruisers for kicks. They taunt police officers, who are prohibited from engaging in high speed chases. In November, four people were killed in one night by joy-riding kids whose stolen cars crashed. In New York City, 430 children under the age of sixteen had been shot in the first ten months of 1992, 73 of them bystanders. In the first seven months, according to city officials, 51 children under sixteen became homicide victims.

• How should police best deal with inner-city males in areas where violence has escalated dramatically? Gun control advocates say there are as many as 150 million guns in America. Scholars and authors like Andrew Hacker *(Two Nations)* and Christopher Jencks *(Rethinking Social Policy)* have begun to document the conditions that overwhelm many urban police departments. The new statistics hardly excuse police brutality, but they at least partly explain why police officers and young males are increasingly confronting one another in violent situations: more kids have more guns and are using them more frequently.

Federal researchers report that by the late 1980s, as the drug epidemic swept America's cities, more teen-aged males in urban neighborhoods began dying from gunshot wounds than from any other cause. Death from guns among all U.S. teenagers shot up by 61 percent from 1979 to 1989, but among black teenaged males in major cities the increase was a staggering 233 percent. A study by the National Crime Analysis Project at Northeastern University found that from 1985 to 1991 the number of sixteen-year-olds arrested for murder climbed by 158 percent, while homicide arrests of fifteen-year-olds more than tripled.

• Can white police officers who live in outlying areas control minority urban communities? Should cities enact police residency requirements, thus increasing the number of minority officers? Should different kinds of policing and patrolling be considered, using neighborhood security aides, social workers, parent-training programs, school-based tutoring, parents, even teenagers?

• Should states of emergency be declared in neighborhoods where children are being slaughtered? Should federal troops or state militias reinforce beleaguered police departments? Should the media deploy more of their own resources to covering violence committed by and upon urban children, thus demonstrating—and pressuring the government to demonstrate—that their plight is as important a story as suburban car-jacking?

The police themselves often aren't much help. Cops may resent reporters, but journalists remain the best and most credible vehicle for exploring and explaining police work. Police departments need to be more forthcoming more quickly when their officers are involved in shootings and confrontations, not wait weeks or months for official reports, as happened in the Garcia case.

As *Cops* makes clear, the more the public sees of their work, the more comprehensible their work becomes. In October, a *New York Times* reporter, trying to explain the pressures that had led to the unruly police demonstration outside of city hall a month earlier, asked for permission to spend a week with the police in a Brooklyn neighborhood. But departmental officials would agree to allow only one night on radio car patrol and one day on foot patrol. Even though the report asked to be assigned to a tough, high-crime precinct, the department insisted that she be assigned to a safe, low-crime precinct. Even there, precinct commanders had to intervene before the reporter was permitted a second day on car patrol. Despite the limitations, the piece was revealing and compelling, in much the same way *Cops* is, belatedly conveying the violence and tensions of urban policing.

Broadcasts like *Cops* are moving into a vacuum that would be better filled by journalists. The press needs to move closer to where it belongs on one of the biggest and most important stories in American life: into the middle, prepared to challenge the police when appropriate, but also willing to capture and put into context the environments in which they work.

THE BIG SLEAZE[8]

It is a sultry summer afternoon on the outskirts of Fremont, Ohio, and Gary Offenburg is making love to a woman named Lynn in a two-tone Chevy pickup truck. She is positioned on the seat; he is standing outside, his pants around his ankles. This is not, however, as uncommon a sight as it would seem. Ever since South River Road became a dead-end street, some five years ago, it has functioned as the town's lovers' lane, much to the irritation of Randy Powers. This day, Powers, who owns one of the houses on the road, becomes further incensed because, he says, his young children can see. He calls the Sandusky County Sheriff's Department. The forty-nine-year-old Offenburg and Lynn, who as it happens is not his wife, are charged with public indecency and disorderly conduct. This is not a national story, and it would never have become one but for two simple facts: There is video, and there is *A Current Affair*.

Having been told by the prosecutor's office that it needed evidence before it could act, Powers videotaped Offenburg's indiscretion. *A Current Affair* bought the tape—folks in Fremont said the show paid $2500—and, living up to the double-entendre of the show's name, aired the footage at least twice, to an average audience of 17 million per show. Gary Offenburg was already pretty upset about the effect this might have on his standing in the community and on his job with the state Department of

[8]Article by Krista Bradford, from *Rolling Stone* 39–43+ Fe 18 '93. Copyright © 1993 by Straight Arrow Publishers, Inc. Reprinted with permission.

Transportation. He had his hands full trying to answer to his wife and children for his infidelity. His wife, Nancy, later confided to me in a quiet voice that her husband repeatedly said to her, "Why can't they just let it die?"

On November 18th, 1992, a little more than a month after *A Current Affair* aired the story a second time, Gary Offenburg decided to pay his debt to society—beyond the measly $150 fine, $33 in court costs and thirty-day suspended sentence. On this dreary, cloudy morning, he descended into his basement. There he committed suicide with a pump-action-shotgun blast to the chest.

Nancy Offenburg blamed the news media for having gone too far. "I'm angry about *A Current Affair*," she said. "I realize it was news, but they didn't have to keep pushing it. It was eating at him so bad that *he couldn't take it anymore*."

You've got to say: "I'm a human being, goddammit, my life has some value!" —Howard Beale in *Network*

Recently, I've felt as if I were channeling the mad-as-hell spirit of Paddy Chayefsky's creation Howard Beale, the raving TV anchor. After nearly five years in the tabloid-TV business, there came a point at which I concluded I was not going to take this anymore. Shows like *A Current Affair* are messing with people's lives—not only the individuals exploited in tabloid-TV stories but the viewers seduced on the other side of the screen.

Beginning in 1987, I worked in the subterranean world of tabloid television, a world where the truth is far less important than the sexy story. I learned that interviews are regularly purchased and that tabloid TV cuts deals, agreeing to cover notorious characters favorably—Manuel Noriega, for instance—and lobbing only softball questions. I've overheard conversations in which field producers have threatened celebrities with damaging information if they didn't cooperate. I have watched reality become fiction in the edit bays as news footage was intercut with movie scenes and music videos and tarted up with sound effects and music.

The world of trash TV is awash in Australian journalists whose perspective on American life is so distorted it's as if they were standing on their heads. I started first as a reporter and substitute host for *A Current Affair*, then later became one of five correspondents for the weekly Fox newsmagazine show *The Re-*

porters. Following its demise and about nine months of unemployment, I accepted a job as senior correspondent for *Now It Can Be Told*, a nationally syndicated show hosted by Geraldo Rivera, which aired for about a year until August 1992. It was my latest tabloid experience. Now I've decided it will be my last.

Granted, the suggestion that tabloid television drives people to suicide seems far-fetched. But the Ohio story reminded me of one I had reported about five years ago for *A Current Affair*. I was sent to see a New York City woman who was one of the first rape victims to reveal her identity in an effort to banish the shame associated with the crime. On the way to the location, we received a series of calls from the assignment editor, Bob Young. The woman was disturbed, it turned out, and her story most likely was not true. But Young said go ahead and shoot it anyway. And it ran. When I later learned that this woman killed herself, I felt ashamed and angry. I felt that we had exploited an unstable woman and shared some responsibility for her death (Young disagreed, since our story was part of a media blitz).

Then I remembered the line that everybody in this business says—as a joke, of course—to themselves and to one another, as a form of absolution: "Don't let the facts get in the way of a good story."

Now, I know what you're thinking: "Hey, lighten up. These shows are meant to entertain, to have a little fun with the news. This kind of TV is all a harmless romp." But is it? Behind its campy humor, its tits-and-ass raunchiness, its rubbernecking at the oddities of American life, there is something decidedly *mean* about tabloid television. Because sometimes *people* get in the way of a good story. And the bigwigs of trash TV don't really give a damn.

As someone who has worked in TV news since the age of eighteen, I fit in the world of tabloid because I was a misfit. At seventeen, I interned for Joan Lunden at KCRA-TV, in Sacramento, California. I cut an audition tape and hit the road, landing at a Monterey station that had just lost its female anchor. I got the job. I later reported for local news operations in St. Louis, Los Angeles, Denver and Boston. Growing up in television news is akin to prolonged high-level exposure to cultural radiation—you don't mature, you mutate. There is something decidedly *warped* about being celebrated for your ability to read aloud or for the way you look on TV. It does something to a person. It made me cranky not being taken seriously as a journalist.

In 1986, some ten years after I started my career, I lost my job as weekend anchor and weekday reporter at the ABC affiliate in Boston, WCVB-TV. My contract wasn't renewed. Looking back, I don't really blame them, and I don't really blame myself for what I did next.

I flew to Manhattan to consider talking a job as a reporter for *A Current Affair*. Back then, even the *New York Times* praised the show, which had not yet gone national: "Forget now the pejorative notions that cling to the phrase," said the *Times*. "*A Current Affair* is tabloid journalism at its best. It is zippy and knowledgeable, and when it falls on its face, at least it's in there trying." But instead of spending the afternoon in the show's Upper East Side offices at Fox TV station WNYW, I was directed to the Racing Club, a dark, smoky bar across the street, where I watched some of my prospective colleagues get pissed—as in drunk, not angry. That's what these journos called it.

It was in this bar that I met producer Peter Brennan, the mastermind who molded *A Current Affair* before moving on to produce Paramount's sleazier son of *Affair, Hard Copy*. There was something lovable about Brennan—the way he affectionately called everyone Bubba, his pink cheeks and graying hair reminiscent of a fellow who preferred chimneys and soot to elevators. He winked knowingly and nodded warmly his approval of me while he nursed a single drink that day. There was something about my WASPy manner that he liked. Later he told me what it was: that I could make the unseemly appear somehow seemly, that I could wade waist deep through the muck of tabloid and emerge unsoiled. Eventually, ABC's *PrimeTime Live* correspondent Judd Rose would give me some more-accurate career advice: "There's only so long you can be a diamond swimming in a sea of shit before you end up a shit-covered diamond."

On my first day at *A Current Affair,* some six months after its debut, I was asked to portray Jessica Hahn in a reenactment of her alleged rape by the televangelist Jim Bakker. I was horrified. I wasn't an actress, I was a journalist, for God's sake. I was supposed to pretend I was the now infamous "bimbo" Jessica—to "act" like I was being sexually assaulted? I refused.

But aside from that hitch in the beginning, I grew to like the wacky stories, the travel and the adventure offered by *A Current Affair.* The show had a delicious sense of humor. The stories often featured a Joe Six-Pack who had gotten his life turned so inside out that it was as if he were wearing underwear for a hat—it was nearly impossible not to laugh at the village idiot. There was the guy who faked his own plunge to his death over Niagara Falls. And the forest ranger who was damn sure he saw Bigfoot. And there was Sheriff Corky, who had rented a video camera to make X-rated movies with his wife. Naturally, they returned the camera with the racy video still inside. Naturally, duplicates were made, providing endless entertainment to law-enforcement officers across the country and grist for *A Current Affair.*

Even the grisly murder stories were fascinating at first. I felt like Truman Capote as he was reporting *In Cold Blood.* I spent weeks psychoanalyzing a murderer and sex offender who was trying to con his way out of prison. I pushed one convict's buttons enough that he broke down and cried (known as "passing the onion" in the trade). I thought that I just might find the key to what caused these people to kill. But after doing enough of these stories, I eventually came to the conclusion that they killed because they were crazy.

I soon started noticing things I wished would go away—only they didn't. *A Current Affair* didn't like doing stories about gays, people of color or unattractive women. I drew this conclusion, as did many of my colleagues, based on the standard questions we were asked when we would propose a story: "What color is he/she, mate?"—followed by "Are there pictures?" to confirm the physical description. Stories that were about these unwanted people generally were not pursued. Former *Hard Copy* reporter Alexander Johnson, who became a correspondent for *Now It Can Be Told* and now reports for *A Current Affair,* is one of the few blacks in the genre. He does not deny that the racism exists. "That's an area I would not want to comment on," Johnson told me. "It's very sensitive."

At *The Reporters,* I worked on a story about violence at the United States–Mexico border. I later discovered that the field producer had negotiated with two brawny young men to videotape American vigilantes beating up illegal immigrants. I didn't know whether this assignment would incite these strapping gents to rustle up some frightened Mexicans for the money. Hell, I didn't know if these men would fake an attack. I urged my superiors to reconsider the story. Instead, they gave it to another correspondent.

Spend any time with the Australians or British Fleet Streeters, and their attitude about race makes itself apparent—for their distinctive vocabulary is rife with racial slurs. And it was my impression that they never felt that there was anything offensive about this. Once, on a flight to Los Angeles, I asked fellow correspondent Steve Dunleavy (known as the Dog) to help me with the *New York Times* crossword puzzle. With all seriousness, he took the paper and puzzled over the clue: a five-letter word for a person of Asian descent. He returned my newspaper with the answer proudly penciled in: *slope*. (For the record, Dunleavy said the slur is "out of character" for himself and that his recollection of the incident "is diametrically different.")

Geraldo Rivera may be tabloid's exception to the racist rule. His staff is the most integrated shop I've seen. And *A Current Affair* may be cleaning up its discriminatory act. A November 23rd, 1992, report in *Variety* said, "Gone, according to a veteran staffer, is the old unwritten rule of what the show wouldn't cover—gays, urban (read black and Hispanic) America." Right. Gone are most of the managers primarily responsible for *A Current Affair's* questionable editorial decisions. They have moved on to the other tabloid shows.

While I was preparing this story, *Hard Copy's* public-relations person, Linda Lipman, sent me a compilation videotape, which struck me as strange, since I had not yet formally contacted the show. Later, Lipman refused me interviews because, she said, the show had heard I was investigating racism in tabloid. With that, I decided to take a look at this mystery tape, and sure enough, *Hard Copy* had sent me a collection of its stories that featured blacks, as if that were proof it did not practice prejudice. (I contacted all the shows requesting interviews; I was turned down by *Hard Copy* and *Inside Edition*. *A Current Affair's* publicist limited my request for interviews, none of which ever materialized.)

I became aware of tabloid's homophobia at Fox when I scripted a story about a woman and two men involved in a murderous love triangle. One of the men was a minister who had been murdered, the other his convicted killer. Peter Brennan told me that he didn't want to reveal that the men were gay until the very end of the story to avoid turning viewers off. But doing that misled viewers into believing the triangle was purely heterosexual.

These managers, however, loved trying to out celebrities to provoke controversy. On *The Reporters*, Dunleavy asked Mike Tyson if he was gay. And George Michael was popped the question. Steve Schwartz, a supervising producer of *The Reporters* who later worked as day-of-air producer for *A Current Affair* and senior producer for *Now It Can Be Told*, explained why: "Because it's a societal taboo in the vast ocean of the American population, it's considered to be aberrant behavior, and any kind of aberrant behavior, especially by a celebrity, is noteworthy to show like this."

Managers at *The Reporters* routinely referred to the powerful Los Angeles Fox contingent as "gerbils"—the rodents rumored to be gay sex toys. But sadly, the most troubling development in tabloid's gay-bashing mentality has been its response to the AIDS crisis. "I had some bad experiences, stories that they forced me to do—like the Robert Reed story," said a field producer for *Now It Can Be Told*. She explained that a contact in Los Angeles had obtained Reed's death certificate, which stated that he had died of AIDS—tarnishing the pop image of the perfect *Brady Bunch* father. "It was Geraldo ultimately who wanted to do it," she continued. "We broke it, and we got a lot of heat. I really felt like shit about it."

At first, I felt liberated by the creative freedom tabloid offered to experiment with longer stories—up to twenty minutes instead of the average minute-and-a-half package you see on your local news. We could use music, sound effects and reenactments, and the possibilities seemed inspiring. But now you can consider me a purist. My trouble with sound effects came after *Now It Can Be Told* producers had edited in the sound of an explosion to accompany pictures of the space shuttle *Challenger* breaking up in the sky for promotional teasers coming in and out of every commercial break.

The story was about NASA's withholding information from family members and investigators about the fate of the astronauts. The producers insensitively played the tape over and over again, never stopping to consider the feelings of family members and friends. And the *Challenger* didn't explode; rather, it was torn apart by aerodynamic forces, as I explained in my report—but now after having heard the blast, I'm sure most of the people who saw it are certain the *Challenger* blew up.

While I was a correspondent with *The Reporters,* the show reenacted the Tampa, Florida, murder of Karen Gregory, showing a photograph of her dead body in the promotional teasers. Her family and friends claimed that the reporter, in order to gain their cooperation, promised them there would be no such sensational scenes. "They told us this was going to be good, respectable journalism; we all fell for it," said David Mackey, a Tampa therapist and a friend of the victim's. Back then, correspondent Steve Dunlop told me he did make that promise, only to be overruled. At the time, Bob Young, executive producer of *The Reporters,* explained Dunlop's promise was out of order. "That reporter misspoke," said Young. "He didn't have the authority to say that. It never should have been said." Young went on to say that the objectionable material was dropped from the story and that he had "no moral problems" with the final version.

And that is my main complaint about tabloid television. Rarely do its producers have trouble sleeping. I never heard discussions of ethical dilemmas. They do not pause to consider the consequences—for the ratings justify the means. Said *Reporters* producer Schwartz, "You can't go into a village of cannibals and say, 'I'm a vegetarian, come and be like me,' because these people have been eating human flesh all their lives."

So I guess I shouldn't have been so dumbfounded when I witnessed a producer stab around a child's feet on an exercise trampoline with a real knife, reenacting how a teenage boy had terrorized his younger brother. This same producer later asked Mexican children selling chewing gum at the Tijuana border to stand in the way of oncoming traffic because she felt the shot behind me was empty.

While working at *The Reporters,* I was given the assignment of flying to Toronto to purchase an interview with disgraced Olympic sprinter Ben Johnson. I was ethically opposed to paying for interviews, and I didn't care to be responsible for the safekeeping of $20,000 in cash; nonetheless, no other reporter was available to take the assignment, so I did it. Accompanied by a woman friend of Johnson's who had helped arrange the contact, I broke through a crowd of journalists who were camped out at his house (Johnson had gone into hiding after being banished from the Olympics for steroid use). I arrived on his doorstep with a basket of fruit and an envelope of cash. Johnson let us into his home, but he then disappeared into a back bedroom and never came out. He did not do the interview and did not take the money. When I asked to see him, I was chased out of the house by a relative of his who was waving a wooden cooking spoon overhead, shouting, "No interviews!" But buying news is a tabloid tradition. Susan Crimp, former news editor of *Now It Can Be Told* and current *Hard Copy* employee, told me she would see suited men at press conferences in London. "And they weren't journalists at all," she said.

"They were called brokers. I was just twenty-one, and I thought naively they were arranging where they could do the interview, but they actually had very large checks on them, and that's where it all started." But that's kids' stuff compared with the level to which tabloid television has taken checkbook journalism.

Tabloid does not like to admit how often it resorts to buying interviews or cooperation, but all the shows have huge war chests just for that purpose. Why else would many of these people talk to these programs? The charges are often buried in expense reports as "location" or "consulting fees" or "reimbursement for salary lost" during the time spent shooting. According to Murray Weiss and Bill Hoffmann, authors of *Palm Beach Babylon*, *Hard Copy* put together an international media consortium and offered nearly $1 million to Patricia Bowman to sit for an interview during the trial of William Kennedy Smith, who she alleged had raped her. (*Hard Copy* disputes details of this account.) In this instance, money didn't talk; Bowman spoke to ABC for free.

But because it is now common knowledge that tabloid pays small fortunes, people offering to betray friends, neighbors and loved ones are "coming out of the woodwork," said a source at *Hard Copy*. Often these monetary arrangements work against other journalists because they lock in exclusives, making it impossible for other reporters to interview, much less scrutinize, these people. Tabloid TV is pricing the news out of the reach of the general public, and the information is further corrupted as it enters Hollywood's movie-of-the-week mills, where the truth is interpreted by screenwriters.

Take the Amy Fisher saga—the classic tabloid tale spun off into three network movies of the week, which were so successful that even the networks were surprised. The movies were vigorously cross-promoted in local newscasts: *Meet the real Amy Fisher! Meet the actress portraying Amy! Find out how the real people felt about the movies! Find out how the actors felt portraying the real people!*

In addition, tabloid has led the trend featuring celebrity interviews to the exclusion of more serious reporting. Said Pete Simmons, a former *Now It Can Be Told* producer: "When Barbara Walters first started her specials, she was interviewing important people who were movers and shakers. Her ratings sucked. She started doing interviews with celebrities, and her ratings shot up. So guess what she does now? Journalism, true journalism, if it does nothing else, should do one thing—it should bring people the hard facts of life." But tabloid television would point to its very success as proof that a large number of viewers don't want that.

In 1990, when I was interviewed by Geraldo Rivera, he promised me that *Now It Can Be Told* would be an investigative news show. I had my doubts but chose to quell them, foolishly telling myself that journalism's premier performance artist at long last wished to redeem himself. My hopes were raised by his first hires, which included, most notably, investigative reporter Roberta Baskin (now with CBS's *Street Stories*) and Pete Simmons, formerly of ABC News. Geraldo named Simmons the show's senior producer. But late in the game, much to Simmons's surprise, Geraldo also named *A Current Affair's* Wayne Darwen a senior producer, claiming the shotgun managerial team would proffer a much needed "yin and yang" effect—in Geraldo's vocabulary, "the meat," or substance, provided by Simmons and "the heat," or sizzle, provided by Darwen.

My heart sank. I had heard stories about Darwen, but not one to believe everything I hear, I invited him to lunch before we even began to work together. At Manhattan's Water Club, on the East River, the bearded Australian drank and smoked heavily and spoke freely. "There's something about you which reminds me of . . . Marilyn Monroe," he said. "We should use that. . . . I've got an idea. Why don't you take a hidden camera and go to a sex therapist? Tell him you're married—haven't been laid in twenty-five years . . . and we could catch him seducing you. That would be fuckin' brilliant, mate!" With that, Darwen dragged on his cigarette and checked my reaction, which at this point I'm certain was a blank stare. (Darwen didn't recall those details, and he took the discussions at this meeting to be hypothetical.)

By the time Darwen came aboard, I was learning how insensitive Geraldo was to concerns of ethics and sexism. Sue Levit, a field producer for *Now It Can Be Told,* reminded me about a staff meeting in which Geraldo said, "Oh, what was that chick's name?" Levit told me, "You and I locked eyes at the same exact moment." Later in the meeting Geraldo gave a pep talk in which he exclaimed to us, his troops, most of whom were women, "You gotta *feel it in your balls.*" Said one woman who still works in tabloid, "You know, where are we supposed to feel it?"

Now It Can Be Told senior producer Steve Schwartz explained that during ratings periods, "it was just understood that we had to 'tart up' the show." National news editor Maury Terry concurred: "We went through a T&A stage, and that bothers me. I thought it was gratuitous." Marc Goldbaum, a former field producer for *The Reporters* and *Now It Can Be Told,* said it was hard to miss: "If somebody did numbers and figured out how to quantify that, I mean they would be shocking. It's *all* tits and ass."

The field producer who often assembled the raciest pieces for *Now It Can Be Told* is a woman. "There were several stories I didn't put my name on," she told me. "A lot of those *A Current Affair*-type stories: bikini girls selling hot dogs in G-strings by the highway in Florida. That was something I'm not going to put my name on."

But I believe T&A to be only the tip of the iceberg—that there is a deeper misogyny at work here. Because tabloid paints in sweeping strokes, women are depicted only as madonnas or whores. Female sexuality is punished—where male appetites are expected or even celebrated. This is obvious in the way tabloid promotes stories: "Cold! Arrogant! Manipulative! The real Lolita!"—tabloid's description of Amy Fisher, a criminal but also a messed-up teenager.

I mean, who gives a shit about Amy Fisher? Well, the little beady-eyed unwashed television viewers do.—Pete Simmons, senior producer, *Now It Can Be Told*

On September 22nd, 1992, at a Massapequa, New York, health club, the young woman who put a bullet in Mary Jo Buttafuoco's head, Amy Fisher, was laughing and talking with boyfriend Paul Makely about sex in jail and the benefits she hoped to gain from her notoriety. Unbeknown to her, she was being videotaped. Also unbeknown to her, *Hard Copy* paid for the betrayal.

The show aired the tape, which damaged Fisher's credibility as the main witness in the case against Mary Jo's husband, Joseph Buttafuoco, for statutory rape. That night, Fisher reportedly attempted to kill herself with a drug overdose.

"I think what [Rafael Abramovitz] did with Amy is outrageous, just fuckin' outrageous—he totally set her up," said John Parsons, who worked in management at *Hard Copy* before joining *Now It Can Be Told.* It is reliably said that Abramovitz negotiated a deal with Makely that he would secretly videotape Fisher with two hidden cameras (one of them failed) for some $6000 to $10,000. You may remember that this bearded fellow with the monotonous voice was involved in the purchase of another infamous tape for *A Current Affair*—that of the so-called preppie murderer, Robert Chambers, twisting the neck of a doll at a slumber party. Parsons explained why he was so offended: "Rafael and I began in the *The*

Fifty-first State [a PBS program], when we were chasin' the real criminals, and now he's in bedrooms for a buck. Everything's for a buck. I told him he made me feel tawdry, made me want to get out of the business. So now he's not talking to me."

Abramovitz won't talk to me, either. I worked with him at *A Current Affair* and *The Reporters,* but he was unhappy that I was writing this story. When I called him at home, Abramovitz said why: "I don't consider you and me on the same level. . . .Never did."

To be fair, Abramovitz isn't the only one with his channels in the bedrooms of the masses. More and more, it seems, tabloid television is leaping at the chance to use hidden cameras, invading people's privacy, regardless of the consequences. As a former colleague at *Now It Can Be Told* confessed: "When I dialed London and hired a private detective to dress up in Salvation Army gear and go shoot the forgotten cousin of the queen in a mental asylum, I realized I had reached the all-time low in journalism."

So why, you might wonder, did I stay in a profession so low, so lacking in dignity? Well, I'll tell you. The pay and the perks were generous. I went to Vietnam, El Salvador, Brazil, Thailand, Cuba and other places. I was asked to do a lot of things, and I did some of them, like trying to buy Ben Johnson's story. I was upbraided by TV critics for hugging a subject on camera. I did a story on strippers. But gradually I learned how to define and enforce my own boundaries. By the time I reached *Now It Can Be Told,* I routinely refused what I believed to be unethical or distasteful assignments. But by then, it was too late. I'd been slimed. I was caught in the tabloid trap. Network executives advised me to go back to local news. And I did.

So maybe my five years in the big sleaze has made me a bit oversensitive. All around me I see tabloid's corrupting influence— in local news, in political campaigns, in movies of the week, even creeping into the staid network newsmagazine shows, which are resorting more frequently to hidden cameras and other tabloid techniques. Not that hidden cameras are necessarily always bad; at least these shows have been known to weigh the consequences of invading people's privacy.

I wonder if viewers should consider the consequences as well. It's easy to chuckle over the poor soul who got caught by the hidden camera with his pants down. But consider this: Orwell might have gotten it wrong, mate. It could be the journos of tabloid television, rather unexpectedly, who have assumed the role of Big Brother, watching our every move.

IV. THE FUTURE

EDITOR'S INTRODUCTION

The Information Superhighway. Multimedia. High Definition Television. Fiber Optics. 500 channels. Interactivity.

These are the buzzwords of the new technology that looms just ahead. Alliances, such as mergers between phone, cable and computer companies, are being formed to bring a new age of technological interactivity. The ramifications of this interactivity, though, remain uncertain. Proponents claim it will provide a wealth of information and choice enabling the public to become a force to be reckoned with in the global economy of the future. Yet, if these futuristic informational devices are mostly used to call up favorite episodes of *Gilligan's Island,* then how enabling will the information future be? Or will heralded potentials—such as a doctor checking on patients in remote locations or a student consulting material from a distant database—become reality?

Furthermore, many questions remain unanswered about this developing information superhighway. Who will provide the information? Censor it? Regulate it? Police it? Who will keep the conglomerates in check? Will the technological treasure trove be available to everyone, or just those who can afford it? Will new technology metamorphose the vast wasteland of television into a fertile garden or just expand its vastness?

The first two articles, reprinted from *Time,* by Philip Elmer-Dewitt and Richard Zoglin, respectively, deal not only with the interconnected world and the technological advances that will bring the information age into our homes, but also with the possible forms this information will take, and the effects on our current communication systems and society.

The third article, by Arthur Cordell, from *The Futurist,* discusses troubling matters raised by the new media: the integrity of information; the creation of facts without context; and the issues of liability, privacy, access, disclosure, and availability. The fourth piece, Leo Bogart's article reprinted from *The Nation* makes the case for a media policy and why this is so imperative.

The last article, reprinted from the book *Of Media and People* by Everette Dennis, is entitled "Can News Survive in an Age of Information?" Dennis suggests that the news might well not survive the onslaught of the information future unless "the media return to their essential public service function, distinguishing news from information, linking news and opinion but maintaining some orderly separations. . . ."

TAKE A TRIP INTO THE FUTURE ON THE ELECTRONIC SUPERHIGHWAY[1]

Everybody knows what the telephone is for. It rings. You pick it up. A voice travels down a wire and gets routed and switched right to your ear.

Everybody knows what to do with the television. You turn it on, choose a channel and let advertising, news and entertainment flow into your home.

Now imagine a medium that combines the switching and routing capabilities of phones with the video and information offerings of the most advanced cable systems and data banks. Instead of settling for whatever happens to be on at a particular time, you could select any item from an encyclopedic menu of offerings and have it routed directly to your television set or computer screen. A movie? Airline listings? Tomorrow's newspaper or yesterday's episode of *Northern Exposure?* How about a new magazine or book? A stroll through the L.L. Bean catalog? A teleconference with your boss? A video phone call with your lover? Just punch up what you want, and it appears just when you want it.

Welcome to the information highway. It's not here yet, but it's arriving sooner than you might think. Already the major cable operators and telephone companies are competing—and collaborating—to bring this communicopia to your neighborhood, while the Clinton Administration is scrambling to see how the government can join in the fun.

Driving this explosive merger of video, telephones and computers are some rather simple technological advances:

[1]Article by Philip Elmer-Dewitt, from *Time*, 141:50–55 Ap 12 '93. Copyright © 1993 by Time Inc. Reprinted with permission.

• The ability to translate all audio and video communications into digital information.

• New methods of storing this digitized data and compressing them so they can travel through existing phone and cable lines.

• Fiber-optic wiring that provides a virtually limitless transmission pipeline.

• New switching techniques and other breakthroughs that make it possible to bring all this to neighborhoods without necessarily rewiring every home.

Suddenly the brave new world of video phones and smart TVs that futurists have been predicting for decades is not years away but months. The final bottleneck—the "last mile" of wiring that takes information from the digital highway to the home—has been broken, and a blue-chip corporate lineup has launched pilot projects that could be rolled out to most of the country within the next six or seven years. Now the only questions are whether the public wants it and how much it is willing to pay.

We won't have to wait long to find out. By this time next year, vast new video services will be available, at a price, to millions of Americans in all 50 states. Next spring Hughes Communications will introduce DirecTv, a satellite system that delivers 150 channels of television through a $700 rooftop dish the size of a large pizza pie. At about the same time, Tele-Communications, Inc. (TCI), the world's biggest cable-TV operator, will begin marketing a new cable decoder that can deliver as many as 540 channels; next week it will announce plans to provide this service to 100 cities within the first year. Time Warner (the parent company of this magazine) is up and running with a 150-channel system in Queens, New York, and early next year will launch an interactive service that will provide video and information on demand to 4,000 subscribers in Orlando, Florida.

The prospect of multiplying today's TV listings has launched a furious debate over what a fragmented and TV-anesthetized society will do with 100—or 500—offerings. Will scores of narrowcast channels devoted to arcana like needlepointing or fly fishing fracture whatever remains of a mass culture, leaving Americans with little common ground for discourse? Or will the slots be given over to endless rebroadcasts of a handful of hit movies and TV shows—raising the nightmarish specter of the Terminator saying "I'll be back" every few minutes, day in and day out?

But to focus on the number of channels in a TV system is to miss the point of where the revolution is headed. When the infor-

mation highway comes to town, channels and nightly schedules
will begin to fade away and could eventually disappear. In this
postchannel world, more and more of what one wants to see will
be delivered on demand by a local supplier (either a cable system,
a phone company or a joint venture) from giant computer disks
called file servers. These might store hundreds of movies, the
current week's broadcast programming and all manner of video
publications, catalogs, data files and interactive entertainment.
Remote facilities, located in Burbank, California, or Hollywood or
Atlanta or anywhere, will hold additional offerings from HBO
and Showtime, as well as archived hits from the past: *I Love Lucy,
Star Trek, The Brady Bunch.* Click an item on the menu, and it will
appear instantly on the screen.

This is the type of system that most of the top cable companies—including TCI, Time Warner, Viacom and Cablevision—hope
to build within the next year or two, at least on a demonstration
basis. Many of the regional Bell operating companies (the so-
called Baby Bells) are trying to create their own interactive networks, either by themselves or in partnership with cable companies. Bell Atlantic is scheduled to begin offering video on demand
to 300 homes in northern Virginia this summer. U.S. West has
announced plans to deploy enough fiber-optic lines and coaxial
cable (the pencil-thick wire used by cable systems) across 14 states
to deliver "video dial tones" to 13 million households starting
next year.

Once the storage and switching systems are in place, all sorts
of interactive services become possible. The same switches used to
send a TV show to your home can also be used to send a video
from your home to any other—paving the way for video phones
that will be as ubiquitous and easy to use as TV. The same system
will allow anybody with a camcorder to distribute videos to the
world—a development that could open the floodgates to a wave
of new filmmaking talent or a deluge of truly awful home movies.

Today's home shopping networks could blossom into video
malls stocked with the latest from Victoria's Secret, Toys "R" Us
and the Gap. Armchair shoppers could browse with their remote
controls, see video displays of the products that interest them,
and charge these items on their credit cards with the press of a
button—a convenience that will empower some folks and surely
bankrupt others.

In the era of interactive TV, the lines between advertisements,
entertainment and services may grow fuzzy. A slick demonstra-

tion put together by programmers at Microsoft shows how that might be so. The presentation opens with a Seattle Mariners baseball game. By clicking a button on a mouse or remote control, a viewer can bring up a menu of options (displayed as buttons on the screen). Click on one, and the image of the batter at the plate shrinks to make room for the score and the player's stats—RBIs, home runs and batting average—updated with every pitch. Click again and you see the Mariners' home schedule. Click yet again, and a diagram of the King dome pops up, showing available seats and pricing. Click one more time, and you have ordered a pair of field box seats on the first base side (and reduced your credit-card balance by about $25).

This is the vision that has the best minds from Madison Avenue to Silicon Valley scrambling for position at the starting gate. The telephone companies, with their switching networks already in place, want to build the superhighway and control what travels over it. The cable-TV companies, with their coaxial systems think they should own the right-of-way. Computer companies such as IBM, Hewlett-Packard and Sun want to build the huge file servers that will act as video and information libraries. Such software companies as Microsoft and Apple want to build the operating systems that will serve as the data highway's traffic cops, controlling the flow of information to and from each viewer's screen. Meanwhile, *TV Guide* is racing against InSight, TV Answer and Discovery Communications to design electronic navigators that will tell viewers what's on TV and where to find it.

"Make no mistake about it," says Vice President Al Gore, who was talking about information highways long before they were fashionable. "This is by all odds the most important and lucrative marketplace of the 21st century." If Gore is right, the new technology will force the merger of television, telecommunications, computers, consumer electronics, publishing and information services into a single interactive information industry. Apple Computer chairman John Sculley estimates that the revenue generated by this megaindustry could reach $3.5 trillion worldwide by the year 2001. (The entire U.S. gross national product today is about $5.9 trillion.)

During the 1992 presidential campaign, Clinton and Gore made building a "data superhighway" a centerpiece of their program to revitalize the U.S. economy, comparing it with the government's role in creating the interstate highway system in the 1950s. The budget proposal the Administration submitted in February includes nearly $5 billion over the next four years to develop new software and equipment for the information highway.

Private industry, fearful of government involvement and eager to lay claim to pieces of the game, has been moving quickly in the past few months to seize the initiative. GTE, the largest independent telephone company, has already built a system in Cerritos, California, that lets customers pay bills, play games, read children's stories and make airline reservations through the same wire that brings them basic cable television and 30 pay-per-view channels. Three hundred fifty miles north, in Castro Valley, Viacom, the purveyor of MTV and Nickelodeon, is building a similar system to test consumer reaction to the new services.

Some of the projects *seem* more impressive than they are. TCI customers in the suburbs of Denver already have what looks like true video on demand. By pointing a remote control at the TV set, they can select from among 2,000 offerings (from *Hook* to old Marx Brothers movies to last night's MacNeil Lehrer NewsHour) and have their choices appear on screen whenever they want them, any time, day or night. But behind the high-tech service is an almost laughably low-tech delivery system. When a customer presses the Enter button, a bell goes off in a three-story building a few miles away, alerting a TCI attendant that he has five minutes to run to the video library, grab the proper tape and slot it into one of a bank of VCRs.

TCI's Denver setup reveals the weakness behind a lot of the information-superhighway hype: for all their posturing, neither the phone companies nor the cable-TV operators are quite ready to build a fully interactive and automated data highway that stretches from coast to coast. But thanks to a number of technical innovations, they are getting awfully close.

The key to the entire enterprise is fiber. Fiber-optic cable, made up of hair-thin strands of glass so pure you could see through a window of it that was 70 miles thick, is the most perfect transmitter of information ever invented. A single strand of fiber could, in theory, carry the entire nation's radio and telephone traffic and still have room for more. As it is deployed today, fiber uses less than 1% of its theoretical capacity, or bandwidth, as it's called in the trade. Even so, it can carry 250,000 times as much data as a standard copper telephone wire—or, to put it another way, it can transmit the contents of the entire *Encyclopedia Britannica* every second.

In the mid-1980's, AT&T, MCI and Sprint installed fiber-optic cable between major U.S. cities to increase the capacity of their long-distance telephone lines. At about the same time, the Federal Government, spurred by Gore, leased some of these lines to give scientists a high-speed data link to supercomputers funded by the National Science Foundation. These two networks, private and public, carry the bulk of the country's telephone and data traffic. In the superhighway system of the future, they are the interstate turnpikes.

The problem comes when you get off the turnpike onto the roadways owned by local phone companies and cable-TV operators. Some of these are being converted to high-bandwidth fiber optic. But at the end of almost every local system—the "last mile" that goes from the local-service provider to the house—you run into the electronic equivalent of a bumpy country road. In the phone system, the bottleneck is that last bit of copper wiring, which seems far too narrow to admit the profusion of TV signals poised to flow through it. In cable TV, the roadblocks are the long cascades of amplifiers that run from the company's transmission headquarters to the home, boosting the signal every quarter-mile or so. These amplifiers are notoriously unreliable and generate so much electronic noise that two-way traffic in a cable-TV system is all but impossible.

It has long been assumed that nothing was going to change much in telecommunications or television until fiber was brought all the way to the home, a Herculean task that was expected to cost $200 billion to $400 billion and take more than 20 years to complete. The breakthrough that is bringing the info highway home much sooner than expected is the discovery, by both the phone companies and the cable industry, that it is possible to get around the bottlenecks in their respective last miles without replacing the entire system.

For the cable-TV companies, the key insight came in the fall of 1987, when cable engineers demonstrated that coaxial wire could carry information quite effectively over short distances; in fact, for a quarter-mile or so, it has almost as much bandwidth as fiber. They pointed out that by using fiber to bring the signal to within a few blocks of each home and coaxial cable to carry it the rest of the way, the cable companies could get a "twofer": they could throw away those cranky amplifiers (giving them a system that has more capacity and is easier to maintain) and get two-way interactivity almost cost-free.

For the phone companies, the breakthrough came three years

ago when scientists at Bellcore, the research arm of the Baby Bells, found a way to do what everybody had assumed was impossible: squeeze a video signal through a telephone wire. The technology, known as asymmetric digital subscriber line, has some drawbacks. It cannot handle live transmissions, and the picture it produces is not as clear as that provided by a well-tuned cable hookup—never mind the high-definition TV signals expected to come on line before the end of the decade. Bellcore researchers say they have already improved the quality of the picture and that with further compression they may be able to accommodate several channels of live video.

The government is the dark horse in the race to the information highway. It got into the business almost by accident: thanks to Gore's lobbying during the 1980s, it funded the fiber-optic links that form the backbone of Internet, the sprawling computer grid that is for students, scientists and the Pentagon what Prodigy and CompuServe are for ordinary computer users. Today Internet has grown into the world's largest computer bulletin board and data bank, home to 10 million to 15 million networkers who use it for many of the purposes the information highway might serve: sending and receiving mail, sharing gossip and research results, searching for information in hard-to-reach libraries, playing games with opponents in other cities, even exchanging digitized sounds, photographs and movie clips.

During the 1992 campaign, Clinton and Gore repeated the information-highway metaphor so often that many voters—and industry leaders—were left with the impression that the government actually planned to build it, to use taxpayer dollars to construct a data freeway that anybody could ride. But the spending proposals released after the election make it clear that the Administration's goals are more modest. Of the $5 billion requested for the next four years, nearly $3 billion would be spent building supercomputers. Most of the rest would be set aside for developing techniques for transmitting different kinds of data over the networks—such as CAT scans and engineering blueprints—and on pilot projects to give schools, hospitals, libraries and other nonprofit institutions access to Internet.

The government is more likely to play a critical role in cutting through the thicket of state and federal regulations that have grown up over the years to keep the local telephone and cable-TV monopolies out of each other's business. White House officials say they want to give the private sector incentives to invest in the data highways. At the same time, however, they insist on preserving features of the current system that voters value, such as universal access to affordable phone and television service and protection against price gouging.

In a speech in New York City two weeks ago, acting Federal Communications Commission Chairman James Quello cautioned industry executives against making all television pay per view. Free TV, he warned, "is essential to a well-informed citizenry and electorate in a democracy." As if to punctuate his remarks, the FCC last week voted to cut the cost of most cable-TV services 10% and to make it harder for operators to raise rates in the future. The commission also issued a ruling in an ongoing dispute between the TV networks and the Hollywood studios, relaxing restrictions that have prevented the networks from owning shows and sharing in the lucrative rerun market. As new ways of packaging and delivering these shows emerge, skirmishes over copyrights and program ownership are likely to become increasingly bitter and complex.

What shape the highway takes will depend to some extent on who ends up building it. The cable companies tend to think in terms of entertaining mass audiences. Their emphasis is on expanded channels, video on demand and video-shopping networks. They admit the possibility of more special-interest programming—such as MTV, the Discovery Channel and Black Entertainment Television—but only if they can be convinced that the demographics are sufficiently attractive.

The phone companies, with their background in point-to-point switching, tend to focus on connectivity and anything that will rack up message units. They emphasize services that will generate a lot of two-way traffic, such as video phones, video conferencing and long-distance access to libraries.

The computer users, and some enthusiasts within the Clinton Administration, tend to see the information highway as a glorified extension of computer bulletin boards. Vice President Gore talks about making it possible for a schoolchild in Arkansas to have access to a book stored on a computer in the Library of Congress or take a course at a distant college. Mitch Kapor, cofounder of a computer watchdog group called the Electronic Frontier Foundation, wants the superhighway to do for video what computer bulletin boards did for print—make it easy for everyone to publish ideas to an audience eager to respond in kind. He envisions a nation of leisure-time video broadcasters, each posting his creations on a huge nationwide video bulletin board.

The technology makes all these things possible. It's easy to imagine families exchanging video Christmas cards. Or high school students shopping for a college by exploring each campus interactive video. Or elementary schools making videos of the school play available to every parent who missed it.

It's even easier to picture the information highway being exploited to make a lot of money. The powers that be in entertainment and programming have their eyes on the $4 billion spent each year on video games, the $12 billion on video rentals, the $65 billion on residential telephone service, the $70 billion on catalog shopping. They are eager to find out how much customers will shell out to see last night's *Seinfeld* or the latest Spielberg. They are exploring the market for addictive video games and trying to figure out how much they can charge for each minute of play. It won't be long before someone begins using video phones for the multimedia equivalent of "dial-a-porn" telephone-sex lines. All these services can be delivered easily and efficiently by the information highway, and they can be backed up by a threat with real teeth. As TCI chairman John Malone puts it, "If you don't pay your bill, we'll turn off your television."

In the end, how the highway develops and what sort of traffic it bears will depend to a large extent on consumers. As the system unfolds, the companies supplying hardware and programming will be watching to see which services early users favor. If they watch a lot of news, documentaries and special-interest programming, those offerings will expand. If video on demand is a huge money-maker, that is what will grow. If video bulletin boards—or teleconferencing, or interactive Yellow Pages, or electronic town meetings—are hot, those services too will thrive and spread.

We will in effect be voting with our remote controls. If we don't like what we see—or if the tolls are too high—the electronic superhighway could lead to a dead end. Or it could offer us more—much more—of what we already have. Just as likely, it could veer off in surprising directions and take us places we've never imagined.

WHEN THE REVOLUTION COMES, WHAT
WILL HAPPEN TO...[2]

Smellovision replaces television, trumpets a newspaper headline of the future, as spied by Elmer Fudd in a Bugs Bunny cartoon from 1944. Elmer, that old fuddy-duddy, is astonished, but the Merrie Melodies folks may have been onto something. The technological revolution about to sweep over TV will not be merely an incremental change—more channels, more choices, more chances to play *Jeopardy!* along with the TV contestants (using your interactive home remote). Ultimately it could bring about a transformation so radical that the medium may scarcely be recognizable as television.

Bruce Springsteen's famous lament *57 Channels (and Nothin' On)* now seems almost quaint. Very soon, the 57 will multiply to 500, or somewhere in the neighborhood. And even that will be only a way station. The final destination is a post-channel universe of essentially unlimited choice: virtually everything produced for the medium, past or present, plus a wealth of other information and entertainment options, stored in computer banks and available instantly at the touch of a button.

A dazzling scenario, to be sure. Maybe a little scary. And definitely fraught with uncertainties. No one involved in the TV industry has a precise idea of what the new world will look like, or how the audience will react to it. When TV offers custom selections to suit every narrow interest, will mass-audience programming disappear? Or will the interactive offerings appeal mainly to an audience of techno-freaks, while the rest of us, at least for the foreseeable future, stick with our favorite channels? Will the traditional networks survive? What about commercials, local affiliates, video stores? Will we wind up watching more TV or less? Or all go quietly mad?

Let's take it one step at a time.

First will come the channel bonanza: a simple expansion of today's cable world in which more and more stations and networks will become available on your box. Yet even 500 points of

[2]Article by Richard Zoglin, from *Time*, 141:56–58 Ap 12 '93. Copyright © 1993 by Time Inc. Reprinted with permission.

light will not necessarily mean a sudden bounty of new home entertainment. "There isn't an inexhaustible supply of talent out there waiting to fill 500 channels," warns Howard Stringer, CBS Broadcast Group president. "The first thing that comes to mind is what Alvin Toffler called the Law of Raspberry Jam: the wider any culture is spread, the thinner it gets."

Many of the new channels will be devoted to information services (your morning newspaper on TV) and home shopping stations (specific ones for designer clothes, health products, sporting goods and so forth). Pay-per-view movie channels will proliferate, and premium services will grab up extra channels to "multiplex" their programming—offering movies on several channels at staggered times to increase the viewer's options. (HBO, Showtime and the Disney Channel have already begun offering such a service in some cable systems.)

Existing cable channels will subdivide or create spin-offs: a battery of sports channels from ESPN, say, or targeted versions of MTV. "My guess is we'll probably do three to five feeds of MTV, much like radio," says Frank Biondi Jr., president of Viacom, which owns the music-video channel and several other cable networks. "We'll do hard rock, rhythm and blues, urban contemporary—right down the line."

But there will also be a fresh batch of original channels aimed at special tastes. Already being planned, or at least promised, are channels devoted to game shows, talk shows, crime shows and soap operas. Also the Golf Channel, the Military Channel, the Television Food Network, Ovation (for fine-arts programming) and the Wellness Channel (for recovering addicts). A major stumbling block to such niche services in the past was the limited channel capacity of most cable systems. Soon these fledgling networks will have all the room they want.

The question is whether they will have all the money they need to survive. Some special-interest offerings may be able to attract related advertising or even blur the distinction between advertising and programming. Others will have a tough time gaining enough advertising revenue to support themselves in the increasingly fragmented TV marketplace. Charging subscribers—either directly as a "pay" service or indirectly through the cable operator—is one alternative, but that might be difficult at a time when both viewers and federal regulators are unhappy about soaring cable bills.

One prospect: cable systems could switch to an à la carte system of billing, in which subscribers build customized cable menus channel by channel, rather than paying a lump sum for an entire "tier." Such a system would probably be a boon for narrow-gauge networks (golf enthusiasts would presumably be willing to fork over a buck or two a month for a channel aimed at them). But many general-interest services, from the Weather Channel to USA Network, would surely see their circulation—and thus their ad revenue—drop if viewers were forced to choose and pay for them individually.

At this stage, the traditional broadcast networks would probably be hurt, but not necessarily crippled. Though their audience will be nibbled at further by a fresh attack of narrowcasting barracudas, they would retain their special role as providers of national news, big sports events and broad-based entertainment fare. "I think it is conceivable that a 200- or 300-channel environment might work in a perverse way to the networks' advantage," says Herb Granath, president of Capital Cities/ABC Video Enterprises, "in that it will be more and more difficult for people to identify what they're watching. You keep flipping with the remote from channel to channel, and after a while it all becomes a blur." Overwhelmed viewers may continue to seek refuge in the networks' old and familiar nightly lineup.

All bets are off, however, when the TV revolution reaches its next stage. As interactive technology fully kicks in, the very concept of channels will start to disintegrate. Virtually everything will be instantly accessible to home viewers hooked into the new "full-service" (TV, computer and telephone) network. Not 500 channels, or even 5,000, but just one: your own channel that can call up anything.

The first concept that seems outdated in this post-channel world is the traditional network schedule. No need to be in front of the set at 6:30 p.m. for *World News Tonight* or at 9 o'clock on Mondays for *Murphy Brown*. Simply call up the show when you want it. The consumer, rather than the network, takes control of the schedule, and TV viewing becomes akin to browsing through a huge library and making a selection.

In a post-channel world, the traditional broadcast networks (and cable networks too) could, if they're not careful, start to look like superfluous middlemen. ABC, CBS, NBC and Fox might want to indicate combination of functions simply turn into producer distributors with a familiar brand name. (Partly in anticipation of that day, the networks are fighting to be freed from government regulations that have prevented them from owning more than a small portion of the programs they air. They won a victory last week when the Federal Communications Commission significantly relaxed those restrictions.) W. Russell Neuman, author of *The Future of the Mass Audience*, predicts: "You'll have a television network that, instead of giving you *The Cosby Show* at 8 o'clock on a particular evening, gives you the peacock instead. Then the peacock turns to you and says, 'What do you want to watch?' And you say, 'Something funny.' The peacock says, 'Something new, or do you want something from our classic archives?' Basically, you'd have a conversation."

Other familiar components of the TV landscape may disappear as well. Local affiliate stations, which have the exclusive right to pick up network shows and distribute them to viewers in their localities, would seem to have no function—except as suppliers of local news and other community-based programming. The video store may be another dodo bird. When any Hollywood release can be called up instantly on the home screen, a cumbersome system in which people have to trek to the corner video store to rent a tape, then return it a day later, seems like a low-tech anachronism. Film studios might even release a major movie as a high-priced pay-per-view offering at the same time it opens in theaters. (Hollywood might then be less likely to target its blockbusters to the tastes of teenage boys, who are currently the chief ticket buyers.)

The same interactive technology that would enable programming to be customized for individual homes could be put to use by advertisers. "If you can deliver a single program to one home, you can also make sure a certain commercial goes into that particular home," says Larry Gerbrandt, a senior vice president of Paul Kagan Associates, a media-research firm. "Another way you can do it is to make sure that no matter what they're watching in the home, your commercial goes into that show." From spending and demographic information, advertisers could determine that one home should see an ad for a Buick while another is getting the soft sell for a Jeep.

Interactive technology could, moreover, give rise to a hybrid of advertising and infomercials. Viewers could order up lengthier, information-packed ads for such products as insurance or automobiles the same way they order up programming. "When you get ready to buy a car," predicts Geoff Holmes, Time Warner's senior vice president for technology, "you could literally call up the showroom of each of the major car dealers and do a sort of 15-minute browse." Video classifieds could be next: simply scroll through the house listings and call up the ones that interest you for a full video presentation.

The options for new forms of advertising are likely to be attractive enough to ensure that a lot of programming will remain ad supported. The question is whether newly empowered viewers will continue to sit still for the traditional 30-second commercial interrupting a show. If not, more programming of the future may be financed instead by viewer fees. The monthly TV bill could ultimately look something like today's phone bill, with message units reflecting the household's viewing.

Some futurists look forward to this brave new world, forecasting a burst of creative programming for niche audiences and a withering of mass-audience pap. George Gilder, in his book *Life After Television*, raves that the new technology will "liberate our imaginations from programs regulated by bureaucrats, chosen by a small elite of broadcasting professionals and governed by the need to target the lowest common denominators of public interests." Other seers are as depressed as Gilder is sunny. "I worry seriously about a world in which it's too easy to simply flip around the dial and think you are gaining access to the world of knowledge and meaning," says Todd Gitlin, a sociology professor at the University of California, Berkeley. "There's a kind of mental and emotional laziness that gets built up."

At this point we should all take a deep breath. The post-channel world may mean the transformation of TV programming, the demise of the mass audience, the death of the networks—or it may not. While technology pushes in one direction, a host of societal forces are pulling in the other. No telling where the point of equilibrium will be.

One powerful countervailing force is corporate America. No matter how many narrowcasting options are made possible by the new technology, advertisers will still crave network television's unique ability to reach a critical mass of consumers at one swoop. For that reason, if no other, there will be pressure to retain some semblance of a network schedule and programming that appeals to a large cross-section of viewers. One possible scenario: a network show such as *60 Minutes* or *Roseanne* will still "debut" each week at a set time. Many viewers will plant themselves in front of the set to watch at that time; others will call up the show on their screens later. Compare it with the typical movie opening today: the biggest crowds rush to see the film on the first weekend, while others catch up with it in due course. In fact, this could end up increasing the potential mass audience for a name-brand show, since more people would be able to watch an episode of *Roseanne* whenever they wanted, without having to figure out how to program the VCR.

Other economic and psychological pressures will work in favor of the status quo. For one thing, not every home will be connected to the information superhighway (even now, 39% of American homes are still not hooked up to cable), which means some form of traditional broadcasting will stick around for at least a decade or two. In addition, pressure from Congress and the FCC is likely to protect the role of free broadcasting and local affiliates.

Video on demand, moreover, will not obviate the communal pleasures of watching a popular show at the same time as everyone else in the country. "The shared experience is the value of television, and of network television in particular," asserts CBS president Stringer. "It's part of the nature of the beast, and that is worth conserving." And no matter how dazzling the home screen becomes, people will still want to get out of the house—to a movie, to the mall and maybe even to the corner video store.

The irony is that the explosion of choices is more likely to reduce, rather than increase, the amount of TV people watch. It will wreak havoc on the TV habit. Turning on the set each evening to see what's on becomes meaningless when "what's on" is essentially "anything you want." Will old movies, sitcoms and talk shows still be viewed as diligently when they are taken off the daily schedule and put in a computer file for instant access? Doubtful. People watch reruns of old network sitcoms mainly because cable channels dust them off and give them a daily time slot. The day *The Patty Duke Show* is put in a computer bank is the day *The Patty Duke Show* will start to vanish from human memory.

Consumers demand packaging: someone to select, present, organize, promote. The networks, or some 21st century transmogrification of them, will probably stick around to do that job. But they may be shrunken entities, offering only a few shows a week while concentrating on news, sports and such big events as the Academy Awards. What is likely to disappear are the mediocre fillers, the disposable sitcoms and the cop shows that exist primarily because there's a hole in the schedule on Friday night at 8:30.

That may be good news for the future video landscape. A TV

world where viewers get what they want, where the good drives out the bad and the mediocre falls away? Now, there's a revolution worth storming the barricades for.

PREPARING FOR THE CHALLENGES OF THE NEW MEDIA[3]

The way we receive and use information will change vastly during the 1990s. We'll have seemingly limitless amounts of facts at our fingertips. But seemingly limitless amounts of information about ourselves may also become part of the public knowledge base available through the "new media."

The new media are the result of technologies combining computers, laser discs, and telecommunications. Information can be stored, manipulated, and processed, then delivered visually to the user upon demand. The new media are fast, accurate, information rich, and responsive. They are based on inquiry and response. Interactivity is prime. So different and so much swifter are they than the old media that they are generically referred to as "hypermedia."

The new media are new in at least two important respects: In the first place, they are interactive. The old media that dominate our lives today are broadcast in one fixed form that is received by a large mass of people. This one-way communication holds true for television, newspapers, magazines, etc. In the second place, the new media combine several existing media, which permit users to select what they want and create a personalized message or program. Existing media—telephone, computers, CD-ROM, video, still photos, audio, etc.—can now be merged, allowing users to choose the material they wish to view in the form in which they wish to receive it.

The new media are interactive. This stands in contrast to all previous media, where the product was a single package whose content and format was controlled by editors. Now, the new media permit the user rather than the publisher to select the style, organization, order, and content of the items.

[3]Article by Arthur J. Cordell, from *The Futurist* 25:20–24 Mr/Ap '91. Copyright © 1991 by the World Future Society. Reprinted with permission.

Because they blend different sources and because they are interactive, the new media raise a large number of policy issues. In addition to such obvious areas as technical standards and protocols to ensure compatibility, there are social, ethical, and economic implications that must be carefully considered by policy makers.

Integrity of Information

Where does information come from? Currently, media as diverse as CNN (Cable News Network), *Maclean's* and other newsmagazines, and the *Encyclopaedia Britannica* deliver news, numbers, information, and photos. We presume that the numbers and other information can be trusted since the television network, magazine, or encyclopedia has used a reliable external source such as Statistics Canada, a journal article, an "expert," or another source as an authority.

The new media will merge many strands of information and deliver it to the user. This merger raises important questions, such as where the information will come from, how it will be collected, who will package it, and whether we can trust the integrity of the information. Will an existing entity such as Time Warner or Associated Press become the delivery agency? One that we can trust? Or will new middle brokers emerge to package and repackage information? If so, they will need to earn our trust if they are not associated with existing brand names.

The electronic publishers of the new media can also select their readers and can differentiate their products across classes of readers. To a certain extent, the old media can already select their audience. *Newsweek* and *Time* magazines, for example, publish domestic and international versions as well as regional versions within both their domestic and international products. Newspapers now include supplements aimed at suburban readers. New media based on electronic publishing will enable finer distinctions to be made among the universe of possible users.

The emergence of the new media raises the question of liability. Locating the "source" of libelous or inaccurate information becomes increasingly difficult on electronic networks. In the "old" media, distinctions between primary publishers, secondary publishers, and republishers were clear, and attributing inaccurate, false, or defamatory information to a specific source was relatively easy. This issue will become more complicated in a new media environment.

One technique of the new media that warrants discussion is hypermedia. Hypermedia technologies, such as Apple Computer's HyperCard™, allow users to develop a rapid and accurate profile of persons, places, and things. It is used by researchers and security analysts, for instance, and increasingly by broadcasters reporting on sporting events or elections.

For in-house and nonpublic uses, hypermedia technology may not pose concerns about the source or integrity of information. If hypermedia are used by a television network broadcasting the Olympic Games or a national election, the network would be seen as a guarantor of the integrity of the data.

A possible policy issue arises when we consider the enormous expense and effort involved in creating a hypermedia program or "stack" of, say, the Olympics. When a stack is completed by one network, will others create their own? Can they afford it? A stack on a particular subject could give that network a unique or even unfair advantage; the lack of a hypermedia stack might bar some information media from the marketplace.

Facts Without Context

Hypermedia, as used in the upcoming Olympics, will allow each on-air commentator to become an instant "expert." In effect, a well-constructed hypermedia stack can mimic a human expert. While we value expertise, excessive use of this technology may trivialize the notion of "the expert" by permitting anyone with access to the technology to barrage us with facts.

Recently, while I was channel hopping on my television set, I learned that 2,000 thunderstorms are occurring on our planet at any given time. I have used this number in conversation, as I am using it now. Where exactly did I learn this? How do I know that it is true? Does it matter?

We are inundated with facts, and they are usually fed to us out of context. The barrage of facts becomes a parody of learning and of education itself. Ted Koppel, the respected anchor of ABC's *Nightline,* has noted that "on television, in place of truth we have discovered 'facts.' For moral absolutes, we have substituted moral ambiguity. We now communicate with everyone and say absolutely nothing. We have reconstructed the Tower of Babel and it is a television antenna."

Koppel's concern is that 60% or more of the American public is getting most or all of its news from television. Of this group, how many will be able or willing to interface with the interactive media? Will the public be able or willing to pose adequate questions? It is likely that they will be deluged with still more facts, and most will be presented without any context.

Koppel notes, "There is no culture in the world that is so obsessed as ours with immediacy. In our journalism, the trivial displace the momentous because we tend to measure the importance of events by how recently they happened. We have become so obsessed with facts that we have lost all touch with truth."

The creation of a growing body of facts without context may be one of the less-attractive aspects of high-tech society. If data or facts without context are taken to be either information or knowledge, then we can take this as a symptom that we have failed to create adequate safeguards to protect the integrity of information.

Privacy in the New-Media Era

When a medium is broadcast in nature (i.e., one to many), you receive an entire package of material (a newspaper, a magazine, television programs, and—of course—advertising), but you are the only one who knows whether you are consuming one item, some, none, or all.

The advent of interactive media changes this. You set the pattern of use: Each item you select can be assumed to be of interest to you. This is especially true in a user-pay system. With the shift in locus of control comes a new policy issue. What you access can be identified very easily. Now imagine someone creating an "interest profile" of people who use interactive media—a profile that can be accessed by anyone. What safeguards can we—or should we—put in place to protect individual privacy?

We currently leave an electronic trail with our credit cards. Telemarketing firms interrupt us with phone calls and even messages on our computers; junk mail pours into our homes and offices, as mailing lists are rented or traded among those who wish to sell us new commodities. It is clear that once our information tastes are clearly identified, the marketing function will be set in motion to sell us more of what we are known to consume. For some, this is a good thing since it saves them the job of "shopping" for the additional informational commodity. For others, the very existence of solicitations on their computer screen or by phone or by mail will be seen at best as an annoyance and at worst as an invasion of privacy.

It takes little imagination to see that hypermedia technology will make amassing personal files simpler and cheaper. It is a user-friendly technology. It is likely to be used by marketing, commercial, and credit interests in the private sector and by a host of agencies in the public sector.

Currently, there are federal laws that protect individuals from having all data about them in federal-government files linked together to form a profile. But the existing legislation may not be adequate to protect against hypermedia matches by zealous federal officials. While courts might interpret hypermedia technology as computer matching when used to link records, they could just as easily see it as something else and therefore not in violation of the existing privacy laws.

If computer matching can catch tax cheats, welfare cheats, and even those who are a threat to national security, then why should we be concerned? Because there is a fundamental conflict between the government's right to know certain things and the individual's right to privacy. Computer matching, now made easier by hypermedia technology, violates a basic privacy-protection principle, which is that the personal information supplied for one purpose ought not to be used by the data holder for another purpose.

Since computer matching often involves searching through many computer records, it is in many ways like going into a neighborhood and conducting a general search of all the houses to see if anyone is concealing stolen or illegal goods. In this way, computer matching can be seen as a type of search and seizure. Unreasonable search and seizure is against the law. A law-enforcement official may search a home only after the appropriate search warrant has been obtained.

The Question of Access

A hallmark of an information economy is that information can have value, depending on who accesses it, when access takes place, and the form in which the information is accessed.

Access to the new media will not be without cost to consumers. If users need a considerable amount of equipment, such as a computer, modem, or CD-ROM, a class of people who are already information poor could conceivably be further disenfranchised because they cannot afford the equipment or are unable or unwilling to acquire the equipment.

Consider the public library. Most of us take the public library for granted. Public libraries were created in a time when goods were costly and information was treated as a free good to be distributed to the people by governments. If the public library were created today, when we know that information has value both in collection and application, it might not be constructed in such a way that access was free and unlimited. New media technologies also may begin to make the public library obsolete as an information repository. This is likely to happen simply because the library cannot afford to provide new media services and because the new media are, in most instances, time sensitive and can be updated quickly.

Another issue is access to the new media by sellers of exotic, controversial, or radical content. Today, we can obtain virtually any publication by going to a well-stocked newsstand. With the new media, offbeat information providers may not be ensured access to potential consumers.

There could come a time when some information is so difficult to obtain on interactive systems that "truth" will be defined as that which is easily available, since selections are costly and must be made quickly. We may tend to assume that information which is not easily available does not need to be known. Since sources other than those available through the new media may be too costly or difficult to access, we may witness a narrowing of our field of inquiry rather than the broadening promised by information technologies.

And what about national content? For example, if an international encyclopedia appears in electronic form and is updated every month, every week, or every day (and allows inquiries in "real time"), would individual nations be able to offer an equally valuable product? Governments might increasingly seek ways to ensure that their nations' ideas do not get lost in an age of global communications.

What about information that is "free" but is delivered by a corporation that combines the information with a commercial message or presents it as a "public service"? What would be your reaction if automobile facts and road-test results were delivered "free" by General Motors? It could hardly be delivered in an unbiased way. Some worry that we will see corporate control over the content of new media develop as it has over the current media, with advertisers covertly or overtly controlling content and rights of refusal. The high capital costs of the new media might forever relegate consumer groups that run on a small budget to the "old media"— i.e., print and paper.

Policy Issues Must Be Addressed

The advent of the new media implies that new forms of publishing and broadcasting will grow up alongside the "mass" communications that we are familiar with today. Individuals will select the information, its format, and manner of presentation. Consumers might do all this processing themselves at intelligent terminals in their home or business. Or the processing may be done further "up the line" by the local telephone or cable company.

Integrity of information, access by providers and consumers, and protection of privacy are just some of the policy areas that must be addressed now so that the new media can evolve in an orderly way—a way in which choices and tradeoffs are made in an open environment, where the greatest good for the greatest number is an ever-present part of the policy gestalt, and where solutions are sought that are compatible with the goals, aspirations, and values of the majority of people.

Choices and trade-offs are being made. New developments and products are announced daily. We must sensitize producers, users, consumers, and governments to the changes inherent in these developments. At the same time, we also must ensure that those who are left behind are also given a chance to catch up.

SHAPING A NEW MEDIA POLICY[4]

Any day now, the White House is expected to announce two appointees to the five-member Federal Communications Commission, one of them its new chair. The Senate hearings on these nominations offer an important opportunity to raise fundamental questions about where the country's mass communications system is headed in an era of rapid and dazzling technological change—change that up to now has taken place in an impenetra-

[4]Article by Leo Bogart, from *The Nation* 257:57–60 Jl 12 '93. Copyright © 1993 by the Nation Company, Inc. Reprinted with permission.

ble maze of rules and regulations. Consider only a handful of recent developments that have added to the mounting confusion:

• The F.C.C. announced a fifteen-year plan to phase in high definition television (HDTV). Shortly afterward, under pressure from the commission, three competing consortiums of companies agreed on a unified approach to producing a high-fidelity system based on digital technology. HDTV will provide an interactive capacity compatible with computer applications, thus making television an instrument of personal as well as mass communication. But HDTV will also make all 193 million existing TV receivers in the country obsolete. As when rival systems of color television vied for F.C.C. approval in the 1950s, policy-makers now face the question of how to introduce advanced technology without depriving the public, locked into an existing system, of its stake in the equipment it already owns.

• Congress passed a new Cable Regulation Act that altered the balance of power between cable system operators and the television networks, allowing stations to demand fees for the right to retransmit programs. The major cable systems are adamantly refusing to pay—at least until a deal is cut. Consumers would likely have to pay a higher proportion of programming costs. Indeed, with the growth of cable and VCR use, the public is increasingly carrying more of the cost of media and advertisers less.

• Xerox announced the development of a television display panel no thicker than a pad of paper. Like similar Japanese products using liquid crystal technology, the device, which accommodates both pictures and text, could be the key to developing a constantly updated paperless newspaper customized to the interests of the individual reader.

• One of the last big independently owned newspapers, *The Boston Globe,* was recently acquired by the New York Times Company. Second newspapers have closed in San Antonio and Pittsburgh—the latter a city in which, under the Newspaper Preservation Act of 1970, antitrust rules had been set aside to permit the now-failed daily to survive by joining with its healthier competitor in a joint-publishing arrangement. Three-fifths of the American population now have only a single monopoly daily that reports local news.

• The *New York Post* was rescued from extinction by Rupert Murdoch's News Corporation, under a temporary waiver (now being contested) of F.C.C. rules that forbid common ownership of newspapers and broadcast properties in the same market. Under the same provision, Murdoch, who owns WNYW-TV in New York City, was forced to give up the *Post* in 1988, in part because of opposition from Senator Edward Kennedy, a target of Murdoch's *Boston Herald*. Few episodes so aptly illustrate the combination of commercial and political pressures that come into play when the F.C.C. or any other government body seeks to apply its regulations.

• Congress may soon authorize the first auction of a segment of the broadcast frequency spectrum. Although the auction is to be limited to personal communication services using advanced technology, it marks the first time that communications franchises have not simply been given away by the government as "licenses to coin money."

• The U.S. Court of Appeals for the District of Columbia Circuit temporarily stopped the F.C.C. from allowing cable operators to enforce rules restricting indecency in public access cable programming, thus highlighting the fact that constraints on content differ between cable and over-the-air broadcasting.

• The Newspaper Association of America and the seven so-called Baby Bells, the regional telephone companies that rose out of the breakup of the AT&T monopoly in 1984, are competing for Congress's favor. The newspapers support legislation that would amend a 1991 court ruling (just re-affirmed) that allows the phone companies to offer new telephone-accessible information services, including news items and "electronic yellow pages." The publishers accuse the phone companies of using their monopoly power as local public utilities to subsidize the price of information services, and thus to undercut classified advertising, on which newspapers increasingly depend. The phone companies retort that newspapers, with their local monopolies, fear competition. Both are right. Meanwhile, some papers are making pacts with the Devil. Times Mirror's *Newsday* has just launched a joint venture with NYNEX, the Baby Bell in the Northeast, with the phone company as carrier and the daily providing content.

• Although the telephone companies have been kept out of the broadcast television business, U.S. West, the Denver-based Bell operation with a local telephone monopoly in fourteen Western states, entered into an agreement to purchase a 25.5 percent stake in Time Warner Entertainment for $2.5 billion. Two-fifths of the money is to be invested in upgrading Time Warner's cable systems to carry electronic information and entertainment services.

• The F.C.C. set aside its financial interest and syndication rule, which had restricted the television networks' ownership and sale of rerun rights. Syndicated programming fills a growing amount of non-network broadcast and cable network time, and reruns are a $5 billion business. The battle between two politically powerful sets of lobbyists—those with the networks and those with the Motion Picture Association of America—demonstrates the highly charged politics that enter into media policy formulation when enormous sums of money are involved. The studios are contesting the ruling through litigation, and Attorney General Janet Reno has announced that the Justice Department is examining the F.C.C.'s ruling.

The foregoing examples only hint at the crazy quilt of regulations that constitute our ad hoc national media policy, one that even its most dedicated interpreters find hard to make sense of, much less apply in any rational way. Not the least of the difficulties is that the executive branch, the courts, the F.C.C. and Congress constantly deal separately with aspects of the same issues, and often in contradictory ways. In the past, for example, the Sherman Antitrust Act has been invoked by the courts, and by the F.C.C., to keep media companies from "cross-owning" newspapers and broadcasting stations in the same market and to keep the telephone companies out of cable TV in their phone-service areas. But these principles are not applied uniformly. Although giant organizations can become powerful players in some arenas, they are arbitrarily restricted from entering others. Broadcast networks can and do own cable networks, which provide content. But until last year, they had not been allowed to own cable systems—the delivery mechanisms—and the new rules set severe limits on their ventures in that field. Foreign companies can't buy control of a U.S. radio station, though the Canadian conglomerate Thomson Newspapers owns more dailies in the United States than any other chain. And large chunks of our magazine, book and recording industries, as well as television and film production studios and cable systems, are now also foreign owned. Any number of newspapers can belong to a single owner, but ownership of radio and television stations is restricted. If the cross-ownership rule is now waived (as it should be) to allow Murdoch to save the *Post* from certain death, why shouldn't any owner of a hugely profitable television station be allowed to start up a new newspaper in the typical town that now has only one?

Along with such inconsistencies there is the matter of enforcement, or lack thereof. The 1934 Federal Communications Act required broadcast stations to operate in "the public interest, convenience and necessity." In applying for renewal of their franchises every three years, they were asked to report on the extent of their news and public affairs programming, past and intended. The act made it explicit that the F.C.C. should not engage in censorship. In practice, the commission was reluctant to police closely the extent to which stations complied with the public service provisions of the act or to evaluate the merits of the programming that owners reported under the category of public affairs. (One station included *Amos 'n' Andy* under this heading.) In almost sixty years, no station's license has been revoked because of low programming quality, and for that matter, licenses have almost always been renewed. When the Reagan Administration began its deregulation march in the mid-1980s, the F.C.C.'s public interest requirement was abandoned altogether, and the "good character" required of prospective licensees was limited to prohibition of actual felonies or broadcast-related misconduct.

The Children's Television Act of 1990 limits the number of commercials in programs directed at children and requires franchise holders to serve "the educational and informational needs of children through the licensee's overall programming, including programming specifically designed to serve such needs"— language sufficiently vague to be effectively ignored. Under the law, broadcasters are required to show "educational and informational" programs. But stations quickly redefined the purpose of existing children's shows— such as *The Jetsons, G.I. Joe* and *Leave It to Beaver*—to fit under this rubric. One station claimed that when the hero of *Yo Yogi!* captured "a bank-robbing cockroach," this showed the virtue of "using his head rather than his muscles." The F.C.C. recently announced such reasoning would no longer be acceptable, prompting broadcasters to complain that their audiences would flee to the unregulated drivel on cable channels.

Clearly, we need some kind of comprehensive national media policy if the present knot of laws, competing interests and technological advances is to be untangled and the much heralded communications highway of fiber optics is to bring us a rich variety of information and entertainment. In a society that cherishes free expression, such a proposal risks conjuring up images of thought control; but other democratic nations pursue media policies in a deliberate fashion without falling prey to Big Brother. Sweden, for example, provides newsprint subsidies that permit the survival of a political minority press. Germany places strict limits on the amount of advertising broadcasters may inflict on viewers.

Whatever the precedents abroad, any overarching media policy is bound to be controversial. Should great multimedia conglomerates like Time Warner be broken up or limited in size? The argument in favor of such a policy is not simply the standard one against monopolistic tendencies in any industry; it holds that the realm of ideas, values and tastes is qualitatively different from the manufacture of biscuits or electric turbines. The opposing argument advances the familiar complaint against government interference with business but also the notion that the intrusion of the state into the exercise of market forces inevitably leads to the control of ideas. At the very least, the media cross-ownership rule should be recast so that it works to discourage monopoly rather than bring it about, as is now the case.

Unless one falls back on outmoded ideological clichés, there is no easy alternative to the present order of things. Implicit in the policy that now exists are some useful principles that:

• encourage a variety of channels for expression and discourage concentration of control;
• insure that the necessity of awarding franchises to use scarce public goods (like the frequency spectrum) does not result in financial exploitation of the public;
• facilitate an extensive and fair exchange of ideas, and that protect society, and especially children, from abuse;
• subsidize forms of expression that enrich the national culture and intellectual resources, but that are not necessarily viable in the commercial marketplace.

In pursuing such goals, any national media policy should reaffirm the doctrine of public responsibility as the price for private use of any public property like the airwaves, and should also establish criteria of acceptable performance. The requirement of the 1934 communications act that broadcast stations operate in the public interest should be revived and extended to cable system operators and program providers. If broadcasters were once again made to acknowledge that they have a social duty, the subject might at least move higher up on their own agendas.

Broadcasters should pay for their franchises. Since the early days of radio, it has been periodically proposed that broadcast channels should be auctioned off to the highest bidder, with the proceeds going into the public treasury and some substantial percentage of the money allotted to strengthen public broadcasting. This reasonable idea has rarely been seriously discussed either in Congress or in the press. Affirming the principle that public goods should be paid for need not mean putting the present broadcasting system up for grabs, which would create chaos and be unacceptable to the public. However, in a time of transition like the present, it is important to have this principle in place.

Communications channels should be recognized as public utilities, and their ownership and control should be separated from control of programming. By strict logic, this rule would force newspaper owners to divest themselves of their printing plants and radio stations of their transmitting towers—not likely or politically feasible. However, the principle of separation can and should apply to all wire-transmitted programming and information—by cable, telephone or even over the electric power grid—and it should apply to microwave direct broadcasting by satellite as well. Why is such separation desirable? Because it would keep the powerful monopoly utility, the carrier, from also determining what ideas and images are fed into the cultural mainstream.

A modest fund should be created to stimulate research into aspects of mass communications technology that are not responsive to market forces. An example might be the development of new low-budget ways to distribute newspapers to match the much lower cost of producing them in the computer era. This would make it easier for new papers to start up in a time of constricted advertising revenues and would restore competitive energy to local journalism. Will the development of such technology emerge from the newspaper industry itself? Not likely from a business that has been investing 0.2 percent of its revenues in research and development and that lives comfortably with its local monopolies.

Funding for public broadcasting should be increased, and its governance system safeguarded to protect it from political interference. The nation's total investment in public broadcasting represents only 2 percent of the annual spending on television and cable. Britain spends thirty-six times as much per capita on public broadcasting; Japan seventeen times as much.

Most important, media policy should be seen as social policy, not just as the legal administration of technical complexities. Broadcasting frequencies must be allocated to avoid chaos on the airwaves, but the F.C.C.'s rulings have consequences for every aspect of national life. Educational policy is made by educators, not left to lawyers. Why should the F.C.C. be a lawyers' preserve? The public accepts enormous expenditures on schools as a necessary social obligation. Television is no less a formative influence than the classroom and deserves to be taken far more seriously as an educational resource. (In many school districts, it is just a commercial opportunity for Channel One, a venture of Time Warner affiliate Whittle Communications.)

Education is a matter of public concern, at both the community and national levels; but mass media policy has not been a matter of widespread interest. As it deals with ever more complex technical matters, it becomes increasingly inaccessible to general debate. Vigorous discussion, and not just by experts, is precisely what media policy needs as we enter an era of powerful new communications technology.

CAN NEWS SURVIVE IN AN AGE OF INFORMATION?[5]

In January 1990, an editorial in the *New York Times* tried to divine the meaning of the 1980s as a prelude to the 1990s. It grappled with such monikers as the "Age of Revolution," referring to Mikhail Gorbachev, Eastern Europe and China; the "Age of Greed," describing the juxtaposition of great fortunes and homeless people; but finally settled on the "Age of Speed" because of the rapid acceleration of information in the last decade as phones and faxes, microchips and personal computers, satellites and cable services, changed the world. It was also an "Age of Convergence," as many forms of communication came together in a single electronically based, computer-driven system. This has most often been called the "Age of Information," a time when a

[5]Chapter 2 from *Of Media and People* ('92) by Everette E. Dennis, executive director of The Freedom Forum Media Studies Center at Columbia University. Copyright © 1992 by Sage Publications. Reprinted with permission.

series of evolutionary technological changes affected the fabric of life globally and, in the process, brought us closer together.

Much has been said about the links between the satellite, the television set and the computer, which are present in most places we go or things we do. For the news media, where once the lines between print and broadcast media were clear and unmistakable, convergence meant a blurring and merging. Some observers spoke of a "united state of media" wherein there was no longer much difference between a newspaper, a television station, and an electronic database. All of them gather, process, and distribute information to a consuming public. As media companies—which often call themselves information companies—acquired broadcast stations, cable services, market research firms, outdoor advertising firms, newspapers, magazines and book publishers, their executives increasingly began to speak about information products wherein news was just one of several commodities to be offered to the public.

Nowhere was this more evident than at the national television networks, which historically had developed different divisions for news, entertainment, sports, and other services. Recently those once distinct functions have shifted, sometimes blurring one into the other, or so it seems. For the networks, the news had been something of a loss-leader that was not required to make a profit to survive. A different standard had been used to measure Edward R. Murrow and his successors in television news than that applied to prime-time entertainment programs, in which ratings and profits had always been king. In the 1980s, some of the special gloss and protected status of television news rubbed thin, as ratings and profits were expected from all aspects of electronic media operations. Well beyond the headlines and industry gossip, it was clear that convergence of ownership was also accompanied by a convergence of many media activities, in which news and advertising became more symbiotically linked, news and entertainment intersected, and sometimes also news and opinion intersected—not that they were ever clinically separated, but certainly they once had more distinctive identities.

In a feverish attempt to retain their dominance, particularly in the face of the declining audience share influenced by cable, VCRs, and other competition, the networks and the television industry turned increasingly to technical pyrotechnics and hype and, inevitably, to a blurring of information and entertainment functions. Recreations or simulations of current and historical events, as well as compelling computer graphics and split-screen transmissions, were some of the ways new technologies were employed to bolster ratings.

These seemingly innocuous innovations actually blurred media functions, more often than not with entertainment values taking precedence over news values. In some instances, thoughtless juxtapositions of news in showy graphic formats actually conveyed unintended opinion that impaired credibility. These innovations, along with quasi-historical docudramas and miniseries, and information-oriented talk shows, disturbed and distressed thoughtful observers. The reason: fewer and fewer Americans can distinguish between what is news and what is entertainment.

As a study by The Times-Mirror Company in August 1989 indicated, public perceptions of news and entertainment are blurred. Although most Americans think of the daily soap operas and evening sitcoms and dramas as entertainment, they are not quite sure about "Geraldo," "The Oprah Winfrey Show," "A Current Affair," "The Reporters," "America's Most Wanted," and other popular programs, sometimes called tabloid TV. I think this criticism merits attention as we ask what, if any, consequences does this trend have for the future of news?

Fred W. Friendly and other critics have warned that dilution of the news with entertainment values can be detrimental. They mention sensational tabloid television programs that run back-to-back with the evening news and thus risk confusing the public about news/entertainment distinctions. Of course this does not differ much—except in audience size—with supermarket tabloids sold on the same rack with mainstream newspapers and magazines. I doubt that the *National Enquirer* debases the *Los Angeles Times* because they are sometimes sold on the same newsstand. The greater threat in the long run is the incremental impact of profitable news programming that may cause television executives to encourage more entertainment-oriented news.

Although it is easy to identify the sins of television, much of the same blurring and merging of functions also applies to newspapers and newsmagazines. Although the newsmagazines were once champions of "hard news," that is, news of public affairs and economics, they now showcase the heroes of popular culture—rock stars, actors, dancers, and even dogs and cats. They, too, are scrambling for an audience in an increasingly competitive advertising and subscription market, looking perhaps for a new identity. Newspapers have hardly been immune from forces of entertainment, ratings and packaging. Throughout the 1970s and 1980s, American newspapers engaged in what I have elsewhere called *creative damage control* as they worried about extinction. The result was special sections, more color, more "soft news" about fashion, food, and pop psychology, as well as other features aimed at capturing the "youth market" or "upscale readers."

The problem goes beyond mainstream media competing among themselves, and now includes other vendors who are selling information. Back in colonial times, broadsides, newsletters, and newspapers were about the only public sources of vital news of that era, reporting on ship movements and markets, town meetings, and taxes. But now there are other competitors actively selling or brokering information. An American Express advertisement puts it plainly:

Our product is information...that charges airline tickets, hotel rooms, dining out, the newest fashions and even figures mailing costs for a travel magazine; information that grows money funds, buys and sells equities and manages mergers; information that pays life insurance annuities, figures pricing for collision coverage and creates and pays mortgages...information that schedules entertainment on cable television and electronically guards houses; information that changes kroners into guilders, figures tax rates in Bermuda and helps put financing together for the ebb and flow of world trade.

"American Express," writes communications scholar Dan Schiller, "is not unique. Companies engaged in information-intensive services in banking, communications, data processing, advertising, law, and so on play an ever more critical role in U.S. investment, employment, and international trade." What we have seen develop in the 1980s is a large business information enterprise that will grow to $12 billion in revenues by the year 1992. This is only the tip of the iceberg, as Ma Bell and other vendors get into the information business. Once Will Rogers mused, "All I know is what I read in the papers." Perhaps this could even be said seriously in the 1930s, but certainly not in the 1980s or 1990s, when information comes from many sources and usually at a price.

There is an unfortunate tendency to link information and news together so that it is difficult to distinguish them, making it all the harder for us to fully understand, appreciate or comprehend our news media—especially newspapers and television, the two dominant instruments of public communication. For that, scholars who take the long view can help. The great social scientist

Harold Lasswell told us that, functionally, the media engage in surveillance of the environment, correlation of the parts of society, and transmission of the social heritage from one generation to another. A tall order, and one done by informing, influencing, entertaining, and providing a marketplace for goods and services.

We ought to remember that a news story, an editorial, and the crossword puzzle render different intelligence and represent different functions. Although both information and news are in, Harlan Cleveland's words, "renewable resources," they are also commodities for sale, but they are different in degree. Information is the raw material on which news is based. It includes facts, numbers, data, observations, sometimes ordered and organized, sometimes not. Pure information is often cold and clinical—such as weather reports, sports scores, directions, and lists. In Walter Lippmann's formulation, "news is not a mirror of social conditions, but the report of an aspect that has obtruded itself. The news does not tell you how the seed is germinating in the ground, but it may tell you when the first sprout breaks through the surface. It may even tell you what somebody says is happening to the seed underground. It may tell you that the sprout did not come up at the time it was expected. The more points at which any happening can be fixed, objectified, measured, named, the more points there are at which news can occur."

The news as we know it, of course, is a report, and a report is generated by people—professional people who gather information, write stories, edit and transmit them to the public. This is the value-added aspect of news that can be distinguished from the pure information of lists and tables. Whether people generally recognize and appreciate this is another question, however. We must ask whether the demand for news is being largely satisfied by information received over the telephone, through word of mouth, electronic mail, or other instruments in this age of speed and accelerating information. The yield from this question may be an important indicator for newspeople trying to determine what should be included in news reports, what not. As telephone companies are poised to provide electronic yellow pages, something the courts once forbade, the public will have more and more sources of information to answer its questions about daily life—and, at least for upscale audiences, the electronic wherewithal to ask questions like "What will the weather be tomorrow?" "Where did that stock end up on the exchange yesterday?" or "What was the score of that game?"

If our information needs can be satisfied by business information and other sources free and paid, why should we worry about the future of the news media? Will they not simply factor in these new information brokers and offer an expanded range of new topics and arenas of coverage? The answer is no. Information economists have demonstrated that people will spend only a fixed amount of discretionary income on information and entertainment. Certainly the new information brokers will severely challenge newspapers and television as well as magazines. Remember that the new information (as opposed to news) media can reach us by television screens, personal computers, telephone, or mail. Public communication in the United States is largely driven by user fees (subscriptions) and advertising. Clearly this is a finite and limited source.

The main characteristic of the Information Age has been the proliferation of information and information sources, ranging from the limited reach of individual desktop publishing ventures to the overpowering influence of giant media companies, many of them with global interests and aspirations. In this bombardment of more information than we can possibly consume, we see thousands of magazines and newsletters come and go, electronic data services getting a new foothold, and scores of cable channels competing with traditional broadcasters. There is continuous buying and selling of these properties as media entrepreneurs pitch their wares to a public that can only consume so much. In the inevitable shakeout that will come in the 1990s, there is no doubt that traditional media, especially those that deliver the news, will face severe threats to their survival.

All this depends on the public, whether it gets sustenance and satisfaction from news as opposed to other information sources that could challenge the present information order, now led by newspapers and television. Thus I think that newspapers and television news need to become more thoughtful sense-makers for their local communities, regionally or nationally, in whatever market is appropriate. This means thinking about and attending to the audience in a much more thoughtful, creative, and calibrated way than they presently do.

If producing news shows and editing newspapers has been somewhat hit and miss, essentially intuitive in the past, it cannot be in the future. We already have the tools of market research, which alone and unguided by editorial values can put news decisions in the hands of accountants. But read thoughtfully, as a strategic guide to news coverage and follow up, research can give cues about the value of vivid language, graphic illustrations and subject matter that really serve the needs of the reader and viewer.

In the 1990s, this will mean paying close attention to our changing demographics. According to *American Demographics* magazine, there will be increasing ethnic and racial diversity, a resurgence of metropolitan growth, more households with fewer people in them, a spurt upward in household income, more older people, more women in the work force, and many other indicators of profound change in the composition of our country and its citizens. Our communities will become increasingly international. In such a world the news has a place—an important one— but probably only if it makes its voice heard above its information competitors.

The news (and information) delivered by competent news professionals must be in a form that respects the inherent intelligence of the viewer and reader. It must not be laden with meaningless buzz words nor be overly simplistic or incomplete, leaving more questions than it answers. Although modern hypertechnology can answer questions and assemble information, neither it nor any business information service or electronic database can provide interpretative reporting that tells stories, analyzes issues and projects consequences with vivid language and pertinent illustrations. Neither can it offer coherent opinion in the orchestrated fashion of the newspaper editorial and op-ed pages.

Though the often tepid editorial pages of the country do not always have many readers, they can restore their purpose and vitality by restoring the art of passionate prose. In the process they can help readers form opinions about public issues. The opinion sections of newspapers, as well as columnists of all kinds, are what give personality and local identity to a news organization. In doing so, opinion sections can build a loyal following that is confident it has received credible commentary that is both useful and pertinent.

Unfortunately, though, while television has created some superb formats and interpretations for news, it has not yet created a comfortable vehicle for opinion, at least not in a way that effectively showcases different points of view. There are, of course, the well-known Sunday morning public affairs shows, but television still has no effective means of direct viewer feedback, as do the print media's letters-to-the-editor and guest columns. Electronic opinion programs may be just over the horizon, however, as various notions about interactive television come into the economic marketplace.

At a time when every person can be an editor (thanks to databases and other information services), people need to know and understand what it is they are not getting. What they are not getting in information are the values the news media bring. Values that give greater attention to one issue over another because it is more important to more people. I also mean values that distinguish the significant from the trivial; values that deliver ordered, quality news rather than aimless quantities of information. It is clear that the news media do not have an exclusive franchise on information. Much valuable information comes to us from the new media sources mentioned earlier as well as the entertainment media, particularly television and motion pictures. Who is to say that a television program like "L.A. Law" does not convey more information about lawyers than, say, a newspaper series on law firms? There is much information in entertainment programming, and even the crossword puzzle has been known to teach readers a thing or two. But remember, here information is only incidental, not central. The essential difference between news and information is that news is gathered, processed, and presented to the public with agreed-upon professional standards, checked for accuracy, and put in an overall context. Although information is the raw material from which newspeople fashion reports, reporters add comments about what these facts or events or processes mean. They find intelligent, well-sourced speculation about what the information means to individual citizens or to institutions. If news is to survive in the Age of Information, we must take some precautions to see that is does, namely:

1. Encourage news organizations to be more forthcoming with information about themselves, until their readers and viewers know what their values are, what standards they operate by, who their staff members are, and why we should trust them and respect their work. It is time to have more visible news staffs with news organizations—even newspapers—giving their audiences a more detailed preview of news coverage, both present and future.

2. Use recent census information to tell local news consumers how coverage will change and why in light of changing demographics. The media need to say to their respective communities, "We know who you are, we are trying to serve you more effectively, and here is how."

3. We need more effective means of public feedback than litigation—
approaches that do not impair anyone's freedom of expression.
Such means could include ethical audits linking media people and
citizens, more open channels for citizen complaint and feedback,
possibly local press councils and databases wherein people's concerns can be gathered together, codified and made openly available
to the public. In the 1980s, after a major credibility crisis and an
explosion of libel litigation, the press settled back once again into
what some have called a "public be damned" posture, often arro-
gantly unresponsive to simple issues of access and understand-
ability, and not always caring whether their readers, viewers, and
sources are accorded courtesy and respect. In the name of our
collective democratic governance and the media's economic well-
being, this must end. The news media need to project a friendly,
caring face, saying to their respective constituencies, "We care
about you and we are open to your concerns."

4. It would also be a public service for the press to promote its own
professionalism in overt fashion, explaining how a particular story
was developed, what ethical issues were involved and how they were
resolved. An interactive approach to this process would be even
more effective.

5. The news media should confront a very difficult, but not insolvable
problem: that of defining the public interest. It is common to claim
allegiance to "the public interest," but when asked to define it we
say lazily, "That's impossible." I believe it is possible; that the concept of the public interest, linked closely with the ancient idea of *vox
populi,* can be thought through, explicated, discussed, and debated.
We have for too long confused what is *of* public interest—matters
sensational or simple morbid curiosity—with what is *in* the public
interest. Philosophers, ethicists, legal scholars, members of the cler-
gy, and others have addressed these issues, and though there is no
universally accepted formulation, there is a rich yield of thought
that can help all of us think through the idea of the public
interest—whether it is a fusion of many special interests and self-
serving pleas or a more abstract and generalized concept. We could
then relate the idea to local issues, controversies, trends and enduring public questions. While there may be no mechanical test for the
public interest, it is an idea too important to be written off with an
arrogant wave of the arm. It requires the kind of hard thought of
which citizens and their communicators are capable.

If the media return to their essential public service function,
distinguishing news from information, linking news and opinion
but maintaining some orderly separation, we will better understand that news embraces information, but with value added: the
commitment of sensitive editors and caring publishers and broadcasters who realize the essence of their public franchise and who

seek to distinguish themselves from other businesses by fostering public trust in the service of the public interest.

Just because we do not all agree what the public interest is at any given time is not a reason to forsake the ideal. Doing so could lead the news media to succumb to information services. That would be a loss for us all, because in opting for easy access to information, some of us will not know what to ask for, others will not be able to afford it, and still others leading understandably busy lives will miss the richness and texture only news can offer. In the end our democratic system is well served by news rigorously acquired and presented that guides, instructs, and gives us the kind of ordered information capital we need to keep freedom of expression well and strong.

BIBLIOGRAPHY

An asterisk (*) preceding a reference indicates that the material or part of it has been reprinted in this compilation.

BOOKS AND PAMPHLETS

Alali, A. Odasuo & Eke, Kenoye Kelvin, eds. Media coverage of terrorism. Sage Publications. '91.

Angel, Dean. How to handle the news media. Betterway. '92.

Auletta, Ken. Three blind mice. Random. '91.

Burns, Eric. Broadcast blues: dispatches from the twenty-year war between a television reporter and his medium. HarperCollins. '93.

Carter, T. Barton; Franklin, Marc A.; & Wright, Jay B. The first amendment and the fifth estate. Foundation Press. '93.

Christians, Clifford G.; Ferre, John P.; & Fackler, P. Mark. Good news: social ethics and the press. Oxford University Press. '93.

Coffey, Frank. 60 minutes: 25 years of television's finest hour. General Pub. Group. '93.

*Cohen, Elliot D., ed. Philosophical issues in journalism. Oxford University Press. '92.

*Cohen, Jeff & Solomon, Norman. Adventures in medialand: behind the news, beyond the pundits. Common Courage. '93.

Corry, John. My times: adventures in the news trade. Putnam. '93.

Cottle, Simon. TV news, urban conflict, and the inner city. Leicester University Press. '93.

Creech, Kenneth. Electronic media law and regulation. Focal. '93.

Dayan, Daniel & Katz, Elihu. Media events: the live broadcasting of history. Harvard University Press. '92.

*Dennis, Everette E. Of media and people. Sage Publications. '92.

Denton, Frank & Kurtz, Howard. Reinventing the newspaper. Twentieth Century Fund Press. '93.

Diamond, Edwin. The media show: the changing faces of the news, 1985–1990. MIT Press. '91.

Dominick, Joseph R.; Sherman, Barry L.; & Copeland, Gary. Broadcasting/cable and beyond. McGraw-Hill. '93.

Eldridge, John, ed. Getting the message: news, truth and power. Routledge. '93.

Fowles, Jib. Why viewers watch: a reappraisal of television's effects. Sage Publications. '92.

211

Gruley, Bryan. Paper losses: a modern epic of greed and betrayal at America's two largest newspaper companies. Grove Press. '93.

Hallin, Daniel C. We keep America on top of the world: television journalism and the public sphere. Routledge. '94.

Harsch, Joseph C. At the hinge of history: a reporter's story. University of Georgia Press. '93.

Hayward, Philip, & Wollen, Tana, eds. Future visions: new technologies of the screen. BFI. '93.

Hausman, Carl. Crafting the news for the electronic media: writing, reporting and producing. Wadsworth. '92.

Lashley, Marilyn. Public television: panacea, pork barrel, public trust? Greenwood. '92.

Lewis, Lisa A., ed. The adoring audience: fan culture and popular media. Routledge. '92.

Maltese, John Anthony. Spin control: the White House Office of Communications and the management of presidential news. University of North Carolina Press. '94.

McQuail, Dennis. Media performance: mass communication and the public interest. Sage Publications. '92.

Morrison, David E. Television and the gulf war. J. Libbey. '92.

O'Neil, Michael J. The roar of the crowd: how television and people are changing the world. Times Books. '93.

*Parenti, Michael. Make-believe media: the politics of entertainment. St. Martin. '92.

Quirt, John. The press and the world of money: how the news media cover business and finance, panic and prosperity, and the pursuit of the American dream. Anton/California Courier. '93.

Raboy, Mark and Bernard Dagenais, eds. Media, crisis and democracy. Sage Publications. 92.

Shrader, William K. Media blight and the dehumanizing of America. Prager. '92.

Signorielli, Nancy. Mass media images and impact on health. Greenwood Press. '93.

Singer, Eleanor & Endreny, Phyllis M. Reporting on risk: how the mass media portray accidents, diseases, disaster, and other hazards. Russell Sage Foundation. '93.

*Squires, James D. Read all about it: the corporate takeover of America's newspapers. Times Books. '93.

White, Barton. The new ad media reality. Quorum. '93.

ADDITIONAL PERIODICAL ARTICLES WITH ABSTRACTS

For those who wish to read more widely on the subject of the media and the public, this section contains abstracts of additional articles that bear on the topic. Readers who require a comprehensive list of materials are advised to consult the *Reader's Guide to Periodical Literature* and other Wilson indexes.

Confessions of a network newsman. Terry Eastland. *The American Spectator* 23:29–31 Ag '90

Fred Graham, a journalist who is best known for his work as CBS's law correspondent during the 1970s and 1980s, has published a bittersweet and well-written memoir entitled *Happy Talk: Confessions of a TV Newsman*. Graham states that CBS had "standards" and "prestige" during its golden years in the 1970s but that "infotainment" became the rule in the early 1980s. Gradually, the major network news shows lost viewers, and Graham left to become a local news anchor in Nashville. He believes that serious journalists should stay in television and try to redeem it. He recently signed on as the anchor of the first full time cable channel devoted to legal affairs, the American Trial Network, which will debut in early 1991. In an interview, Graham discusses his career, the relationship between the media and government, and the difference between television and print journalism.

Soviet journalists: starting to dig. Steve Weinberg. *The Bulletin of the Atomic Scientists* 47:22–25 Jl/Ag '91

Soviet journalists are becoming increasingly aggressive in their exposure of government incompetence and corruption. Prior to glasnost, much of the material that could be published in Soviet newspapers and magazines emanated from Tass, the Soviet telegraph agency, and much of what a journal wanted to print had to pass an elaborate censorship bureaucracy. This changed in 1986, when tough investigative reporting began to appear in the Soviet media and became more frequent as Mikhail Gorbachev's glasnost policies took effect. Until 1989, most of these efforts concentrated on petty local corruption, but since then, journalists have felt free to tackle the larger issues of national security and foreign policy. Despite a new crackdown on investigative journalism by the Kremlin, it is doubtful that the Soviet media can be forced to return to their pre-glasnost docility.

Television journalism in the '90s: stay tuned. Or will you? Ben Bagdikian. *Television Quarterly* 25/2:21–8 '91

A need exists for more reforms in television journalism. Programming is now fueled solely by the desire for ratings, which produce advertising profits. Television, however, should serve the public good to some extent. Public service requirements, including the Fairness Doctrine and equal time, should be reinstated, as should local community programming during good viewing hours. As is done in some European democracies, national civic groups should be given regular free time. Paid political advertising should be replaced with generous free air time provided two months prior to an election to all parties that have polled five percent or more in the previous election. Commercials should be limited in number and frequency, cross media ownership should be forbidden, and licenses should once again be easily challengeable by dissatisfied communities.

Rise and decline of mass culture? Stanley Rothman. *Society* 30:29–35 Jl/Ag '93

Part of a special section on America's mass culture. The media have contributed to the spread of tolerance and the increase of cosmopolitanism in America, but they have also encouraged a corrosive fragmentation that threatens the very democratic order and that already has bred violence and discouragement. The trend, which was not initiated by the media, reaches back to the origins of the American work ethic. Specifically, the roots of gradual decline go back to the mid 19th century, when America's economy was first beginning to expand with the technological innovations of the telegraph and the railroad. The Calvinist ideal of early American society—hard work, frugality, and achievement—became undermined by the success of the middle-class marketplace. An ever-expanding array of goods and services weakened the American sense of self-control, and achievement was replaced by power as the ideal. Academia and journalism also contributed to this trend.

Everyone hates the media. Joe Saltzman. *USA Today* [Periodical] 121:55 Ja '93

Americans have developed a profound distaste for the news media, a perception that is creating a dangerous situation. This attitude can be attributed to the contemptuous way in which reporters have been depicted on television and in films during the past few decades. In contrast to earlier movies, in which journalists were treated with some affection and with a true understanding of their role in a democratic society, Hollywood now portrays them as biased, arrogant, and ruthless muckrakers who care about no one and will do anything for a story. As a result, the public's estimation of journalists has dropped substantially in 10 years; only politicians, lawyers, and psychologists are held in as much disdain. If the public continues to view journalists as untrustworthy and to believe that the media are presenting biased, inaccurate information, then opportunities will abound for the proliferation of disinformation and demagoguery.

The "New News" and the old. Donald Baer. *U.S. News & World Report* 113:34+ Jl 27 '92

The once familiar rules of public discourse have been transformed, as is apparent in the media coverage of the Democratic National Convention.

Unlike "Old News" coverage, which is characterized by straightlaced reporting and serious analysis, "New News" ranges from infotainment to talk show politics to pop culture treatment of breaking stories. For example, reporters at the convention included MTV's floor correspondent, Dave Mustaine of the rock group Megadeth; Comedy Central's Al Franken; and the team of Tom Brokaw and Jay Leno. This new journalism addresses some of the basic questions of good journalism that have been ignored by Old News in its pursuit of increasingly sophisticated instant analysis. MTV's "Choose or Lose" coverage, for example, tries to bring disaffected younger voters into the fold in the realization that the vernacular of politics tends to drive them away.

A pox on Dan and Murphy. John Leo. *U.S. News & World Report* 112:19 Je 1 '92

Dan Quayle's comments about television character Murphy Brown's status as a single mother are bothersome to many people who care about family values and who do not wish to be lectured on the topic by an administration that has done almost nothing to help. However, family disintegration and the dramatic rise of single parent families are a major social disaster for the United States. According to sociologist Amitai Etzioni, the overwhelming bulk of studies indicates that single parenting is harmful to children. Nonetheless, the U.S. elite, particularly the media elite, considers single parenthood a nonissue. The noncensorious attitude about other people's choices and lifestyles results in an ocean of feel-good journalism and programming that is intended to raise the self esteem of single mothers, which amounts to cheerleading for the unraveling of the social structure.

The right wing targets public TV. Laurie Ouellette. *Utne Reader* 44–5 My/Je '92

Articles in the November/December 1991 *Columbia Journalism Review* and the February 25, 1992, *Village Voice* discuss right wing criticism of public television. Conservatives are targeting public TV in what promises to be an intense battle against "subsidized cultural dissidence." Right wing critics, including David Horowitz of the Committee on Media Integrity and Lawrence Jarvik of the Heritage Foundation, claim that public television has a "leftist bias" and misuses public funds. According to the alternative news service Alternet, these critics have attacked a number of PBS programs and are against the public funding of public TV in general. They are also attacking the Independent Television Service, a new arm of public television. Critics from all parts of the political spectrum question whether public television is meeting its goal, but public television does offer virtually the only controversial and unconventional programming that is available on free TV.

The buck stops here. Diane Keaton. *Women's Sports & Fitness* 13:48–9 N/D '91

Part of a special section on women in sports journalism. Coverage of women's sports receives scant attention in both print and broadcast media. According to a study by the Amateur Athletic Foundation (AAF) of Los Angeles, major television networks devote only about 5 percent of their sports coverage to women. Gene Policinski, managing editor of USA Today, says that women's sports account for perhaps twenty-five percent to thirty percent of the newspaper's overall sports coverage, but most newspapers do not come close to that figure. Newspaper editors and television producers assert that as long as men's baseball, basketball, and football dominate, all other sports, including all women's athletics, will play second fiddle. Recent AAF reports have criticized print and broadcast media for their limited, low quality, and trivialized coverage of women's sports. Efforts to improve the profile of women's sports in the media are discussed.

All over the press Down Under. Brendan Trembath. *Washington Journalism Review* 14:11 D '92

Stuart Littlemore, who anchors the Australian Broadcasting Corporation's Media Watch: The Last Word, inspires fear among Australian journalists. His program criticizes questionable reporting from both print and broadcast sources, using what Littlemore calls "the techniques of modern journalism to criticize modern journalism." Several media figures have accused the show itself of unethical tactics and sensationalism.

TV news & the neutrality principle. John Corry. *Commentary* 91:24–7 My '91

The performance of U.S. television reporters in Baghdad during the Persian Gulf War confirms that neutrality has replaced objectivity as the central principle of American journalism. Instead of striving to gather, analyze, and present relevant facts, these journalists reported selectively, censoring themselves to avoid expulsion from Iraq. Most of them seemed to believe, however, that the content of the news coverage was less important than the fact that reporters were on the scene at all. Moreover, they insisted that their duties as American citizens did not supersede their supposed duties as journalists. These attitudes probably contributed to the low opinion of the news media that many Americans expressed during the war.

Is it fact? Or is it fiction? Deborah Baldwin. *Common Cause Magazine* 19:25–9 Wint '93

It is becoming increasingly difficult to differentiate between fact and fiction in the media. Critics who monitor eroding standards in the broadcast and publishing industries blame a number of forces, including the media owners' obsession with the bottom line, advertisers who cheapen the language, academic "relativists" who question the truth of virtually everything, politicians who cannot distinguish between truth and fantasy, and a public with an insatiable appetite for celebrity gossip that substitutes for knowledge in today's culture. Concern about the reliability of the news media frequently focuses on television because the medium tends to value entertainment and immediacy at the expense of accuracy and context. The contributions of "docudramas," TV "newsmagazines," journalism ethics, digital photography, Oliver Stone's JFK, and the airing of the Clarence Thomas-Anita Hill hearings in blurring fact and fiction are discussed.

Money and reporters: a conflict of interests? James S. Doyle. *Current* 324:35–40 Jl/Ag '90

An article excerpted from "Has Money Corrupted Washington Journalism?," which appeared in the Winter 1989 issue of Nieman Reports. The results of an informal survey by the writer, a vice-president of the Times Journal Company of Springfield, Virginia, of some press corps members on the growing affluence of their Washington peers. The writer says that increased wealth among journalists has led to complacency and indifference toward the problems of average Americans. Survey responses presented discuss the journalist as a performer, the elite among media figures, talk shows, the authority derived from television, the potential for corruption, journalistic specialization, the new posture of the press, what passes for political analysis among reporters today, the quality of modern reporting, and the exaggerated sense of importance among media staffs.

A walk through the Garden. Christopher Lydon. *Columbia Journalism Review* 31:9–14 S/O '92

This year's slick, predictable Democratic National Convention revealed the decline of the U.S. political media. Despite the lack of news at the convention, there were three media people for every delegate. Most of the journalists at the convention were in fact wondering why they were there, given that the big three networks, which used to own or at least host the conventions, are broke and have reduced coverage to as little as an hour a night. The article discusses the challenge that Ross Perot's campaign has presented to traditional journalism; Larry King's style of "chummy" interview journalism; how political journalism has become divided into the Old News of network shows and metropolitan newspapers and the New News that is made up mostly of the pop media, and the effect that these two approaches are having on the 1992 presidential campaign.

Collateral damage to network news. Jon Katz. *Columbia Journalism Review* 29:29 Mr/Ap '91

Part of a special section on media coverage of the Persian Gulf War. The war's implications will be far-reaching for much of U.S. journalism, particularly broadcasting. With its ubiquity, mobility, and hustle, Cable News Network (CNN) appears to have overwhelmed its network competitors regarding the presentation of traumatic or significant world events. For the news divisions of ABC, CBS and NBC, the war has been an economic and editorial disaster. The networks were faced with an excess of air time and no advertisers to pay for it. News divisions, isolated and manipulated by the military, were left to their own devices by indifferent owners and preempted by independent affiliates, who often sent their own reporters to cover the war or aired hours of CNN. Ultimately, the war has proved that the networks can no longer afford to be in the breaking news business.

Newsdom's number-one dirtbag. Robert Sherrill. *The Nation* 256:613+ My 10 '93

In only the latest sleazy acquisition to his crudely capitalistic media "empire," Rupert Murdoch has apparently won the right to buy back the financially troubled New York Post, which he turned into a bizarre, rightwing tabloid more than a decade ago. William Shawcross's biography, Murdoch, reveals that such behavior is representative of his entire career. According to evidence that Shawcross supplies in abundance, Murdoch, who controls newspapers and television stations around the world and is probably worth more than $2 billion, is a professional liar and cheater, a disloyal bully, a vulgar hypocrite, and the ultimate symbol of the shamefully greedy and unethical business practices of the 1980s. At the New York Post, the London tabloid Sun and other papers, he perfected journalism as crude entertainment. Sadly, Murdoch's style may represent the future of journalism. Many of his activities are detailed.

Reliable sources. Peter Shaw. *National Review* 45:63-4 Je 21 '93

Part of a special section on American journalism. The mainstream media use ideologically inspired euphemism and misrepresentation to systematically distort the decline of civility in American society. In newspapers, perpetrators are presented as victims of disadvantaged upbringings, and on television, rioting thugs are said to be reacting to the middle class's indifference to their own plight. Political correctness also distorts the truth in movies. Media consumers can find objective presentations and assessments of individuals unrelated to race, ethnicity, or supposed social disadvantages in sports pages and in tabloid journalism, which are characterized by a vivid directness and accuracy that are lacking in the news pages of prestige newspapers. The writer analyzes a well-known headline and story that was published in the April 15, 1983, issue of the *New York Post*.

Drowning in a sea of cliches. George Bain. *Maclean's* 105:52 S 21 '92

Cliches continue to dominate both print and television news reporting. Because television as an oral medium could not be expected to express itself with the same originality and precision demanded of print, the result has been a reduction in originality and precision in the news media in general. Magazine and newspaper editors and publishers are increasingly concerned that they are losing their audience and that print media as a whole may become "a niche player." To slow this trend, editors and publishers should first concentrate their efforts on that part of the public that has not already switched altogether to television. They should then focus less on what they write about than on how they write it, because the public still reading print is most likely to recognize and be put off by dull, tired, lazy, formulaic writing, of which cliches are the most obvious example.

A zombie nation inhabiting two worlds. Fred Bruning. *Maclean's* 106:11 Mr 15 '93

Increasingly, Americans seem to be having trouble distinguishing between illusion and authenticity. Flooded by entertainment and information, Americans have come to inhabit two worlds that are wildly out of sync: In one sphere, the World Trade Center has been bombed, the president is trying to sell a tax plan, AIDS continues to claim lives, suffering pervades Somalia and Bosnia, and the Mideast situation remains tense; in the other sphere, Americans are tuning into radio, television, and tabloids that herald every nutty theory ever proposed. According to experts, junk journalism is harmless in small doses, but, as media psychology professor Stuart Fischoff notes, a constant diet of tabloid newspapers, right-wing radio call-ins, and voyeuristic talk shows is not healthy. Americans must get a grip on reality.

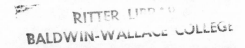